To call this story a roller-coaster ride is [...]
Sandra Lacey walked through a journe[...]
pain, miracles of healing, and the ultin[...]
honesty and uncompromising prose. Sandra's writing mirrors her dancing: it is passionate, committed and raw. It does not dodge the bullets of pain and suffering, but neither does it surrender to despair. Most moving of all is the sense of Rob's surviving legacy in his two beautiful children, in his writings that continue to bless thousands and in the brilliant Lacey Theatre Company, going from strength to strength. None of these treasures would be with us now without the courage and perseverance this book recounts. Rob, if you're reading this on your Kindle-in-the-clouds, we love you, we miss you, and we want you to know the garden you planted is growing, growing, growing ...

Gerard Kelly, *co-director of The Bless Network,*
member of the Spring Harvest Theme Group

A moving story of adversity and breakthrough, pain and hope, tears mixed with joy, where God's presence and light are tangible and real. Rob's life is carved by the Master despite the darkness and mystery of cancer. Humour is a constant thread and this Lacey legacy is a treasure not to be missed.

Rachael Orrell, *executive director of Saltmine Trust*

This is a profoundly beautiful book. Intimate, honest, faith-filled, real and pulsing with hope, this traces the story of an epic journey. Please don't miss this—your heart will be warmed, and your faith strengthened.

Jeff Lucas, *author, speaker, broadcaster*

Rob Lacey was extraordinary. I feel like I am who I am and I do what I do because of him, so reading this book was always going to be emotional. But as much as I giggled and sobbed, I delighted in how beautifully this remarkable story is told. Sandra's hugely generous honesty make every moment rich; that so much can be contained in so few pages is astounding, and much like the life Rob and Sandra have led. Lovingly wrapped inside Sandra and Steve's storytelling skill are Rob's words, and they will dance through your soul like light on water.

Abby Guinness, *actor and writer, heads up arts for Spring Harvest*

Books by Rob Lacey
The Word on the Street
The Essential Word on the Street
The Liberator
Street Life (Rob Lacey and Nick Page)
We Are Getting Through

Books by Steve Stickley
In Drama
Footnotes
The Drama Recipe Book
Street Theatre

People Like Us

Life with Rob Lacey

Sandra Lacey
& Steve Stickley

ZONDERVAN.com/
AUTHORTRACKER
follow your favorite authors

We want to hear from you. Please send your comments about this
book to us in care of zreview@zondervan.com. Thank you.

ZONDERVAN

People Like Us
Copyright © 2011 by Sandra Harnisch-Lacey

This title is also available as a Zondervan ebook.
Visit www.zondervan.com/ebooks.

This title is also available in a Zondervan audio edition.
Visit www.zondervan.fm.

Requests for information should be addressed to:

Zondervan, *Grand Rapids, Michigan* 49530

Library of Congress Cataloging-in-Publication Data

Harnisch-Lacey, Sandra, 1972–
     People like us: my life with Rob Lacey / Sandra Harnisch-Lacey and Steve
Stickley
       p. cm.
     ISBN 978-0-310-31904-7 (softcover)
     1. Christian biography. 2. Lacey, Rob. 3.Bladder—Cancer—Patients—
Religious life. 4. Harnisch-Lacey, Sandra, 1972- I. Stickley, Steve. II. Title.
BR1700.H365 2010
274.1'.083092—dc22   2010024267

Cover design: Curt Diepenhorst
Cover photo of Sandra: Barb Dicker
Cover photo of Rob: taken at the Spring Harvest Festival 2004
Interior design: Michelle Espinoza

Printed in the United States of America

---

11 12 13 14 15 16 /DCI/ 21 20 19 18 17 16 15 14 13 12 11 10 9 8 7 6 5 4 3 2 1

For Lukas
and
Magdalena

with all my love
— SL

For Mark

... thank you for looking
around the next corner
— SS

Contents

Foreword

The last months and weeks of his life, Rob was working on another book ... his life story, our story. Back in 2004 the publishers commissioned Rob to reflect upon his life with cancer, the miracle healing and his creative response amid pain and suffering. Rob always wanted the two of us to write the book together and was very keen for me to be actively involved, in order to create a fully rounded picture. So, of course, after he died I felt strongly that I needed to tell 'our story' in his place.

To look back on our life together fills me with an overwhelming sense of gratitude and deep joy to have been loved unconditionally and to love unconditionally in return. Two soul mates had found their match. No matter what life threw at us, together we were strong, and with God on our side we knew we couldn't lose. Even though the amount of physical and emotional pain felt so unbearable so often and the darkness overwhelming, we walked this journey choosing to focus on Hope, following its light, which was somewhere ahead; ... to bring Heaven on Earth into our daily circumstances became our anchor point, and this reality of Heaven is what carried me and the children through these past few years. The prospect of Heaven is so much more tangible and important now than it ever was, and with eternal life ahead of us, the great stuff is all yet to come!

So, here I stand, four years on, holding my boy's hand in one and my little girl's in the other, looking up and ahead, knowing that there is a new part of the journey to be walked, a new adventure to be lived—resting assured in the loving arms of our Almighty God.

> *Then everything changes. New. All of it brand new. All heaven, all earth—new. Nothing of the old heaven or the old earth left. Gone: all of it including the oceans. Woah! This pure, perfect city—The New Jerusalem—is floating down out of heaven direct from God. It's like a bride, perfectly turned out for her loving groom. A loud shout, coming from the throne. 'From now on, God's living down here with them. They'll be his kind of people; God'll hang out with them and be God to them. He'll collect all the tears they have ever cried, he'll cancel death, there'll be no more grieving, no crying, no pain—all that was in the previous system and that is history.*

> *The Word on the Street,* Revelation 21:1–4

Chapter 1
Alien Safaris

So, Rob and me. Our story.

I prepare myself to set out on this new and strange journey to gather up and express in words as much as I can about our life together. For normal journeys I am accustomed to arranging clothing, toiletries, towels and personal effects into a suitcase. But this trip is unlike any other I have ever taken, and I am overwhelmed by all that I may need. Journals, photographs, email print-outs, poems, fragments of Rob's life lie scattered around me as I sit on the floor. Of course, I have had to sift and sort so much other stuff since he died. At first I was reluctant to strip my home of him. I still needed the evidence of him within these walls. I wanted the very brickwork to sing of Rob's talent with words, the doors on their hinges to signal his onstage skills, the tiles in the hall to trace the beautiful design that was Rob. I have recently reduced the huge number of photographs of his smile around the house, but his laughter is still enfolded in the curtains. I have sent his shoes off to charity shops, but his rhythm still sounds in floorboard clicks. I have dispatched his coats and jumpers to who-knows-where, but his warm embrace still meets me in the arms of my children.

The bladder cancer nearly killed Rob once before, in 2001, and afterwards he wrote a poem for me. So this is where I want to begin, with Rob imagining himself in heaven. If everything else he wrote had to be shredded as a result of me losing some monstrous Shred-Fest Lottery and I was permitted to keep just one piece of paper, this is the one I would rescue. He wrote it on a large sheet of dark-patterned paper, and every time I unfold it, his wit and wonder are there to greet me. Much of it is too personal, so here is an excerpt:

> *... There may've been solar systems to tour, alien safaris to see,*
> *There may've been reminiscing to be had, locked emotions*
> *   breaking free.*
> *But to do all this without you would break heaven's 'no*
> *   pain' policy.*
> *How can it be perfect if you miss out on some eternity with*
> *   me?*
> *Though even if we both begin eternity together, it's still*
> *   enough I know,*
> *So I lay hands on your wedding finger, ask God to make it*
> *   grow,*
> *So you can wear two eternity rings and then everyone will*
> *   know that*
> *After the year God's just brought us through*
> *Having nearly lost you*
> *I want two eternities with you.*
>
> Rob Lacey, 2002

As alien safaris go, the one upon which I have since found myself on this earth would beggar belief, despite the warnings in the brochure. Would we have chosen not to go on that treacherous and deadly journey? Of course we would, but now it is done. I have no choice and I am here. Here to tell the story.

'They said the cancer might be back.'

The backstage dressing room door closed behind Rob automatically with the muted *shush* that fire doors have. In that moment between his words and mine, his eyes and my eyes, his arms and my arms, his breath and my breath – buried deep within that small and mundane silence, that insignificant pause – a seed of knowledge began its inevitable germination, the fruit of which would not show itself for some time yet. How could I have realised that this signalled the beginning of his last ten months? And so much more besides. It was July 2005. I had just finished teaching a dance class at The Gate Arts Centre in Cardiff, our hometown. Rob had returned from seeing his consultant. We held on to each other – my body still fuelled with adrenaline, his fresh with summer air.

Dancers like me are used to seeing their bodies in mirrors. It comes with the territory. Your body is your everything, your voice, your syntax, your expression, your spirit. At every point, you need to know precisely what shape, what stance, what flow, what energy you are communicating to those who watch. For Rob, words were everything. Written or performed. Any husband having to deliver this possible death sentence to his wife would hesitate how to order the words, what type of voice to use, whether to come straight out with it or to prepare her first. For a wordsmith and a performer, the stakes would surely have been higher. I wonder even now how he rehearsed it to himself as he was driving back. We all do it all the time, don't we? The rehearsing. Playing a scene over and over in our mind's eye, again and again, as if training our subconscious not only to get our lines right but our body language and tone of delivery so that nothing else will get in the way. Rehearsing and assimilating. Repetitively. Good news, bad news, what I did or where I went or whom I met today ... but especially the bad news.

Over Rob's shoulder I see the dancer holding her husband. Mirrored. And as I imagine this scene again, I wonder what it would communicate to an audience. What strange inert performance piece is this? And how long will they stay there like that? What kind of soundtrack does it have? A melancholy cello? No, that would be too much like 'Truly, Madly, Deeply'. A lazy tenor saxophone in a minor key with glissando trails? Rob loved jazz. Or, perhaps, simply 'the still sad music of humanity,' as a poet once penned. Then again, maybe just the ambient sounds of the Arts Centre around us, muffled voices as the last of the dance students wander down the stairs, the tiny creaks here and there that any building emits if you stay still long enough to listen, or just the sound of us breathing as our bones and muscles sustain their gentle task of loving and supporting.

I still see that reflection of us holding on to each other. For dear life, as they say. It wasn't even a long hug. But now that I replay it, perhaps it slips out of time, even moving imperceptibly backward. Two bodies pressed together against time and inertia, despair and heaven, life and death. Each desperate to place our hands upon the humanity that is the sum of us, whilst anointing each other with innocence. Maybe we could make it go away. Maybe the words would disappear back into Rob's mouth. Maybe we didn't want this word to become flesh. But we were both in the business of incarnation. It's what artists do. An idea emblazons itself upon you, startling and eye-popping in its audacity or charm or challenge, and then you have to find a way to bring it alive. After all, that's what God does. Words become flesh. Of course, we had no idea then how this last chapter would write itself. We just didn't know the words' worth ... which also happens to be the name of the poet I quoted earlier. (You see, Rob, even I am learning wordplay!)

The day that Rob told me the news might even have been the day after his birthday. Forty-three. Nine years after the bladder cancer was first diagnosed ... and ten years since we got married. During that Easter of 2005, when Rob had been to Spring Harvest with our theatre company, it felt like a really good time. The sales of *the street bible*, which was reprinted as *The Word on the Street*, had topped 50,000 and won the UK Christian Booksellers' Book of the Year Award and was now selling in America. Audiences had bought into Rob's unique approach, his skillful turn of phrase, playful use of words and his endearingly cheeky onstage persona. The theatre company was established the year before to relieve Rob of ever-intensifying tour itineraries that soon rendered him weak and prone to infection. They had already performed the new stage version of *The Word on the Street* dozens of times up and down the country, always to great acclaim. And so, by the time he and the theatre company, which comprised three young female actors (more of them later), arrived at the biggest Christian conference in the UK, we seemed to be surfing on a huge tide of gratitude, interest and excitement.

Around that time, my parents came over from Germany to look after Lukas and his cousin so that my sister Katja and I could take a ten-day trip to Bangalore, India, to see some friends. We visited orphanages and also witnessed first-hand the creative response of indigenous workers to harsh and changing industrial developments which threatened their livelihood. We went into the jungle for three days and had quite a wonderful experience which became a God-centred metaphor for me. We found ourselves waiting to witness wildlife and becoming more highly tuned to the flora and fauna around us, eager not to miss out on that special something. And inevitably, we missed it because we got distracted or bored! It was a salutary lesson to be still and to recognise what is already around us. Combined with the sights, sounds and smells of old and new Bangalore and the exuberant, colourful Bollywood films we saw, there was an overwhelming sense of earthed spirituality. I have always loved to travel, and this was an experience I am glad I didn't miss. But Rob couldn't come.

Encroaching illness and trepidation had cast a shadow over both his Spring Harvest experience and my Bangalore trip. Rob missed being the quintessential performer. He found he had become the revered author who did short appearances here and there, while the theatre company engendered the type of response and applause he loved. Performance was his heartbeat. He was always gracious and selfless about it, but I could see what he was truly missing.

Whilst at Spring Harvest, he started to have quite a few physical difficulties. The preceding year had seen a series of kidney infections which would respond to treatment but always reappear.

Upon my return from India that May, Rob became quite ill and started to have repeating pain. During a family day out to Longleat Safari Park, he experienced a particularly sharp bout which was different from the kidney pain – it was in the bladder region and more severe than before. He didn't feel well and looked quite bad. Later, when I would talk to Lukas about 'when Daddy got ill,' he would always remember that it was after that Easter, when I went to India, that the illness returned. But it heralded a period of time when Rob became very focused and quite on the ball.

'Let's do some tests, let's not let this hang around.' He was determined and, very quickly, we explained everything to the consultants, and they responded with equal swiftness. The urine sample revealed nothing. But by July the X-ray results exposed abnormalities in the lymph nodes. They could not be certain what it was, although there was some speculation that the cancer had returned. So began a trip into the unknown, into the alien landscape of possible secondary cancer, as if we had taken a very wrong turn in Longleat.

Two weeks before Rob opened that dressing room door with the news, we had booked a holiday in Greece for the end of August. Aware that Rob would now need to have more tests, we had to cancel it. Our spirits sank as we lost all of the money. I was livid with the travel company. I laugh with embarrassment now at my indignation but, of course, much of it had its root in my deep-seated anger at the cancer. We very reluctantly let go of our holiday in the sun. It felt so unfair, especially as we knew we really needed it. But if Rob had become ill in Greece, as tourists unable to speak the language, the difficulties could have been enormous. So we didn't want to take that risk. Instead, we would go to my parents in Germany for a week during late September.

But it wasn't only Rob who had news. About halfway through August, I didn't get my period. We did a pregnancy test and it proved positive. Ever since the first round of chemotherapy three years before, we hadn't stopped trying for another baby. Even with the recent prognosis, perhaps in spite of it, we carried on, almost as an act of defiance. Rob and I laughed at the speculation that his sperm was, at last, off drugs, rehabilitated and back to a quality performance. To quote from Rob's prophet Malachi in *The Word on the Street*, it was 'gutsy and going for it!'

We were thrilled. Over the moon. But the timing shook us. Such joy and such sadness together. In one breath we'd tell people, 'We're pregnant, but the cancer's back,' and it became a strange incantation for the rest of that year. Two of life's extremes in one message. Not for the first time I felt I was holding contradictory loads, one hand overflowing with God's goodness, but the other harbouring disease. The promise of life and the threat of death.

And then it was as if a gear shifted. Over the next two or three months, a few things happened that empowered us and lifted our spirits. Of course, being pregnant was the first and biggest of them all. The thought of new life inside me became a promise. A promise from God that all would be well. And in all the hundreds of thousands of small moments of life ... taking Lukas to school, emptying coffee grinds, brushing my hair, talking to my sister on the phone, carrying dirty clothes to the washing machine, opening letters, tidying CDs, walking to the shop, sending text messages, finding keys in my bag ... in all these actions, words percolated up inside me like a repeating chorus: 'I'm pregnant, which will mean the cancer's going to go away.' It seemed to become a walking prayer, a mantra, as well as a kind of holy dance. The positive handful would overcome the negative handful. It just had to. The disease would trickle out between my fingers like dry sand, while the rich and refreshing new life from the other hand would flood the emptiness. Every action of every day was a determination to banish the dead with the living. It was such an absorbing physical focus for me that I finally wondered whether I had become the prayer itself – all of the day and all of the night, falling asleep at the end of each day holding onto Rob, with life's promise growing between us.

By the middle of September, we had a meeting with the consultant together with an oncologist and a urologist. (Rob would probably make a joke here about having too many 'gists' … 'getting an overdose of understanding' or something. Even when things became bleak, I could always rely on that irrepressible humour to surface somewhere unexpectedly.) There was no doubt. The cancer was back 100 percent. They had a few options they could offer to us, but there was really nothing they could do.

We started to thrash out what would be the best way forward. It was as if a light had come on. Ping! Suddenly we were involved in a dialogue, whereas previously we had just been told, 'This is your diagnosis and this is what we're doing.' There had always been that sense before that Rob was nothing more than a conglomeration of limbs and organs. Diseased flesh in need of repair. But I think we had built up a history with them, and they kept on saying, 'But you are different and things are very different with you … our prognosis is you've got a year to live if we do chemo. But you've proven us wrong before, so who knows what's going to happen? You might respond really well again, you responded remarkably well to chemotherapy before.'

But we knew the bigger story.

I watched those health professionals going about their job. Furrowed brows, neatly manicured fingernails, identity badges swinging from lanyards, wristwatches pulsing seconds. As a team they imparted information carefully and impartially. They too had woken up this morning and had breakfast, they too have family and friends, they too know the frustrations that life can deal – the unpredictable nature of events, the fragility of life. They understand more than most people, but that's not really surprising … they have little choice. Human fragility is the rationale for their professional existence. Despite the life-changing nature of their words, or perhaps because of it, humanity found its way through their medical terminology.

'We can prolong life. We can offer you chemotherapy again, but the likelihood that it will work as well this time round is very small. The other option would be to do an operation, which we normally wouldn't offer to anybody because it's the second time the cancer has appeared; we'd normally just give chemo. However, in your case, Rob, it has been different. Last time the cancer developed differently than we had expected, so we would be happy to do an operation first and then chemotherapy.'

Though their words and syllables carried the sort of meaning to which I should have paid the utmost attention, deep inside me the young girl with her fairytale dreams in Germany, the eager and energetic dancer, the mother clutching her baby boy, the wife holding on to her dying husband, all the different facets of me and of our history as a couple slowly whirled and mixed together, forming a prayer. *What now, oh God? Dear Lord, what now? Does Rob have to go through all that again? Is this how you want your glory to be shown in us?*

Meanwhile, the doctors continued, 'We don't know what's going to happen if we do operate on you. Due to all the treatment you've had in the past, particularly the radiotherapy, we can't be sure whether some of the organs are scarred. If the scar tissue is too severe, we may not be able to take the bladder out or take the tumour out. Therefore half of it would be left in place.' It became clear that even if they opened Rob up, they didn't know what they were going to be able to achieve. And it would take a long time to recover from an operation like this. So the doctors simply gave us these two options, and then Rob and I went into the waiting room to talk.

I think they knew us quite well by then. They understood we were the kind of people who didn't just want to be told what to do. We were very much involved in the decision making. It was hugely gratifying to hear them say, 'This is your decision, this is your life. We need to know what you want to do. The prognosis is not good. No one ever survives bladder cancer, so what do you want to do?'

Suddenly there was no talk of him being in remission – the cancer had come back and we were shell-shocked. Who knew what to do? The scan had revealed a tumour behind the bladder and something on the lymph nodes as well, so nothing was straightforward. Rob and I just looked at each other. His warm, playful eyes. He smiled, and I remembered the long, never-ending weariness of before. Our lives had been dominated by hospital visits, blood tests, urine samples, waiting to receive test results and then having to have more and on and on. And none of this would compare to the pain he would have to endure.

'I don't want chemo again.'

'I don't want you to have chemo.'

It was then that our moment of liberation arrived. Unannounced. No treatment. The thought didn't even knock on the door, it just waltzed in, and its simplicity and clarity embraced us like a welcome friend. We didn't need words; the look between us decided it. When we did speak, it was to consolidate our determination.

'Let's not have any treatment.'

This heady mix of audacity and excitement distilled quickly into a prayerful resolve. It was exhilarating. 'Either God is going to heal you ...'

'Or I'm going to die. And heaven's not a bad option.'

'So why waste a year of going backwards and forwards to hospital?'

'Getting infections, having a shit life and not spending any quality time together.'

So maybe God would heal him again, and it would be fine. We just wanted any credit or glory to go to God, like the last time around. It felt radical, especially faced with the expertise built into the walls surrounding us. Walls that put their faith so firmly in drugs and medical procedure.

'Let's make the most of the time we have.'

'And pray like mad!'

'Insane Pray-ers Unlimited?'

'Let's do it.'

A pause.

'The praying insanely or not having treatment?'

'Both.'

Feeling quite rebellious, we went back to the consultants, who suggested yet another option. But we both said that we didn't want to do anything.

'I understand totally. I think I would do the same in your position,' the oncologist said, smiling warmly. 'We always hope that the chemotherapy shrinks the cancer before it shrinks the person, because it does shrink the person as well.'

It is also true that many people who have chemotherapy for primary cancer choose not to have it for secondary cancer. Who wants to repeat a poisonous nightmare and ruin what life is left? The counting down of the days and hours, shelling out the minutes and seconds to buy nothing but uncertainty. We had too many memories of all that.

MIXED TONES
Well, they've just poisoned me again!
The Chemo countdown has dripped through to empty
The counter clicked down six seconds a time
'Til the real countdown begins
'Til it kicks in.
No counter to view
No set time by which it'll wear off you.

Only experience counts here
And it talks with mixed tones:

Pros and cons
Take aways and add ons.
Maybes and possibles
Unlikelies and probables.
Short terms and long terms
Benefits and concerns.
Pay off and prices
Calmness and crises.
Knowns and unknowns
In organs and bones.

Mixed tones.

Rob Lacey, 2002

'You don't have to come to see us.' The consultants slotted pieces of paper back into files and clipped pens back into pockets. Small, simple actions bearing a significance beyond their intention. The patient had decided, and what will follow, will follow.

'If you experience pain or if you feel you want to see us, you can make an appointment anytime. Apart from that, we'll put in a date for January to see how you're doing.'

That was mid-September 2005. We left the hospital feeling quite weird.

No treatment. We couldn't easily get over the crazy thrill of the idea. It was as if all three of us, four counting the baby, had launched out on a bike across a tightrope suspended hundreds of feet above Niagara Falls. A pyramid of acrobats clinging idiotically onto each other whilst pedalling a bicycle unfeasibly small for one, let alone four. And none of us with any previous tightrope experience! But then, what is life without risks? The death sentence had been delivered into our lives again, but now we stood over it instead of it looming over us. I held Rob's arm as we walked, both of us discovering power in the face of powerlessness. Each step we took into that alien landscape of nontreatment brought huge excitement, which grew from an anticipation of what God might do. How strange the sense of strangeness is.

Then came the challenge of telling family and friends. Aware that our decision might, for some, appear as just giving up or opting out, we felt very strongly that we needed to tell both sets of parents immediately so that there could be no doubt or ambiguity. If Rob did die, we didn't want anyone to say, 'Why did you do that? Why didn't you try?' Perhaps we wanted to make a statement of our faith, an expression of the positive view we were taking or just to clarify our position. It was particularly important for Rob's mum and dad to understand our course of action ... or medical inaction.

We needn't have been concerned. Both Rob's parents and my parents responded very positively and stood by us unequivocally. Rob's dad has been ill all his life and is well acquainted with hospitals and extended treatments, so it was reassuring to know he empathised entirely. Some of our brothers and sisters understandably wanted to know why we wouldn't have treatment. It couldn't have been comfortable for them, but after careful explanation and a little time, their love and support joined that of our parents.

So that was it. We had a life to live. We didn't know how long it would be, but then none of us ever do. Why do we human beings so readily entertain complacency and uphold the assumption that the status quo of health and well-being must somehow be intact for all of our time on earth? We assume our invulnerability is somehow guaranteed by right. But then we do aspire to transcend our frailty and weaknesses almost all day, every day. Isn't that why action movies are so popular? The following months revealed how it is possible that strength can be made perfect through weakness – a lesson we learned many times before, but still a vital one that I will return to later.

Rob was very keen to make my second pregnancy as normal as

possible because the first time around, with Lukas, he was undergoing treatment involving nephrostomy tubes inserted into his kidneys. It was extremely unpleasant and proved to be a much worse time for me. I will never forget the effort of having to carry heavy shopping and so on because Rob was too sick to help. I know lots of single mums have to cope, but I was also carrying the worry of whether he would die. I just couldn't enjoy the pregnancy.

By contrast, the last year of Rob's life was good. We had time together. Rob wasn't depressed; in fact, he was quite positive and fighting for wholeness and goodness every day of every week of every month. I think he particularly wanted to give me a good pregnancy because he knew how it had been for me before. The focus shifted, and people would say, 'How's Rob? How's Sandra? How's Lukas? How's the baby?' It wasn't all about The Cancer Victim. Maybe it was because there was no treatment to ask about. It felt good, really good, that friends, family and colleagues asked to have a description of the whole picture of who we were.

For Rob too, the significance of this new life within me became a source of hope. I remember that we had a little time, a break almost, when Rob had finished quite a bit of his writing for *The Liberator*, and he was doing some of the proofreading, which hardly filled his days. I didn't have much to work on either. Lukas was at school, and so we tried to have lunch together and go for coffees in the daytime. It was wonderful. We were just able to be with each other. Just be. Our unborn baby steadily and healthily grew during every precious minute of every precious hour, as if she helped eradicate that possible pit of despair. I look back and see us sipping the froth on our cappuccinos in Coffee 1 on Albany Road or the deli nearby, Rob animated with ideas and future projects and me smiling and listening, one hand on my tummy.

So, not unsurprisingly, life felt almost normal. I remember walking around Roath Park, Rob and me and Lukas, and imagining people watching us and thinking, 'Oh, look at them, what a lovely couple, she's pregnant and they look so happy. They have everything to live for.' And, of course, they couldn't know. So now, when I walk in the same park, it is easy to be jealous of these other families with their husbands and dads. But no sooner has the thought struck me than I correct my attitude. Who knows their story? Most of the time, none of us has the slightest clue what is really happening in other people's lives. Appearances can be very deceptive.

June 2004

Before we had children, in the latter half of the 1990s, we lived in London and used to travel on the tube. Quite often we would pretend we didn't know each other and get on the train using different entrances. During the journey we would flirt across the aisle to each other, slowly moving closer. At the stop where we were supposed to get off, he would invite me for coffee, and I would recklessly answer, 'Yeah, okay, why not?' We giggled to ourselves as we left our bemused and somewhat shocked audience behind. Another time we actually ended up kissing passionately before hopping out onto the platform. This was my husband, the man who had once been advised to leave his job in banking when his boss discovered him doing a headstand on an office swivel chair. These small, and some would say insignificant, examples of Rob's behaviour aid the understanding of a personality shot through with creativity.

It knew no bounds and, combined with Rob's impish humour, would make for some memorable moments. I have always loved chocolate spread. When we were still newly married and having breakfast one day, I set down the knife I had just used to spread Nutella on my toast. While I went out of the room briefly, Rob dipped the knife into some Marmite and replaced it exactly where it had been. Upon my return, true to my habit, I innocently sucked the knife, expecting to finish up the chocolate residue. Yuk. This didn't disappoint Rob, who roared gleefully for a full half hour. I can still see him laughing, his head thrown backwards, his whole body pulsating with pleasure. I was mystified by Marmite ... it took quite a while to understand the quirky English taste for salty brown gunk.

Rob's incurable playfulness was key to his creativity. He even played jokes on himself. Once, whilst touring on his own, he stopped to eat at a service station. I think he must have been pretty fed up and tired because he loosened the lids to the salt and the pepper so he would 'accidentally' sprinkle a pile onto his plate! Yes, touring on your own for weeks on end does get to you. Is it any wonder that some people view us artists slightly askance at times.

These are the kinds of fragments of life with Rob which I am immensely grateful to be able to access so readily in my memory. Rob made himself unforgettable, even to the slightest acquaintance ... so how much more then for me? He and I worked, lived and loved as one. It is quite possible that if somebody were to compare the amount of time Rob and I spent together with that of a couple who work apart from each other, week in and week out, our ten years of marriage could equal their twenty. Every aspect of our lives was intertwined with the next. His respect for me as a professional dancer was second to none, and he often expressed great pride in referring to me as 'My International Dancer/Choreographer.' Few people realised how much input he had into my dance pieces. We utterly respected, trusted and supported each other's work, he in the Christian sector and me in the more secular Arts sector. We each became the other's outlet, which made for a very fulfilling professional life.

Of all the things that I have written in my notebook since Rob died, most of which is far too personal to share publicly, I find one telling section: 'Rob, you helped me find the real me. I became more me when I was with you. Together we both became the best we could be.' Unquestionably, we were made for each other. It was the sort of combination that could easily give credence to the popular phrase 'a marriage made in heaven.' I now realise, though, how much Rob had turned that the other way round, as he so often did. He made heaven in our marriage.

Rob had an insatiable appetite for the life God gives, and he wrung out the very last drop of goodness that he could. Our daughter Magdalena was three weeks and three days old when Rob died on 1st May 2006. We had wanted a girl so much. I had wanted a husband so much. Rob had wanted a better body so much. But his selflessness and optimism would still surface despite his physical condition. Breastfeeding Lena every three hours that first few weeks of her life became exhausting. I would often find myself crying and praying for Lena to sleep longer. Of course, throughout that time there was the constant concern over Rob's well-being. I didn't know how I could continue to cope, feeling so drained and so wretched. Once when Lena was a week old, just before Easter that year, Rob came tottering down the stairs at two in the morning and sat next to me on the settee. I couldn't believe my eyes; he was too weak for this kind of exertion. As I held her to my breast, he lowered his head gently onto my shoulder. His voice was soft.

'Now I'm getting better, I want to help you,' he said. Neither of us could know that he would die just a fortnight later.

One of Rob's journal entries during October 2005:

'I'm going to die anyway, so what's the point? I want to die fully alive so my soul's got extended capacity for heaven.'

So, slowly now, I will pick up the fragments from the floor and start to assemble them into the full story, but to do that I must go back, back much further. To Germany and Sweden just after I had finished school, age nineteen.

Chapter 2
Half the Story

*Think of a number, add a trillion, and times it by the number of
trees and we're getting there: we're talking huge!*

The Word on the Street by Rob Lacey, page 27

Ludwigsstadt is a beautiful small town that can't help behaving
like a village. Google Earth doesn't do it justice; you need to have
your feet firmly on the ground and look up at the hills clothed in
deep pine tree green. The first time Rob visited me and my family
there, he spread his arms wide at the view, simply smiled and said,
'Millions of trees!' This was where I was born and grew up. Ludwigsstadt is on the east side of northern Bavaria in the middle of
Germany, level with Frankfurt and almost halfway between Berlin
to the north and Munich to the south.

Rob made this his home as much as it was mine, and for that
I will always be deeply grateful. Perhaps it was because the green
rolling hills reminded him of mid-Wales, perhaps because he loved
the whole idea of mountains bringing you closer to God. Or perhaps he had very little choice in the matter, since the place is so very
much a part of me. If he loved me, then he had to love my home!
When I was growing up, the train line stopped at Ludwigsstadt.
This was before the Berlin Wall came down and East Germany was

very close, just five kilometres over the hills. But as far as everyone on our side of the border was concerned, the world ended in Ludwigsstadt. No need to go any farther. And who would want to? My town was the best place in all the world: a rich countryside valley that was hot in the summer and boasted an outdoor swimming pool, plus thick snow in the winter and a ski lift on the mountain that stood opposite our wood-clad blue and cream house on one side of the valley.

My parents have lived in this big house with its big garden all their lives. You can't drive right up to it; the final approach is by foot up a path. As you pass my mother's wild and pretty garden, the unmistakeable aroma of a wood-burning stove welcomes you, just before you step in from the well-used veranda.

When I finished my A levels at the Kaspar-Zeuß-Gymnasium in Kronach, in June 1992, at age nineteen, I didn't know what to do. Should I become a PE teacher or a physiotherapist? Basically, I was a gymnast. That summer I stayed with my older sister Katja who, being five years my senior, was living as a student in Nuremberg. I worked as a shop assistant there in Benetton selling clothes and really enjoying my almost grown-up status. It was during those weeks of invigorating city life, walking the warm streets, taking in the smell of new fabrics as I sorted garments on rails, that I formulated adventurous ideas—ideas that, unknown to me, would bring Rob and me together. I had already decided to do a gap year in Sweden starting that September. It was with a Christian organisation, Kreativ Mission, which provided opportunities for imaginative outreach. They ran a one-year discipleship course called Dropparna involving Bible training, mime, dance, theatre and other artistic means of expression and communication, equipping its gap-year students with outreach ideas.

It was all very new to me, and I wasn't very confident. I was especially unsure whether people would understand me. We all spoke English, but my schoolgirl attempts couldn't reflect the real me. How could I make jokes? How could I do funny voices? Of course, I needn't have worried. The team I worked with were great fun, and we enjoyed the creative challenges given to us. A group of us devised and rehearsed about fourteen different short performance pieces to take out around Sweden, Finland and Norway. There was also a three-week trip to Romania. Most of the performance pieces had to transcend language difficulties, so a more physical expression was required, and this suited me very well. One of the Kreativ Mission leaders, Vibeka Muasya, said I ought to think about becoming a professional dancer because I was talented. It was the first time that somebody whose opinion I respected professionally had seen dance potential in me; I didn't even know I had it. All I was certain of at that time was that I was a gymnast and that physical performance work was something I enjoyed.

Following weeks of anxious prayer about my future, I discovered the phrase 'movement theatre' in my head. I didn't know where I got it from, but it seemed to nestle into a comfortable corner of my consciousness, enticing and exciting me with possibilities. Finally, someone told me about a mime and physical theatre school in London run by Desmond Jones.* *Ah,* I thought, *so that's where I need to be.* The fact that even as I had this thought, Rob was already taking the course has, in retrospect, always seemed tantalising. It was as if our search for each other began with both of us exploring physical challenges—a significant theme which would manifest itself in more ways than one, so positively and so negatively, as time would roll on.

My whole experience of God during that gap year in Sweden was rock solid, a firm foundation. Now, looking back, I realise it needed to be, given all the cancer crap that was to follow. So that's where I was heading, to Desmond Jones in London.

But then, there was the dream.

---

* The Desmond Jones School of Mime and Physical Theatre closed in 2004 after 25 years.

I saw Rob and loved him for six months before I knew of his existence. The dream came to me at Easter 1993. It was so strong, so unmistakable ... so Rob. Just after Christmas that year, we had been performing again, and I started thinking about wanting a husband. I'd had boyfriends – not very many, but enough to realise that there was now a need in me to marry, to have a husband. It wasn't enough anymore simply to have a boyfriend, like an accessory. I wanted to share my whole life with somebody. A husband. The thought had a certainty about it. I have, after all, always been someone who knows her own mind.

At the end of a performance that Easter, an older man who had been sitting in the front row came up to me and, after offering praise and thanks for what we had just performed, started pouring out his life story. His wife was mentally ill and confined to an institution, his life was a struggle and so on. Being the diligent, obedient, nice Christian that I thought I should be, I was very sympathetic and understanding. We were standing in a hall with a staircase, just the two of us. I completely missed the danger signals, so determined was I that perhaps I could lead this man to the point of accepting Christ into his life. But instead of opening up his heart to God, he opened up his trousers. Suddenly I was trapped, and he was pressing in closer and closer. Of course, I freaked out, ducked under his arm and ran to where all the other people were, taking shelter with the guys on the team.

Distraught and disturbed, I cried bitterly. The sense that I was a piece of meat in a cattle market was overwhelming and dehumanising. I needed to feel safe, I had to be safe. All I could return to were those thoughts about being loved and cherished. Thoughts about a husband. And so that night, still shaky and vulnerable, I fell asleep and then fell in love with a man who, quite literally, turned out to be the man of my dreams. Where do dreams end and visions begin? I don't know. All I do know is that God gave me this very precious and important experience of Rob six months before I met him: A young curly-haired man with round glasses cycling on a red racing bike. His wheels swish, passing lots of big trees along a beautiful track or road. He has blue eyes and dark hair and is wearing a striped shirt and blue dungarees.

And that was it. Simple. Clear. Uncomplicated. It was sharply focused and very filmic. As I was having the dream, I realised that this was my husband-to-be, and I was getting a sneak preview.

It was as if God said, 'Look, this is who I've got for you. Relax.' When I awoke, the reassurance and refreshment were tangible. Once I actually met Rob, I had forgotten all about the dream. It wasn't until after our honeymoon some weeks later when I remembered it. All the facts fell into place, and every one of them, except one, was true. During Rob's year at Desmond Jones, he did cycle on a red racer down a tree-lined route through Ealing Common to Shepherd's Bush in West London every day. The hair, the eyes, the glasses, the striped shirt were absolutely perfect. Rob's jaw dropped when I told him. The laughter of amazement when he corroborated the facts was matched only by the hoots of derision at the mention of dungarees. No way would he have been seen dead in dungarees! We liked to think of that as God's joke. Rob's taste in clothes was always on the adventurous and colourful side, but he had some limits ...

But why had I forgotten the dream? It is unusual for me to forget important and life-changing occurrences such as that. Perhaps it might have added undue pressure to our relationship in those early days. Rob's first marriage had ended very painfully; he needed an opportunity to get used to the idea that he might want to get married again. So it was good to give him the time and space to do that, even though I didn't realise at the time that this was why the dream had dropped off my radar. Sometimes there may be a very good reason why we can't see the obvious.

By May 1993, I had written to Desmond Jones and had been offered a place starting in September. My mind was made up. I said good-bye to the friends I had made in Sweden and travelled back home to Ludwigsstadt. I went ahead and made arrangements. The ferry was booked. I had inherited my sister's unwanted car, which was older than I was. And Kreativ Mission put me in touch with Carina Persson, a Swedish dancer living in London, who sorted out some accommodation for me with a couple from her church in Ealing. Mum and Dad were not exactly keen to see me going off to England on my own.

'Sandra, it's such a long way, you can't drive it all by yourself.'

'I can, I can. I know I can.'

'No. Look, the ferry to Dover leaves at five in the morning. You'll have to drive through the night. It's not safe.'

'I'll be fine ...'

'You'll get lost and you could even miss the ferry. It's not as easy as you think ...'

I could tell that their objections to all the practical implications ran deeper for them. Their youngest child, already having spent a year away in another country, was now going off to a different foreign place. Also, the prospect of earning a living from mime is rather different from being a qualified physiotherapist. But they knew my mind was made up.

'Okay, at least let us come with you to Calais, to make sure you don't get lost.'

I picture the scene in monochrome, the camera barely finding the beautiful young German woman through the torrents of rain on the windscreen, a droning double bass and a sonorous clarinet wail as her wheels spin rhythmically through the spray. Perhaps a Herzog scene – no, Truffaut. Of course, the film is sliding from Germany into France. Maybe it would turn into a Hitchcock over the English Channel, although hopefully not, perhaps more David Lean. Brooding skies surround the small car battling on, its young driver hooks her hair behind an ear. She narrows her eyes, as if searching for more than the wet road stretching out ahead.

What will become of her? As she drives, what's driving her? But, as always, I must swap the cinema in my head for the real world ... and I'm never quite as beautiful as she is. And, anyway, it was my brother at the wheel.

Frank drove my car and my parents drove theirs. I was about to turn twenty-one and had always wanted to visit London. Now I was going to live there. So Mum, Dad and my brother were my escort, despite the fact that I now owned one made by Ford in bright yellow and rust. The four of us set off on the first long leg from Ludwigsstadt to Calais. I was heading towards an exciting new adventure in the big city, an adventure in physical theatre and, later, dance. I remember there were huge rain showers, and one of my windscreen wipers broke. Somehow my brother was able to fix it, and I remember watching that wiper for the rest of the journey with eagle eyes, every *swish* and *swoosh*, praying it would hold out. Which it did. I think it was especially hard for Mum to say good-bye, but I left all three of them there on French soil ... or Calais concrete. Mum said later how traumatic it was watching the large ferry swallow up her little girl.

I was exhausted, but couldn't sleep on the boat; everything was so new to me, and I was worried about driving on the wrong side of the road, getting lost in London and missing my appointed time to arrive at my digs – nine o'clock that same morning. Driving off the ferry saw the start of my nightmare: I forgot to put my lights on, I was instantly on the wrong side of the road, there were roadworks, confusion. I got lost. Then, fleetingly, I saw a lorry which said, 'London to Munich – Munich to London'. Thankfully, I chose one that was going the right way. It was an answer to prayer on wheels. I stuck to it like glue, and it went exactly the correct route, the M25 onto the M4 and into West London. I wonder to this day what the driver thought about the blonde girl following him in a bright yellow car all the way from Dover.

Just when I thought everything was going to be okay, I got

lost on the Chiswick Flyover roundabout. If I failed to meet my landlord by nine to pick up the key, I'd be locked out all day. Time was ticking by, but could I find the correct exit off that horrendous road system? I shouted to anyone and everyone as I tried each road, the level of panic rising. Every exit I attempted was the wrong one. Even the right road seemed like the wrong road; all I had was a photocopied map with a highlighted route. Eventually I found it, more by luck than judgment. Not surprisingly, the correct route is now emblazoned upon my memory.

With seconds to spare, I found the place. David and Wendy Kennett-Brown and their family proved to be lovely hosts. Wendy gave me the key that morning and left me to it. I decided to get some fish and chips after I had unpacked, simply to experience something typically English. It gave me very bad food poisoning. My introduction to the whole family involved crawling to the toilet and moaning for a few days. It was not a good start. Being ill in someone else's house – particularly someone you've only just met – is not the best plan. It also meant that I couldn't begin the mime school straightaway.

When I did, the course was fantastic. I also settled into St John's Church, in Ealing, very quickly, and one Sunday I spotted a rather handsome young man among the pews. It turned out that he was an actor who had done the same course at Desmond Jones the previous year. So of course we had plenty to discuss when we eventually found the courage to talk to each other. As I said, you can sometimes not notice the hand in front of your face. His name was Rob Lacey.

He told me later that when he saw me around the same time, he thought, *Hmm, how do I get to know somebody like that?* It would be nice to think that it was the exact same moment that I spotted him.

There was lots of small talk. He explained how he had been in a theatre company, but was now starting to perform on his own, having done the mime school the preceding year. I talked about Sweden and the performances in prisons, schools, universities and so on. We established a lot of common ground, and I thought it was great that he was doing similar outreach work. But there were so many things I didn't see, quite apart from the fact that this was the man from my dream. I couldn't know how hurt he had been by the breakup of his marriage together with the theatre company he had founded. I didn't see the vulnerable Rob whose depression was only just leaving him after two years of separation leading to a divorce settlement. I had no idea of the struggle within him and the heart-searching worry whether he could ever have a relationship again. All I did know was that this man had sparkling eyes, a great sense of humour, a lovely voice and was a great performer with a captivating presence.

That Christmas I went back to Germany and naively left my car parked by the tube station for two weeks. When I got back, it had been broken into, the battery was flat and nothing worked. Staring up at the rain, I wondered, *What am I doing here?* I'd left my family in the picturesque snow-covered mountains of Bavaria, and here I was stranded on a dismal and sodden foreign street. To make matters worse, my father had developed a lump in his groin, and there was the suspicion that it was cancer. I felt wretched. Dave Kennett-Brown rescued me, and that same night I went to see Rob performing solo *The Twelve Days of Christmas* in St John's Crypt. My spirits lifted. He was so alive, so entertaining and engaging. For just a second or two, I looked around at the rest of the audience enjoying this funny and lovable man. I felt proud of him. And then I knew: I was falling in love with him.

I loved him? My smile felt broader than all the smiles, all the laughter that the small audience could generate that night. But I had to keep my distance. This wouldn't do. I couldn't possibly throw myself at him. That wasn't how it was supposed to happen. How could my romantic girlhood dreams of being rescued or swept off my feet come true if I made it too obvious how I felt? And so it was that my Keep Your Distance Campaign kicked in. I wanted him to notice me. After that performance, I decided that I would just go and talk to him, calmly, as a friend. It worked just fine. When I left him, I didn't see his very big smile as he watched me go.

As time wore on, I became more shy and apprehensive and far too nervous to talk to him. I felt silly because I really did want to get to know him. By February the following year, it had become ridiculous. All I could think about was Rob. I became the dumb blonde starring in my own inconsequential romantic comedy, blundering around in a dream. Everywhere I seemed to go, I bumped into Rob – a musical montage of me unexpectedly seeing him across the room at a party, or finding myself next to him at a concert, or suddenly walking towards him in the street and not knowing what to do. Whatever was the screenwriter doing? It was far too contrived to be believable. I even burnt myself on the oven once because my head was filled with nothing but Rob as I drifted around the kitchen. It had to stop. I certainly wouldn't part with good money to watch this 'eye candy' film. So I said to God that either he should take away these feelings for Rob or at some point he needed to bring us together. I wanted to be normal; I didn't want to pretend that I was this stupid, shy little airhead. But I became more and more shy to the point where I didn't even talk to Rob! He mustn't know I was in love with him. I couldn't surrender my romantic ideal.

Then Rob's friend Dale, who had been on the mime course with him, asked me out to the cinema. Being from a different culture, I wasn't sure how to interpret this, so I asked Carina, with whom I had struck up a friendship, how to interpret it.

'Don't worry, Sandra, it doesn't necessarily mean that you'll be going out.'

'It could be tricky because I'm interested in someone else.'

'Oh, really? Who's that?'

I think I might have blushed when I replied that it was Rob. Carina's reaction was astonishment.

'Rob? Really? Rob? No!... ROB?'

'Rob.'

'Rob?'

'Rob.'

I wondered momentarily whether we had been robbed of every word other than *Rob*. Carina's incredulity eventually gave way to her explanation that he was still getting over a long-term relationship. I assumed immediately that he had been engaged; little did I know at that stage about the marriage and divorce.

'Please don't tell him,' I said, regaining my composure. 'I don't want him to know.'

I think that perhaps my instinct was telling me that Rob might be my other half – my life partner – and I didn't want to risk spoiling everything at that stage. It had to happen properly. It couldn't be half-baked.

From then on Carina and her husband, John, tried matchmaking us by contriving opportunities for Rob and me to be together. Being performers, they were rehearsing a mime-dance piece and asked if I would come along to watch and give some feedback. They had already asked Rob to watch it. But what did I know? Carina was an accomplished dancer and John was a very good mime. I was a bit surprised they asked me, only being halfway through the mime school course and a novice, but it was a relaxed and positive discussion and, of course, I got to be with Rob. On another occasion, Rob needed a lift because he had left his bike somewhere. He told me afterwards that I was very chatty and relaxed, slapping his knee playfully as I drove. I thought nothing of it, being quite tactile, but Rob responded, 'Ooh, that's nice ...' and laughed.

Then Rob's other friend from church, Colin, started showing an interest in me. So there I was, Dale on the one hand, Colin on the other, both of them Rob's close friends, and me in the middle with eyes only for Rob! By this time, Rob had already discovered I was keen on him, but I still didn't know that he knew. Then both Colin and Dale left the country, Colin to France and Dale to Sweden. Who could believe it? Almost as though it had been orchestrated. Rob later told the story with great comic effect of how his apparent competition simply evaporated, 'Almost unbelievably, the two of them just vanished! Swallowed up somewhere in mainland Europe.'

In reality, however, it wasn't that straightforward for him to have a relationship with me. There was some painful history for him to come to terms with. His first wife had unexpectedly left him, and the hurt had run very deep. Understandably, Rob shied away from entertaining the thought that anything serious could be happening between us.

I'LL HAVE THAT

You saw my hardness
And you said,
'I'll have that.
Collect it.
Melt it down.
Smelt it into an iron nail—
Reckon there's a good six inches in there.
Then I'll let them drive it through the hands of my
*   carpenter son who made it.'*

You saw my sharpness
And you said,
'I'll have that.
Collect it.
Graft it onto the tips of a local thorn bush.
Reckon there's a good crown's worth in there.
Then I'll let them press it into the skull that hosts the radical
*   mind of my son who invented sharp.'*

You saw my bitterness

And you said,
'I'll have that.
Collect it.
Press it down.
Liquidise it into vinegar.
Reckon there's a good sponge full in there.
Then I'll let them thrust it into the sweetest lips ever to smile
   on the earth.'

Rob Lacey, November 2001

On the night of Colin's good-bye party, Rob and I chatted and arranged that he would join me at a gymnastics class for actors and performers which I had been attending at Covent Garden. When we met up the following Wednesday, it was raining and Rob was holding an umbrella. Almost without thinking and very naturally, I slotted my hand into the crook of his arm. We started attending the class regularly, and he eventually learned to do a back flip. Hmm, I thought, any guy who can learn a back flip has automatically got this gymnast's attention!

On the day of Dale's good-bye party, which was a picnic at the beginning of May, Rob arrived late and could only stay for about half an hour. After he left, Dale shouted to me across the crowd of people, 'So, you fancy my mate then?'

My shock and embarrassment were obvious.

'What!' My annoyance kicked in. 'How do you know?'

'Everybody knows! Even Rob knows!'

I was fuming and left immediately with a friend, ranting all the way home. It was all the wrong way round. I wanted him to love me first and then me to love him. So I started playing slightly hard to get and turned down some of Rob's invitations to meet up. I reasoned that if he wasn't interested in me, if he didn't like me, he would just give up. I decided not to panic and just wait to see what would happen. I didn't have to wait long. Rob was very friendly and wanted to spend time with me.

I had brought a little cappuccino machine from Germany because, back then, it was extremely rare to find good cappuccinos anywhere in Britain; it was all instant coffee everywhere I went. After church one Sunday, I wondered whether the prospect of a proper espresso or a latté would appeal to Rob. If I was going to invite a man back for an actual cup of coffee, I was determined it was going to be a very good one! Afterwards we decided to go for a riverside walk from Kew to Richmond. Setting off in the car down Gunnersbury Lane, we hit heavy traffic. Normally it would have taken only ten minutes to get to Kew, but it actually took almost an hour. I don't think it was the caffeine that caused us to chat animatedly and jokingly as my sister's yellow jalopy carried us towards the Thames at less than walking pace.

Sometimes there are those special days that seem quite exceptional. Sometimes those special days require no effort of imagination at all to transform into entrancing filmic adventures. Sometimes the heightened awareness, the physical sensations and the knowledge of the importance of what is unfolding around you create a whole new level of exhilaration and perception. Sometimes it is nothing short of being life-defining, as if destiny has taken a grip. And gripped we most definitely were. It is also the case that relating every moment of what happened between us would, in so many ways, only serve to diminish the beauty and the wonder that we discovered in each other. So I will create just a snapshot or two … stills from the film, I suppose you could say.

We told each other our life story, all about our families, our upbringing and so on. It was honest, relaxed and natural. It took an hour and a half to walk to Richmond in the May sunshine. Puddles on the path caused us to move apart and then back together every now and then. Sometimes our shoulders touched. The longer the walk went on, the more we wanted to stay together. At Richmond we had an ice cream, then a beer and then we walked back, all the time delighting in listening to one another. On our return, I got blisters on my heels, so I took my shoes off and walked barefoot.

Before finally getting into the car, we went down some very narrow steps that led to the Thames so I could wash my feet. Squashed side by side, we sat and, as that ancient river gently lapped the glistening stone, we kissed.

Rob was shaking with joy. We held hands back to the car.

'So ... are we going out then?' I was biting my lip.

'Yeah ... maybe.'

We looked at each other and laughed.

'Why don't we go out tonight? To celebrate?'

'Yeah, yeah. Let's have a meal.'

'Why don't we drive into town? Right into London. I've never driven right to the centre.'

'Okay, it'll be great.' Rob beamed. 'I'll direct you ... let's do it!'

Later on we arrived at Leicester Square, parked for three hours, which took a large chunk out of our meagre resources, and went into Chinatown to eat. The antics and drumming of the performers and street musicians created the sort of vibrant London evening that lives up to tourist expectation. So we stood and watched, Rob behind me with his arms around my tummy. It was perfect. I wondered then whether this was the start of something wonderful. It was a thrilling end to a thrilling day, although, to be honest, we were so taken with each other, we could have stared at a brick wall all night and been delighted.

Three weeks later Mum and Dad came to visit me in London for the first time, together with my sister and her husband and my brother. It was a Sunday in June. Mum and Dad knew a little about Rob because I had talked about him at Christmas time. Of course, that had been long before we started seeing each other, so I hardly knew him at that point. My family had followed the story to some degree, but were taken aback completely when I introduced them to Rob after church. 'Oh, that's Rob, look ... I have to go and rehearse now, but why don't you go to the pub together, and I'll see you after rehearsal. Bye!'

I almost shoved them through the door and ran off. Rob didn't speak German, Mum and Dad didn't speak much English, and my brother and sister and her husband could only manage their school-taught versions at that time. Two hours later, I returned. I heard the laughter from outside before I ran into the pub. Ten glasses of Guinness stood on the table, and everyone was roaring, tears of joy rolling down their cheeks. For a second or two, I stood there with my mouth open wondering how on earth I had thought that they might not get on.

My father, incredibly, was speaking his six-week correspondence course English, making an absurd speech about the proletarians of all nations uniting under Marxism. Dad liked talking about politics, but doing it in a foreign language was another thing. Every single member of my family and Rob was helpless with mirth. They could hardly contain themselves. It was wonderful. Rob joked afterwards that it hadn't been so bad meeting 'the in-laws', after having feigned such nervousness at the prospect. In fact, he made the rather remarkable discovery that Germans do have a sense of humour after all. But clearly, he had disarmed and charmed them and, somehow, managed to share jokes and stories as only Rob could. I would have willingly parted with an immense fortune to witness those two hours as a fly on the wall.

Despite really liking each other and despite this new status of 'going out together', there was still an uncertainty between the two of us. Of course, we talked a lot. Mainly in the pub. Talk talk talk. It was brilliant, but whenever we said good-bye to each other, it was always, 'See you then,' the casual nature of which naturally implies that you might not.

About three months in, we were talking (you know where), and I said to this wonderful Welshman, 'I really like you, I really want to be with you, I feel ...' I didn't want to talk about marriage or getting engaged, but just from a commitment point of view, I said, 'I really think we should ... be together properly. You know, not just see what happens.' I realised it was a really big thing for him. His eyes still reflected the hurt from the divorce and, coupled with all the worry and scariness of what another relationship might bring, it was no wonder that he moved tentatively towards me.

I went back to Germany that August.

'Why don't you come?' I knew he wanted to, and he smiled. In those early days Rob always used to say, 'There's something wrong with you.' Of course, I'd pretend to be a little shocked.

'Because you are just perfect. Everything's so right, but there must be something wrong, there must be.' My invitation served as a way to complete his picture of me, and he knew it.

'Why don't you come and see where I'm from?' So he flew out to join me later that month. Clearly, my parents were keen to meet him again. I think my dad shopped far and wide to get some Guinness in. Amid the beauty of the trees, the mountains and the flowers, Rob grinned.

'Now I know why you are who you are. Because you know you are loved, by your family, your land and ... I don't know ... Everything!'

Our relationship shifted towards commitment. Rob held me. *'Ich liebe dich.'*

To tell me for the first time was wonderful. To tell me in my own tongue moved me deeply.

'I love you too.' We had each found our other half. Our separate stories could become one. And for Rob, his past hurts could be healed and new life could grow.

HALF THE STORY

He died to save me
But I don't want half the story:
He rose again to bring me life.

Half the story ...
Like a play called Romeo
Like a book – Tale of One City
Like a joke with no punchline
Like a story with no point.

Like a light with no bulb
Like a clock with no arms
Like a cello with no strings
Like the land with no farms.

Like a flower with no petals
Like a tune with no notes
Like an unlived-in home
Like a marina with no boats.

Like chewing on powdered milk
Like pushing a taxi home
Like unfermented wine
Like an unfinished poem.

Rob Lacey, 1997

I knew at this point that I wanted to marry him. I thought,
If he asks me to marry him, I'd say yes right now. We went so well
together, enjoying physical and sporty activities such as volleyball,
squash, gymnastics, even climbing trees. Both of us were fit and
healthy. Rob was ten years older than I was, but that seemed fine
too. I was used to growing up as the baby of my family, and I had
friends who were much older. So I reflected on why I wanted to
marry him, counting all the reasons, from his performance skills to
his silliness. From his depth of feeling and thought to his frivolity.
His character, who he was and not just what he did. And as I continued this wonderfully gratifying line of thought, I found myself
realising something I hadn't expected at all. One particular thought
arrived with great clarity.

There was no mistaking it. It was conscious and it was true. I
wanted to make a marriage that really counted for the two of us,
of course, but especially for Rob. Whatever it took. His heart had
been broken once before, and my determination rose up like the
mountains surrounding Ludwigsstadt. As I look back on it now, I
am still amazed that I arrived at the thought the way I did. Perhaps

it was my first inkling that God might have something remarkable in store. Perhaps it was a prayer. Perhaps it was simply an innocent expression of a newfound love. Perhaps it was an understanding of the cost of bringing heaven down to earth. Or perhaps it was all of these things mixed together. The thought, which was unexpected and unusual, was this:

I would marry this man even if he was in a wheelchair.

Chapter 3
Big Moments

Eight years old and far from tired, a mischievous Robert Lacey sat
on his bed one night trying to sell his bedroom wallpaper to his
mother ... in a German accent. The bold swirls and colours of the
late 1960s design clearly fed his imagination, quite apart from his
avoiding the issue of going to bed. But the fact that he decided on
a German accent is something I find hilarious. And so did most
other people as the story entered family folklore.

Young Rob could charm and entertain audiences of all
ages even then, and some of the tactics he employed were unexpected – such as running from his primary school teacher, racing
around and around the classroom to avoid capture after having
done something naughty. Or putting on a girl's swimming cos-
tume at age nine in order to enter a girls-only event at a swimming
gala – and winning. Or, on the day before his tenth birthday, when
traditionally his family gave a treat for turning double figures, perhaps a big ice cream or something similar, Rob piped up, 'Today is
the last day of *not* being in double figures, so can I have something
now as well?' Or knitting a jumper out of plasticised waterproof-
ing material at age sixteen and wearing it in the shower to test it.
Or disobeying his father's wish that he should not play rugby and
finding great success on the school team as a try-scoring winger
because he ran extremely fast in order to avoid being tackled and
sustaining injuries that he might have to explain. Or, on A-Level
results day, telling his father on the phone, 'I've got two Apples and

a Dog' – instead of 'two As and a D' – so he could evade the issue of getting a poor grade in maths when academic expectations were high in his family.

Born in Cardiff, Wales, on 25th July 1962, Rob was the third child of Brian and Win Lacey. His brothers, Derek and Peter, were four and two years older, respectively, while his sister, Gill, was four years his junior. Rob's family history already carried a legacy of public speaking, which would manifest itself in him. In the 1930s Rob's grandfather, Harry Lacey, was very well known and respected as a captivating preacher among the Brethren community. He even received invitations to preach in the US, which, in those days, was remarkable. Harry was father initially to four boys, including Rob's father, Brian. As a result of rheumatic fever at age sixteen, Brian suffered heart damage and was left with a lifelong condition preventing him from leading a physically active life. Rob's memories of growing up included a dad whose lack of energy caused him to sit in a chair most of the time. Later in life, Rob's own illness helped to foster a greater understanding of his dad, and their relationship deepened.

Harry's first wife had died suddenly, and a second marriage gave him two more children. As Rob grew up in the 1960s, his step-uncle David became close to him, giving Rob time and treats when Brian wasn't able. Later on, Rob's older brother also fulfilled the role, so he experienced three important male role models within a loving and supportive family.

Rob also developed a keen sense of justice. At school he would often get into trouble for telling the truth in difficult situations and standing up for other children who were blamed for misdemeanors that were not theirs. This didn't go down especially well when the teacher was obviously at fault.

At the age of nine, Rob was the Welsh junior swimming champion at backstroke. He saw the funny side of this: 'Most people get prizes for going forwards. I got them for going backwards.' He would train three or four times a week and attend lots of swimming galas. He loved to swim and, in later years, when cancer prevented him, he would always hanker after the joy of being in the water. Rob also played cello for the Cardiff County Youth Orchestra, but always managed to hide himself in the back row, perhaps the only example of any performance shyness on his part.

December 1969,
Rob at seven

Summer 1971, Rob, aged nine,
sells coat hangers from his father's shop

Sundays were always spent at Bethesda Gospel Hall in Rhiwbina, Cardiff—morning, noon and night. It was an encouraging youth pastor who urged Rob to first have a go at drama, and Rob's early attempts at performance were eye-catching, sometimes for the wrong reasons, perhaps, knowing Rob. But it was here too that he later found himself in trouble for the sake of others. An unmarried teenage couple who were part of the Brethren youth fellowship found themselves ostracised because they had conceived a baby together. Rob stood by them despite their being banned from the church, whilst he remained resolutely part of the fellowship himself.

After earning his two Apples and a Dog in 1980, Rob went to Canterbury University to read economics. In those early Thatcher days, his course was well known as being left wing with a strong socialist heritage—and served as yet another example of Rob flying in the face of popular opinion. He studied Third World economics and issues of globalisation and, again, found himself in hot water siding with the marginalised. He also became an active member of the Christian Union, where a friend of his became pregnant. In almost identical circumstances as before, a religious body with which Rob was affiliated rejected the young woman. And once again Rob stood up for the 'accused', supporting her through her finals in her third year. If there was one quality of Christ's behaviour and teaching that Rob embodied, it was favouring the oppressed. Although, of course, there were many other qualities too. One lasting memory of his student days was the visit of the now legendary U2 to Canterbury University. An unmissable opportunity, one would think. But Rob, like a good Christian boy, went along to a Christian Union meeting scheduled for that same night, their prayers no doubt accompanied by distant rhythmic thudding. He did become a great fan of U2's music in years to come and would regale friends with his self-deprecating tale of 'The Day I Didn't See U2'.

Then there was the time Rob did some apple picking in Kent with his friend Richard Mattheson from Cardiff. They stayed in a cottage next to an orchard, all of which was owned by two old ladies who lived next door. For four long weeks, they picked apples and received from the ladies gifts of plum pies, plum jam, plum tarts, plum cakes ... all manner of plum provender, on and on it went. It was an endless supply due to the dozens of plum trees around the perimeter of the orchard. Some of the fare tasted a little dodgy because some of the plums were unripe. Rob and Richard eventually got very fed up with it all, but didn't want to offend the women by refusing the gifts. Late one night, towards the end of the third week, slightly tipsy after probably drinking some plum liqueur, they went walking in the orchard and encountered the offending plum trees.

'I curse these plum trees in the name of Jesus!' joked Rob, and then the two of them sniggered their way to bed. During the night there was a violent thunderstorm, and the next morning revealed broken plum trees, with branches and squashed plums strewn everywhere. The two of them stood agog. Years later, tongue in cheek, Rob would relish telling the story as proof of his divine authority to rewrite the Bible.

After Canterbury, Rob secured a job as a clerk at Lloyd's Bank back home in West Cardiff. Unfortunately, the copper and nickel in the loose change caused eczema to erupt on his fingers, and much later he would quip, 'I was allergic to money, so I became an artist instead.' But health and poverty were not the only reasons he eventually left banking. During one lunch hour, perhaps thinking that his fellow workers might be as bored with their jobs as he was with his, Rob explored the qualities of his revolving office chair. The bemused audience watched as Rob's demonstration of the various things one can do with a swivel chair culminated in his performing a headstand, his tie flopping down over his face as the chair rotated. But the entertainment factor was about to increase a hundredfold when the manager entered the room at that precise moment. An inevitable intake of breath could be heard.

'Perhaps, Robert, you are not suited to a career in banking.' The manager's words ceased as the revolving chair squeaked, slower and slower, into the uncomfortable silence that followed. Rob eased himself down, with a futile smoothing of his hair and tie. The manager left the room shaking his head. Clearly, this young man he had in line to train up as a manager couldn't even manage to keep himself the right way up. Realising that his talents lay elsewhere, Rob escaped from the bank.

Released into the wild at last, Rob turned his thoughts towards performance on a more professional basis. Together with a friend from his Brethren fellowship days, Rob had already done drama as an amateur enterprise for local church-based events. Later, as part of the Trapdoor Theatre Company, Rob and his friend toured a show called *I Spy*, and seeing that they had quite a few bookings for 1987, they decided to launch the enterprise professionally. Also that year Rob was married and his wife subsequently joined Trapdoor, but their relationship lasted only four years. The separation and divorce spelt the end not only of their marriage but also of the theatre company. Trapdoor split up, with one of the members, Diana Parsons, remaining a close friend. Years later Rob wrote in his journal about the marriage breakup: 'I'd have left me if I could have.'

Rob found work with a finance company with a Christian ethos based on Barry Island. He found it extremely difficult reconciling himself to single life after his ex-wife left him. Every time he saw her, he wanted to hide, sometimes becoming sick with the stress. Other friends, already running their own professional theatre company,* advised Rob to train at Desmond Jones School of Mime and Physical Theatre in London, where Rob subsequently studied during 1992 and 1993. During this time his unhappiness

---

* Philip Hawthorn and Rachel Hannyngton of Primary Colours Theatre.

ate into him, and it seemed that he was heading for a breakdown. But the tide was about to turn. He had counselling for that year in London and took a couple of weeks out of his course to holiday in Greece. Lying on a beach, he listened to Van Morrison's 'Brand New Day' and something clicked into place. Rob knew he could make a new start in a new place. He imagined himself as a solo performer somewhere away from Cardiff. And so he began the slow journey to find himself again.

Hindsight does indeed provide many benefits, and one of the greatest in my life is the recognition that Rob and I needed each other so very much. Rob nurtured the emerging dancer in me, and I encouraged a hurt and wary man to emerge more confident and less troubled. Those first endless conversations of discovery about each other's background, family, education, adventures, views and opinions established the foundations for a strong relationship. Our mutual trust, understanding and respect grew quickly. I could not have become the dancer and choreographer I am today without Rob's utter and complete belief in me.

Perhaps in those early days, I was attracted to Rob's fragility as much as to anything else. He was hurt that his best friend and co-founder of Trapdoor married his ex-wife. But Rob was full of grace and forgiveness and, to his dying day, would not lay blame at their feet. It wasn't a conscious recognition. I am sure that when any one of us looks into someone's eyes and regards the face and then adds together all that can be gleaned consciously about that person, there are as many, if not more, unconscious criteria that are also taken into account. Dancers, of course, read physical signs and indications very carefully – we can't help it. Each body holds the story of its past locked into its posture and kinetics. In particular, the face contains within its muscles and features that wonderful mix of genetics and experience that gives each one its unique identity. What I read in those blue eyes and the contours of Rob's face suggested a blend of humour, profundity, kindness, thoughtfulness, depth of understanding, playfulness and vulnerability that was very attractive to me. Whatever had happened in his past that had hurt him, I felt he didn't deserve the circumstances surrounding the failure of his marriage and the ensuing divorce.

During that summer while I was in Germany, I realised that there was no reason to remain in England except to be with Rob. I had finished three terms at Desmond Jones and wondered whether to do a fourth, but Desmond had written to the small number of prospective students saying he would have to cancel because there was not enough interest. So why go back to London?

I had only done one year, and somehow it hadn't yet satisfied my aim to do 'movement theatre'. Yet I didn't feel ready to launch myself into the world as a performer. Rob was brilliant as he listened to my frustrations and doubts. The mime school had come close to equipping me, but I just couldn't suddenly start creating material and, anyway, I had always wanted to go to university. We teased out the elements of 'movement' and 'theatre' as I saw them.

'Which do you want to concentrate on more?' Rob studied my face. 'Which is more fulfilling and gives you the greatest pleasure? You know, what really does it for you?'

'I want to move. I need to move.'

'Your body rather than your house?' Rob looked at me cheekily. I was discovering that he was brilliant at defusing tension whilst still respecting its importance. I couldn't help releasing a chuckle. This man was so good for me.

'My body!' I slapped his knee playfully.

'Why don't you apply to a dance school?'

'I do really miss moving my body ...'

'What is there to lose?'

'Okay ...'

The idea instantly generated the heat of excitement. Rob was right and I knew it.

'There's a place called the Laban Centre,' I said, having noticed it a couple of times.

'Go and knock on their door then.' His smile was more than enough to spur me on.

Had I fully realised just how difficult it is to get into Laban and just how highly respected it is across Europe and the world, I might not have bothered. I would have set my sights somewhat lower. In all innocence, I phoned them up and asked about their intake beginning that September, less than a month away. The reply was informative and efficient, but not unfriendly.

'We audition a year in advance for the three-year degree course. You must realise that people apply from all over the world, but tell me what you've done. What's your background?'

I told her about my gymnastics, my performance experience, the year in Sweden and the mime school. I said a little about when I was a child and always wanting to dance, but never feeling that I could. I was very honest. I accepted her reply readily and gratefully, as if it was to be expected somehow, although I subsequently realised it was little short of a miracle.

'Well now, you've certainly got the experience behind you, and we don't have time for an audition because it's only two weeks before the start of the year. Look, why don't you come along on the day, for the levelling class. This is when new students get put into the different levels, and we'll have a look at you. That can be your audition.'

I think Rob was more excited than I was.

Red as a tomato, I stumbled and tripped my way through the class. My gaucheness was matched only by my embarrassment. Again innocently, I had placed myself on the front row as the tutor led us through the exercises and steps. I had no one in front of me to follow or to hide behind, and it soon became obvious that I was about five moves adrift from everyone else. The first session was contemporary dance. There had been talk of 'contemporary dance' in the changing room, but I had only a few basic ideas what that was. I'd seen a few dance shows, but that was all. The second session was ballet. What on earth was a *grande battement*? What did *frappé* mean? Physically I was able to do what was being asked of me because I was strong and very flexible as a gymnast, but my brain couldn't process the demands quickly enough. It was going dreadfully; there was no way they were going to accept me. I tried desperately to concentrate, battling with my reactions. *Please, floor, open up and swallow me right now.* As the class finished and everyone mopped up the copious amounts of sweat, I imagined Rob consoling me, playing out the scene in my head.

'You did your best.'

'It was dreadful. I was dreadful.'

'You could never be dreadful. That's impossible. Don't worry, it was only the first ...'

'Sandra Harnisch?' I turned to look at the tutor. She was smiling. 'Can we offer you a place?'

The description 'stunned silence' didn't come into it, I was utterly dumbfounded. Had she confused me with someone else? No, she had called my name.

'We can see you haven't done any dancing, but you've got great potential. We like the raw material we see in your body and believe you will respond well to training. So we'll give you a chance. All right, we'll have you up until Christmas as a trial. Three months and then we'll reassess you. I hope you're ready for some very hard work?'

I must have mumbled something positive and full of gratitude. I could already hear Rob's gleeful laughter and imagine his ensuing celebration. Somebody must have dropped out and they were down on numbers, but that logic was as remote for me as were my chances of entry to Laban itself. Suddenly I could be a degree student! A degree student doing dance! Me! Rob would already be leaping round the room if he knew.

'You do realise that the first year fee is £7,000?' She looked at me kindly. Thank goodness that the audition relied on my physical and not verbal dexterity. I fumbled for a response. A shadow of doubt clouded her expression slightly.

'Are you able to pay?'

'Er, yes. Yes!' Mum and Dad had been putting money aside for my higher education, and I hoped there was enough in this Harnisch pot. It was September 1994, and now I had another reason to stay in London. Rob embraced my new opportunity as if it were his own, and I did move my body . . . and house. I settled into a shared house in Catford.

Rob's and my relationship deepened, and we spent Christmas that year with my family in Germany. Rob returned on his own for the New Year because one of his close friends had become engaged and there was a party. Amid the celebrations, his friend had an argument with his fiancée, resulting in his clashing with her parents. The party guests found it difficult to avoid the scene. Rob thought, *Wow, they seem to argue a lot and they're getting married, and yet Sandra and I don't argue and are really good together – so perhaps we ought to get married!*

I was due to return from Germany, and Rob had the idea that he would hold up a sign at the airport saying, 'Will you marry me?' In some ways, I wish he had – it would have made for a very funny story – but his sensitivity and his understandable caution at handling our relationship correctly persuaded him otherwise. This is one of those few examples of Rob's good sense triumphing over playful impetuousness. Of course, I now know that if he had harboured more confidence, he might have fixed the sign to his feet, done a headstand on a swivel chair and asked passersby to gently rotate him as I cleared customs.

When he did ask me, it was a low-key, almost missable moment. He drove me back to Catford, and we simply sat on my mattress arrangement on the floor (I'm not sure it qualified as a futon) having a quiet cuddle.

'Will you marry me?' It was almost as casual as if he'd said, 'Shall we have a coffee?' or 'Shall we get a takeaway?'

'Yes!' My response was instantaneous, no room for breath, as if I had been ready with my answer for a long time. Which was true. But then it hadn't fully sunk in, so I kept saying it in German to make sense. *'Heiraten! Heiraten! Hochzeit Hochzeit!'* This was my girlhood dream coming true. I had to make it count. 'I'm getting married, I'm getting married!' Rob gurgled at my incomparable delight and giggled as I 'made it true' for myself in German, as if I was impressing it upon my brain with a huge rubber stamp. The very best cappuccino or tikka balti could wait. I was getting married!

THOSE BIG MOMENTS

Thank you for those times
Those tingle times
Those hearing the hidden rhyme times
When eyes watch on action alert
Rendering the body inert
As all the energy rallies to support
The sense of import that just ticked into Now
It hovers, and demands our reverential bow to a Big Moment.

We pull up two chairs and share, commune, consume,
Ignoring all other calls from busy or banal rooms.
Because we know
We're as old, as mature, as grown
As the sum of the Moments we've known.

Rob Lacey, 2001

By now, Laban had decided that I had enough natural dancing talent and the determination to work very hard, so a second and a third term lay ahead of me. As I arrived at the Laban Centre the next day, I still couldn't believe the thought: *I'm getting married!* In through the door. *I'm getting married!* Change into dance gear. *I'm getting married!* Warm up. *I'm getting married!* My dance that day was buoyed by my utter exhilaration, and my fellow students soon found out why I was beaming so unstoppably.

For Rob too the thought was entrancing, although for slightly different reasons. I knew he loved me, and I knew that love would grow even stronger with time, but Rob was moving on from past disappointments. This new chapter of his life now promised a wife as well as a solo career. Having decided on an early September wedding in Germany, Rob was adamant that he wanted to ask my father formally for my hand in marriage. I tried to persuade him that it wasn't protocol anymore, things had become far more relaxed. But Rob held fast.

'I want to do it in German. Can you help me?' He got his dictionary and wrote it all out in German, but it was a literal translation from the English and clumsy, so I helped him rearrange it a little.

'Darf ich Ihre Tochter heiraten.'

Rob rehearsed it many times, and then I picked up the phone. This is how the conversation went, all in German, of course:

'Hi, Dad. It's just Rob and me here, and we've got something to tell you. Hold on, Rob wants to talk to you first.'

'Okay.'

'Mr Harnisch?' Rob's well-rehearsed German phrasing kicked in fine. 'I wonder if I might ask permission to take your daughter's hand in marriage?'

But, of course, it's one thing learning phrases, it is quite another being able to understand the reply.

'Oh, well ...' I could hear my father laughing. 'Ha ha ha! "Oh, well" ... that is what Sandra's grandfather said to me when I asked for the hand of Anneliese, Sandra's mother. "Oh, well!" Can you believe it? Of course I didn't know what to say and my mouth must have dropped as wide as a mountain tunnel. I mean, what on earth is a young man supposed to think? I well remember that look he gave me when ...' My dad had launched into a series of anecdotes, as was his wont.

After a minute or two, Rob covered the mouthpiece and whispered, 'I don't know what he's saying! But he's talking a lot.' On and on went my dad's stories, and Rob didn't know what to make of it. After all, his only words in German were *ja, nein* and *danke*. That was it. I couldn't contain my mirth. All Rob could do was grimace nervously and shrug at me, which made me laugh until my eyes watered.

'What's he saying?' he urged me quietly, waving the handset at me.

But I was of no help whatsoever. I was rolling on the floor clutching my stomach by then. Eventually I spoke to Dad, drying my eyes and trying to hide my amusement.

'So, what did you say?'

'Oh, of course, I said yes!' I relayed this to Rob, whose relief was obvious.

'Oh Lord, thank you!'

None of my family expected our engagement, and I hadn't either. We had talked just a few days before at Christmas when a German friend of mine had asked if we were going to get married.

'I think it's going to take a while; Rob's got a lot to work through ... We are really good together, and if he asked me tomorrow I'd say yes, but I don't think he's ready yet.' But, of course, Rob caught me and everyone else out. He was very good at doing that in so many different ways.

In the spring of 1994, Rob had devised *Oops, There Goes My Mission* with Michèle Taylor and toured it to every Spring Harvest event in the UK that Easter. The show was a fast-moving farce using physical-mime theatre, loosely based on *A Comedy of Errors*. The hectic two-week tour culminated in their car rolling into a ditch somewhere between Skegness and Nottingham very late one foggy night. Both were unharmed, which is much more than can be said of the car. Nonetheless, the success of this show gave Rob the boost he needed to have a go at something solo.

And so *People Like Me* was born. It was to prove his most significant piece of performance work, continuing for nearly ten years and clocking up over 350 engagements. Rob involved me in the thinking, and we spent lots of time in the park juggling and messing around as we discussed the show. It was cheap rehearsal space. He was bubbling over with ideas and, in the early summer sun, I delighted in our shared creativity, but even more in the confidence and growing self-esteem I saw in Rob the performer. *People Like Me* was superb, and audiences were often astounded at his talent, intelligence and, of course, his comedy. The show was actually about having a breakdown – not the cheeriest evening out on the face of it – but Rob soon had audiences delighting in his characters and their conundrums. With every rehearsal and performance, his confidence continued to grow. This was a show that relied on nobody but him and his understanding of performance and, particularly, solo performance and its challenges. Devising the show was important too. Rob's need to write began to surface more assertively, and as he toured the show to various summer festivals, churches and community events around the country, his contact with audiences helped him to realise how much he had to offer as an artist. The title of the show was intentionally ambiguous; it could be read as an expression of our collective humanity, as a statement of fact about the performer, or as a desperate plea. All of which were true. Rob was honest with his audiences about his need to perform, but also about his need to encounter God's love and nurture as he grew. The show was entertaining and very moving. Audiences came away with a clear sense of a performer knowing how much he is loved. And, bit by bit, his sense of self-worth grew, not only because audiences did like him but because his real talent began to shine through. And he began to truly believe in himself.

To tell Rob's story and not include sheep would be doing Rob an injustice. He loved any stories or jokes about all things ovine, and one crept into *People Like Me*. Audiences were very amused by Rob's Welsh shepherd who would proclaim, 'Hey, hold those two sheep while I count them, would you?' I began to see the wonder of the man I had become engaged to—his wit, creativity and charm seemed to grow by the day.

A handy legacy of his 'sensible days' in the banking world was some insurance cover and, as a result of an earlier accident on his bike, he received £5,000 compensation for loss of work due to an injury to his shoulder. Part of his decision to marry was based on knowing that he could look after me financially while I was studying. When I discovered this, I was bowled over. It was very sweet of him. Incidentally, the end of my first year at Laban also signalled a severe lack of funding for me to do the remaining two years of the course. I had managed to impress the tutors and was doing very well; the last thing I wanted was to give it up. But my family's fund was empty, so Rob and I wondered what to do. Wonderfully, we discovered at Lewisham Town Hall that a fund existed to help foreign students studying in London. Being a local resident I qualified, my application was successful and I received a discretionary award for my remaining time at Laban. We did shout for joy quite literally, but I think Rob's added delight was knowing that his £5,000 could now stretch even further. Sometimes arriving at a point in your life can be surprising, not only because it seemed improbable but because the route to it seemed a little quirky, to say the least.

DIRECTIONS

Turn left after the empty crisp packet, right after the coke can on the wall and straight on past the bloke in trainers smoking a ciggie. Soon as you see a red car going the other way, take a sharp right at the next green hedge. Then you'll see some chewing gum on the pavement—you can't miss it—keep going down there till you pass three parked cars. Just after the third car turn right and you'll go into a street with houses on it. Left at the next sparrow, left again at the abandoned shopping trolley, keep going down there for about three verses of 'Cwm By Yah, My Lord', and you'll get to a car with a three-legged cat on the bonnet—it answers to the name of Fuzzy, if that helps. You'll find what you're looking for in the house with the seagull on the roof and a black plastic bin bag outside. At least, that's the way I went when I found it.

Rob Lacey, 1996

Our really big moment of 1995 came on the second day of September. Twenty guests came over from Britain and stayed with my family in the Place with a Million Trees. Mum cooked breakfast, lunch and tea every day for these twenty family and friends of Rob's as well as being involved in all the many preparations for the wedding. I think she must have found herself questioning her sanity at times. Generally, it was a very happy atmosphere. Rob's family weren't used to spending time together, and suddenly they were all amassed, playing board games and cards or going off with Dad on sightseeing trips to places of local historical interest. The whole of my family gave a hand too—everybody was there to help and support—it was very moving.

Weddings are a big thing in Germany. The whole town gets presents for you. A table is set up in a local shop, and people make their selection of gifts. But then as bride and groom, you provide small gifts in return. Traditionally, it's cake, perhaps a whole plate of cake; however, we chose bottles of wine, which had to be delivered to homes with a message of thanks. It was a lot of work because we received a mountain of presents.

But on the Friday before the wedding, the weather turned unpredictable and so did my nerves. Sheets of rain poured down all day long, and the weather outlook was for more rain.

'No! This can't be happening! I'm getting married! This is going to be terrible!'

My Uncle Ingolf had found an open-top Trabant for hire. This is a small car which was produced in the Eastern Bloc countries during Soviet rule. They are quirky and endearing . . . and the manufacturers never made an open-top version. This 'Trabby Deluxe' my uncle had hired was a little limousine that had been adapted by having its roof cut off, plush leather upholstery added, with purple alloy wheels and bright metallic green paint. There was no roof to cover us in the event of rain.

'It's going to be terrible!'

'Just wait and see.' Rob, as always, was reassuring. 'You don't know yet what tomorrow will bring.'

I was awoken by torrential rain and thunderstorms. Roads had turned into rivers. My uncle was racing round getting umbrellas to fix onto the car, but he didn't seem to notice that some of them had huge holes. The car itself was a disappointment. The paint was patchy and flaking and the engine smoked terribly. Then the wedding dress arrived and it was blue! And far too short! I just couldn't believe that I'd been sent the wrong one. With tears of desperation, I grabbed at the net curtains and tried to wrap them round me like I used to when I was a child playing at weddings. Added to this, my mother was barbequing sausages and making sauerkraut for twenty while my father was telling stories in German to Rob's family, all of whom were engrossed in Snakes and Ladders. To crown it all, Rob was juggling with bottles of wine over a stone floor without a care in the world.

Then I woke up properly.

Thank goodness for reality and sunshine . . . well, at least a lack of rain. With the memory of my anxiety dream fading and the reassurance that we were unlikely to need a boat instead of a car and that my dress was indeed as beautiful as ordered, I sat smiling as the hairdresser drew up my hair and created a beautiful series of ringlets. My wedding dream was coming true. I remembered a list I had made in Sweden, sitting in the back of the van with two friends while we were touring.

'What about you, Sandra?'

'Yes, Sandra, it's your go ... what will your husband be like?'

'Um ... well, he has to have a heart for God. He has to be sporty, funny, good-looking of course ...'

'Of course ...'

'He's got to have ... blue eyes and dark hair. And, if at all possible, he has to be able to do a back flip.'

'You're joking!'

'Nope. Seriously.'

I smiled at the memory. Then my smile turned into a laugh, and I think, for a moment, the hairdresser thought she'd done something wrong. Rob had now mastered the back flip in gymnastics. Yes, Mr Rob Lacey ticked every box for me. He always did and I hoped and suspected that he always would.

'Mrs Sandra Lacey?' a beautiful young bride in the mirror asked me with her eyes, 'are you ready for your close-up?' It was my big moment, and I couldn't believe it was me. For once I saw myself fulfilling my filmic fantasies.

I feel as though I could write a whole book just about our wedding day. Every moment, which of course I have played over and over throughout the years, still seems tangible. Rob was brilliant, making a special effort to learn all his vows in German, and even though I hadn't yet remembered that prophetic dream I'd had way back in Sweden, this wonderful and special man made my day perfect. Although there were a couple of moments which threatened perfection, even so, I must contain this account to the headlines.

At the appointed time, just before setting off in the gleaming Trabby Deluxe, which now had balloons tied to it, we saw each other in our finery. I thought for a moment that Rob might faint; it took him a while to catch his breath. Naturally, we were both thrilled to be wearing these particular 'costumes' for this one-off 'performance' in such a beautiful setting ... and with a chosen and loving 'audience'. This was the one traditional event in our lives that we knew would remain with us forever. We stood on a small balcony staring in awe at each other's beauty and laughing and chatting for almost ten minutes, our smiles stretching our faces. Just the two of us at the start of a whole new adventure. The car was waiting in the parking bay by the side of the house, which did not afford much room for manoeuvring, even with such a small vehicle. My dress brushed the stone wall, which was covered in moss, and it left a large green stain.

I swore loudly. I couldn't help it. We'd hardly stepped out of the house, and I felt my dress was ruined. So far, only close family had seen me looking perfect. 'It's ruined! It's ruined!' Rob's mum was standing nearby on the pavement waving the car out and heard my swearing. Rob couldn't help laughing, knowing how much she would disapprove of my colourful outburst.

'If only you'd sworn in German, she wouldn't have understood.' He giggled.

My mum, meanwhile, looked as if she was going to have a heart attack, not because of my expletives, regardless of whether she understood, but because she knew that moss marks on white are very bad news.

In Germany, couples who wish to marry in a church must also have a ceremony in the Town Hall to legalise the marriage contract; religious ceremonies are not recognised by the state. Some guests at the Town Hall might have wondered why my mother came sprinting up the stairs with bottles of cleaning materials and cloths; perhaps the Brits concluded it was another German tradition. But a mixture of her vigorous elbow grease, determination, prayer and a squirt or two of her potions fetched the mark out, and the guests were none the wiser. The mayor made an uninspiring speech, we signed the books and that was that, as far as our statutory obligation was concerned. Our guests and public applauded as we emerged and took the Trabby to the little Lutheran church where I was nurtured as a new Christian. Its old thick stone walls, wooden ceilings and fresco paintings enclosed the maximum congregation possible ... just eighty people, all squashed in happily cheek by jowl into this picturesque place of worship.

The service was conducted in German and English. Rob's German vows were complete, not just the 'I do.' He'd learnt the whole thing. I was very moved and almost cried. I knew I couldn't look him in the eyes or I'd melt into an uncontrollable heap of tears, so I stared at his forehead like actors do on stage if they suspect a shared stare will break their concentration.

It was all over far too soon. We kissed, hopped back into the pimped tin can on wheels and set off for our reception at Burg Lauenstein, a fairy-tale castle with pointed turrets, set on top of a steep hill.

The crane camera circles from a bird's-eye view, down through the ornate castle window, spiralling lower onto the wedding guests, clapping and laughing. In the middle of the celebratory clamour dance the bride and groom, each having carefully practised a waltz, but now caught out by a tempo change. They both improvise dance moves, much to the delight of the crowd, who whoop and cheer as their movements change from doing the Twist to becoming more wacky and wild. The music climaxes, the young couple bow and curtsy ostentatiously, then collapse into each other's arms to riotous applause and more cheering.

The whole wedding and the party was a fabulous day characterised by so much laughter and, of course, we were stars in our very own romantic comedy with a fabulous supporting cast of family and friends for those extraordinary twenty-four hours. Rob and I now belonged to each other. It was glorious ... and a distant memory was stirred for Rob by his sister's husband, Tony. During a picnic as a young boy, a red setter dog stole a bar of Bourneville chocolate that Rob had received as a gift. For years afterwards, Rob harboured a fear that good things would always be taken away from him. That day of the wedding, Tony said, 'Guess what I dreamt last night, Rob. You shot that red setter.'

Lots of people initiated games and told anecdotes about us. Rob and I both made speeches, but mine fell apart because I cried copiously, I was so moved by my family and all they had done for us. The whole day was a heartfelt celebration of us as a couple, and the partying went on well into the early hours. Just before two o'clock, as Rob and I were setting off for our stunning bridal suite in one of the towers, complete with a spiral staircase, my father put his arms around us.

'You have given so much today. Your love for each other and for God has enriched everyone. This has been such a wonderful, beautiful day. You gave back to people, and that is so very important.'

Even our flight back to Britain was made special. A friend of mine who worked for Lufthansa alerted our flight crew, who announced that some newlyweds were onboard and served us with champagne. Our fellow passengers applauded as Rob and I slipped into our mock VIP roles, proposing our own toasts with silly voices.

But there was one significant person who was absent from the German celebrations. Rob's dad was not well enough to make the journey, so we decided to have a blessing of our marriage in Wales after our honeymoon.

WEDDING VOWS – ROB & SANDRA

S – For richer, for poorer
R – For better, for worse
S – If you become a snorer
R – If you don't support Spurs
S – In sickness
R – In illness
S – In tiredness
R – In touchiness
S – In just-under-the-weather-ness?
R – Yes, and in health
S – In strength
R – In strident

S – In vibrant
R – In crazy, when I want to be quiet
S – In a muse, when I want a riot
R – In rage?
S – In every stage
R – In stumble, fumble, foible and fault?
S – Indestructible, invincible, impenetrable vault
R – So, in sickness
S – And in health
R – 'Til death, us two part
S – So help us God
R – So help us God
S – What God has brought together
R – Taught to float
S – Set to sail
R – And sent to sea
S & R – Let no one   put   us   under.

Rob Lacey, 1995

Rob and I wrote our alternative vows for our Welsh blessing while we sat by a pool at a quiet resort in Tenerife a few days after our wedding. During our honeymoon, we always seemed to do the opposite to all the other guests. When they were by the pool during the hottest part of the day, we were at the beach. When they were at the beach later when it was cooler, we were by the pool. Despite trying not to read too much significance into events, there is the suspicion, even then, that our life together was not going to conform to predictable or traditional patterns. For a start, we were both performers and both Christians, and we had already discovered that the church doesn't easily or comfortably embrace those working professionally in the Arts. Often it may think it does, but more on that later.

Towards the end of September, our marriage was blessed in Glenwood Church in Cardiff, with Rob's father able to be present, along with one hundred and fifty other friends who couldn't make it over to Ludwigsstadt. We had a few days touring around the beautiful Welsh countryside for what we referred to as our second honeymoon, except it included my mum and dad and my sister's husband, Rainer, who drove for us.

Our small rented flat in Lewisham with its tiny roof garden and views of the Cutty Sark and Greenwich delighted and charmed us the day we moved in. It was only a six-month rental, and its arty style suited us perfectly. Of the many things I had discovered about my gorgeous husband, one was that he had a tendency to work very hard. Sometimes too hard. Taking time off for himself was something Rob had to pay careful attention to; otherwise he wouldn't stop.

'Sandra, I've made a decision.' I looked up at him from my coffee and toast, still finding it difficult to believe that we were a married couple in our first home. 'I really want to give time to our first three months of being married, so ... I'm not going to work. I'm just going to be at home and support you.'

'Oh. Are you sure?'

'Yup. I can start booking shows after the New Year, and there's enough money to live on until then. Besides, this is the one and only chance you and I get to be newly married, so I thought ... let's make it a good one.'

'Okay. We can enjoy being Mr and Mrs.'

'Sounds like a good game. Shall I be Mr, or ...?' He struck a camp pose, licked his finger to stroke his eyebrow provocatively, which made me splurt my coffee back into the mug. Out came his mock American drawl, 'It means you can concentrate on Laban while your house-husband is tossing all those dreadful secondhand clothes into the garbage. From now on, girl, it's Dolce and Gabbana all the way!' We laughed and held each other.

'Thank you.' I kissed him. I was holding my dream come true (and not a pair of dungarees in sight). Being short of money, we often bought clothes in charity shops, and this gave way to a shared joke. 'You're brilliant. And, as secondhand husbands go ... you're the best I've ever had.' Rob gurgled with delight.

'And as wives go' – his eyes twinkled impishly – 'you're the most recent.'

I slapped him playfully, grateful at how much more whole he had become in this last year. I couldn't believe life could be so wonderful. A minute later, he was mincing across our bedroom towards the wardrobe, apparently talking to himself. 'Girl, those drapes just gotta go! And will you look at those shoes! Soooo last season!'

Inevitably, those three months turned out to be far from idyllic. My second year at Laban was extremely rewarding, but very demanding, with me often working all day and into the night, getting home around nine. Weekend rehearsals also kicked in here and there, so I saw less of Rob than I had wanted. My househusband was also encountering the unexpected. A series of bladder infections struck him throughout those three months and, tracking backwards, we realised that he had suffered his first bout with cystitis just three weeks after we had started going out together, followed by some repeated infections here and there. By Christmas that year, he was having tests to find out why these infections were becoming more persistent. As Easter 1996 drew near, the hospital carried out a biopsy on the bladder. When the results came back, we were stunned to learn that there was an early form of cancer in the bladder wall. We immediately phoned Rob's best man, Stefan, who worked as a manager in another hospital, and asked if he could help us find out more about cancer of the bladder. These days, of course, anyone can Google for more information in an instant, but we had to wait to see what Stefan could find out in the medical library.

'It doesn't sound very good.' Stefan's voice was controlled and calm on the phone, his compassionate nature always evident. 'It's a really terrible form of cancer, I'm afraid. I'll get this stuff to you.'

His envelope delivered not only a sheaf of photocopied papers but utter devastation. One sentence in particular stood out: 'Bladder cancer kills one 100 percent of people who contract it.'

For some reason, Rob was in the bathroom reading the statistics. After a while, his stillness and quietness drew me to him. He simply passed a piece of paper to me.

'Nobody survives it.' His whisper drifted on the air as I scanned the information. When I looked up, his eyes were filled with tears. The outside world made its faint noises on the other side of the window. A tap dripped. My heart thudded and my breathing became shallow. This was unreal. It could not be happening. My hands started shaking as we held on to each other. We wept. Inconsolably. Sinking to the floor, we clutched at the life that was each other as the implications of the facts tumbled around our brains. No one survives bladder cancer. Treatment might involve being unable to have children. We would have no family of our own, no grandchildren. Pain and ongoing treatment lay ahead. Rob might die. We would not grow old together. Our sobs filled the small flat, and we stayed there for some time on that bathroom floor, just holding on.

Only a few months before, the happy bride and groom marvelled at God's great goodness filling every part of their lives. Now their faith would be tested. Rigorous, unforgiving and very painful testing.

Chapter 4
Roller-Coaster Role

The ragged-haired man in his early thirties did not look as though he had been severely smacked in the face as he calmly browsed the shabby little Greenwich bookshop. The slender dancer sitting on the studio floor holding her ankles while listening carefully to her tutor did not look as though she had been severely smacked in the face. But both felt as though they had. And very severely. The man found a secondhand book whose title, *Living With an Incurable Illness*, drew his focus into its pages. The dancer regarded the other healthy bodies sprawled around her and wondered briefly whether any cancers lurked there too. For the man and the woman, cancer's lingering sting had forced them both to look in a new direction to see their path ahead as a couple. Cancer's brutality, Cancer's insulting behaviour, Cancer's bullying tactics had left them bruised and confused – and it had gate-crashed in with its capital C, brash and impudent.

Those first few days after receiving the news, we felt as though we bore a stigma, like red welts on a bruised face publicly advertising the shame of physical abuse. The unreality of the nightmare that seemed sure to follow seeped slowly into our consciousness. How to tell people? Who to tell? We were having enough problems telling ourselves. Shouldn't people with shock sit down and drink sweet tea? Should they be allowed out? Should they be allowed to go into bookshops and dance rehearsals? The evening of the same day Rob bought the book, I was performing in a dance piece at

Laban. It was the end of my second term in my second year, and the performance was one of the rawest pieces of dance I have ever done. Along with the select audience, Rob sat in the semidarkness and watched a very physical and highly energetic show. It involved smacking bodies against the studio walls, its percussive frenzy perfectly expressing much of the fear and anger I had inside. Buckets of water stood on stage, and we splashed our heads in them as part of a tumultuous dance, spraying the wet from our hair across the floor, making the dancing dangerous to do and very edgy to watch. In the core of me, as I flung myself around with the other dancers, I screamed and railed. At Cancer. At unfairness. At being insulted. At something wonderful now ruined. At dreams turned to nightmares. At injustice against Rob. We had learnt the facts: Cancer of the bladder is more common in people over the age of fifty and rare in those below the age of forty. Rob was thirty-three. More insult heaped upon injury. If only it could all have been left behind with the fading of the stage lights and the final applause. As Rob kissed my cheek afterwards and told me how brilliant I was, I couldn't help but entertain the thought that this beautiful man was spoilt by Cancer. This man. *Mein Mann.*

'I bought this today.' Rob slid the book towards me later that night. 'Stupid, isn't it? I realised it's not just a cold. It's not something I will just shake off ...'

'It can't stay.'

'It seems to have taken up residence.'

'No, I mean we must want it to go away.'

'Absolutely.'

'Lord, take it away.' Hope started to flicker somewhere deep inside me. Rob took both my hands in his and looked into my eyes.

'Well, God made the miracle of you happen for me. So anything is possible.'

'Just take away the cancer, Lord.' The threshold between conversation and prayer seemed negligible.

'Yes! Go for it ... Take it away!'

'Take it away ...'

'Amen.' There was a pause, then Rob smiled. 'Adds a whole new meaning to "going for a takeaway", doesn't it?'

The treatment started quite soon after that. From the Easter term into the summer, Rob was touring *People Like Me*, my dance training demanded all my time and the hospital visits continued. Gradually, however, Laban allowed me time off to accompany Rob for his treatments, and I managed to be with him for all of them.

Rob was starting to write his first book, *Are We Getting Through?* which was a compilation of ideas for better communication. Even before he started working on *People Like Me*, Rob had expressed a desire to write. Before we were married, he bought one of those self-help books called *How to Be a Successful Writer in Six Weeks* or something like that. In reality, it was nearer six years before he could claim such an accolade. His first writing contract was a great boost for his confidence, and the subsequent devising process for all the shows that followed further strengthened his writing skills. But during these earlier years, the struggle with primary cancer predictably coloured everything.

'Immunotherapy is a newer treatment.' The Irish consultant looked from Rob to me and back again, his soft accent intoning our uncertain future, as if a casting director had matched his voice perfectly to this moment in our script. 'It is a different form of chemotherapy. It's non-invasive. No operation. We use a catheter and fluid with live TB bacteria, which is the same used for the BCG vaccine you get as immunisation against TB. So what we do is introduce this into your bladder, which kicks the immune system into action – that's why it's called immunotherapy. And then' – Rob and I followed his words carefully, alien phrases which we suspected would become all too familiar to us as time went on – 'the immune system will fight those TB cells, but at the same time take the lining of the bladder away. It strips the lining, which is where the cancer is, so it achieves the result of an operation without being one. It will be sore for a while, but then you'll be fine again. And it's very early, so there's no need to worry.'

There was a pause and the word *worry* hung in the air. This scene was one of those unpredictable ones where expectation may be entirely thwarted.

'Bear in mind that this procedure is very effective at preventing recurrence in a large majority of cases.' His friendly smile seemed to belong elsewhere, as if we were choosing wallpaper from a salesman's book of samples. Rob and I looked at each other. In that glance, in that momentary silence while we thought about our response, we were standing at the altar again in my small church back home. Rob in his finery, me with my gleaming white dress. In sickness and in health. But how easy would it be for this stain to be removed?

Both consultants we saw were extremely positive. We learned later that in Germany the treatment would have consisted of removing the bladder completely, along with the kidneys and the prostate because all three are genetically linked and prone to the same cancer. The thinking is that this gives the best possible chance of survival. But the implications are drastic: a lifetime of dialysis and infertility. We did consider it briefly, the snippets of conversation now playing in my head like an accelerated and tense montage.

'But you'd have to give up touring ...'

'Ugh ... the thought of constant dialysis ...'

'It's our only income – your performances ...'

'And they did say the immunotherapy gets good results ...'

'Besides, I don't want to lose the chance of having children.' Rob cupped my face.

'Me too.'

In the end it became obvious that the immunotherapy would hopefully catch the cancer at an early stage and the prognosis, in all probability, would be good.

QUESTION MARKS

The seconds crawl along
And the darkness makes like it's beginning to belong.
But the eyes accustomise to the keyhole-shaped shaft of light
And I see every 'Why?' 'Why?' 'Why?'
And many more 'Whys' replayed
Have ricocheted off the ceiling and walls.
And my question marks?
I find them strewn across the floor of my prison cell.
Unanswered.
Broken.
It's only then the keyhole whispers,
'Harness the darkness
And hear it hum the hymns of how to cope.
Saddle the sadness
And then sit astride the kaleidoscope of hope
And ride
Wide-eyed
In the roller-coaster role of life
The roller-coaster role of life
The roller-coaster role of life.'

Rob Lacey, 2001

Trying to sustain touring a one-man show, spending what little time there was with his new wife and attending clinics for tests and treatment, Rob soon found himself under a lot of pressure. His performance work was vital to him, not just because it was earning much-needed money, but because it signified a new him. He was being released into a creative arena, the likes of which he hadn't known before. Slowly, his skills deepened and broadened, and he began to find his unique voice as an artist. But, of course, the cancer was there too. The stakes had been raised. There were two new areas of growth – one extremely good, the other extremely bad. Our prayers became fuelled with faith; this co-existence could not be allowed. Creative potential had to have the upper hand. One particular episode illustrated Rob's struggle.

It was in between biopsies, before the cancer was finally confirmed. Removing a sample of the bladder lining via the urethra is quite uncomfortable, and Rob was advised to rest for a few days after the procedure. This biopsy was on a Thursday. Rob was due to perform in Birmingham three nights later and, feeling fine, he set off on the Saturday morning by car. During that period, the need to urinate could hit him quite frequently due to infections – sometimes as often as every half an hour or fifteen minutes – so when he was driving he would take a bottle with him for that purpose. The prospect of visiting every service station en route from London to Birmingham seemed bad enough, but the possibility of being stuck in a traffic jam was even more worrying. So a trusty bottle was by his side, together with a coat to put across his lap in case any passenger in an adjacent bus might look down to chance upon an intriguing discovery whilst perhaps taking a break from leafing through a magazine proclaiming 'True Life Stories – filthy goings-on in cars!'

Unfortunately, Rob's timing was bad. He didn't even make it out of London. At the start of the A1 at Archway, North London, he hit very heavy traffic. Inching the car forward, his bladder screaming at him to find a toilet, he understood all too well the meaning of travelling at a painfully slow speed. He resisted resorting to the bottle with so many other drivers looking on, but he became desperate as the queue of cars seemed to go nowhere. He reached for his bottle and the coat, but it was no good. The bladder went into spasm and, bent over in pain, he eventually edged the car into a garage forecourt and phoned for an ambulance. The medic attending him did not have the correct catheter, so improvised the best he could. Unfortunately, the tube the medic inserted into Rob's urethra was about three times the diameter it should have been.

Much later, Rob and I stared in disbelief at the size of that tube. It didn't seem possible that it would ever fit inside such a small opening as his urethra. Much later, whenever Rob told the story to an audience or to friends, elaborating in graphic detail, much to their dismay and consternation, it was often the case that any male members (Rob wouldn't have let me resist using that phrase) would wince, moan and cross their legs. Rob's relief was glorious, he said, both on that garage forecourt and at having shared his experience through storytelling.

The immunotherapy worked. Following the treatment during May, for about six weeks Rob was in pain, but it wasn't as severe as before. His toilet visits were quite frequent, not unlike severe cystitis for a few weeks, but eventually they diminished. By the end of June, it was all over. Life resumed, and the whole episode seemed dealt with quite quickly. It was all pretty easy. He didn't lose his hair because it wasn't chemotherapy. He was sore, but it wasn't terrible. We were quite happy, the result was good and the doctors were positive because we had caught the cancer early.

'Everything should be fine' – the consultant's face broadened into a warm smile – 'just carry on and we'll check up on you every six months.'

Walking out of that consultation room lifted our spirits. Rob had the checkups and, for a while, he didn't even have cystitis. I came to the end of my second year at Laban. The course was very exacting, and I had learnt so much. Together we spurred each other on. Rob knew what an extremely steep learning curve I was engaged in, making up for many missed years of dance tuition and practice. He worked very hard too, sustaining his tour of *People Like Me*, deriving huge satisfaction at being a published author (*Are We Getting Through?*) and looking forward to ideas for his next show to build on his successes. At the end of the summer term that year, with my dance commitments starting to ease, I spent many weekends accompanying Rob to his performances. We both felt strong. Focused. Inspired. Loved. This was the blossoming of our creative and artistic work, which would soon bear so much fruit in our lives.

'I've got problems with plumbing!'

Rob was scratching his head. In his other hand hung two long lengths of one-inch-diameter white plastic piping, while at his feet lay copper fittings and spanners on our living room floor.

I laughed. 'Shall I fetch a catheter?'

He saw the funny side and immediately improvised a pastiche of his garage forecourt experience, becoming the medic, who somehow transformed into an impersonation of John Major.

'Hello there. Urine trouble?' 'Yes, I certainly am!' 'Well, pipe down then ...' He was rolling on the floor with white tubes sticking out from every available gap around his drawn-up legs.

'Let's try this one, shall we?' 'ARGH ARGH!' 'Oh, dear, maybe not. Let's try the biggest size of all then ... and use this axle grease shall we?'

And so it went on, the two of us ending up in tears from our hysterics. The reason for all the piping, not to mention extensive rolls of green garden netting and literally hundreds of balloons, was *Prodigal Grandson*, his second one-man show.

Rob devised the piece with Steve Stickley, artistic director of Footprints Theatre, with whom he had worked back in the Trapdoor days. It was now autumn 1996, and Rob and Steve had come up with a refreshing yet quirky take on the Prodigal Son, set in a balloon factory. It looked at how family history can repeat itself, progressing to the next generation and comprising dozens and dozens of large balloons in a big circular pen made of plastic plumbing pipes and netting. The show set creativity and playfulness against authoritative repression, so hundreds of frivolous balloons seemed a good choice. The whole spectacle was fabulous, and audiences were wowed by the ingenuity of the staging, which involved Rob, at one point, diving into the midst of the waist-deep pool of large purple and blue balloons. Many people have since said that this show was Rob's magnum opus as a solo performer. It was a strong and power-ful statement as much about the nature of creativity as it was about spirituality – as well as a resounding challenge to consider family dynamics, especially male relationships. It also equipped Rob with a new and unlikely sphere of knowledge. Apparently, in the inflat-able latex trade, there are 'pub'-quality balloons and 'wedding'-quality balloons. *Prodigal Grandson* was always wed to quality, and so our small flat bulged with boxes of good-quality blue and purple balloons for many, many years. In fact, as a testament to Rob's enthusiastic purchasing strategies, I still have some to this day.

So I started my final year at Laban. Rob was quite healthy, only getting slight infections here and there during times of stress and tiredness. We weren't too worried; it just seemed this would be his thorn in the flesh for the foreseeable future. Generally, life was good, and by the time Christmas came along that year, we looked into buying our own flat near Streatham, South London. While we were in Germany with my parents for the festive season, Rob spent many hours on the telephone chasing banks in the UK in order to secure a mortgage. It was very frustrating, explaining to financial institutions that it was impossible to provide accounts for the preceding three years of income as they insisted. Rob had only been working as a self-employed performer for a little over a year. It felt as though we should have to practically beg them for money. But Rob's persistence paid off, and by Easter the following year, we moved into our own little place in Furzedown. Our gratitude for God's goodness (and influence through prayer upon certain bank employees, no doubt) was infectious as we heaved our suit-cases and bits of furniture up the stairs to our very own first-floor

home. Standing among balancing boxes containing various belong-
ings, books and balloons, we raised our glasses and toasted our new
home together. Life had a definitive buzz as its pace picked up. For
me, the student dancer, my course continued to issue its never-ending challenge to play catch-up, and I rose to it with determination.
For Rob, the increasingly experienced performer and writer, ideas
for new projects began spilling out in every direction.

This clear focus for both of us grew out of our nurturing of
each other. Our appetite to find and grow our potential was insatiable. Even if something seemed completely against the odds, like
getting a mortgage, we realised our kindred spirit and fought for
it. Rob wrote me a particular poem after we had heard someone
speak about feeling uprooted and recognising the need to be nurtured. When we had first got married, I was quite conscious of my
German-ness.

'How am I going to live in Britain?' I would ask. 'Can I live
in Britain? Can I find my home in this country? Can I make a life
here? Can I give birth in a hospital here? What if I want to scream
in German and ask for things in German, but have to do it in
English? Could I do that? It wouldn't feel natural. I don't want to
be chopped off, but if I have to, then dig me up and plant me over
here – with my German-ness, ready to grow in this soil.'

Rob frowned, obviously feeling for me and understanding my
perspective. When he spoke I knew his words came from deep
inside. Even so, his playfulness was never far away.

'I want to be your bucket, your pot you can grow in, so you
can feel safe.'

It was exactly what I needed to hear. So then he wrote this for
me, probably around the time of our first wedding anniversary.

SANDRA
*The girl from the town of a million trees and the home of a
thousand works of art.*

The daughter from the fullest field and grown and flown
   the nest.
And I must tend her now and protect her from the city smog,
which would clog her memories of where her roots first grew.
Lord, keep me pure, give me green fingers.
Soften them from fist, to applause, to touch and prepare my
   heart
so it won't burst with pride when I stand back and see first
   the blossom,
then the fruit which you have wombed and warmed and
   watered and watched and soon will use to bring colour
   to so many broken branches.
I wait and I wonder at what one day you will bring to be.

Rob Lacey, 1996

Even now I wonder at the phrase 'bring colour to so many broken branches'. The poem is about my fragility at that time, and yet, given all that has passed since, it seems quite possible that it could refer to so much more. Sometimes it is possible to read too much meaning into words, events, relationships and so on, but every now and then it seems that there could well be prophecies and promises woven intricately into the fabric of who we are. If we want it to, if we are brave enough to allow ourselves, perhaps we can be filled with wonder that God's hand plays a part in shaping who any one of us might be. Perhaps it is a little like watching the final scene from Peter Weir's film *Dead Poets' Society*, when the significance of schoolboys standing on their desks to say good-bye to their teacher and mentor hits you, and you realise that there are so many reasons, sometimes too many reasons, to be moved by acts of love. It was one of Rob's very favourite films.

And so the time came for my degree finals at Laban. After having never done a contemporary dance class in my life, I was awarded a first in technique. It was a long three years to get there and extremely hard work. Rob and I were thrilled with what I had achieved, perhaps he even more thrilled than I. Throughout the constant challenge to my brain and body, the knowledge that this was where God wanted me to be had given me the drive I needed. And of course, I had a loving husband who understood entirely the need in me to satisfy that imperative to do 'movement theatre'. It wasn't long before we started looking at opportunities for me to get out there and perform professionally. Rob knew I still needed to have a go at this movement theatre thing, and so he encouraged me to act as well as to dance.

'Don't worry about earning. This is your time to experiment. I want you to be free to experiment.'

'But the mortgage ...'

'Really, don't worry about the money, I'll look after that.'

So, again, Rob made it possible for me to find my feet in the early stages of my dance career, where you often work long hours with little or no pay. He worked extremely hard fulfilling bookings for both of his shows. Ask any solo performer how hard it is to sustain regular earnings in the precarious and unpredictable world of performance art, and you'll hear tales of penury, frustration and disappointment. Steadily, churches all over the UK were learning about Rob's shows, and Christian organisations started to show interest in what he had to say. He was commissioned by the Baptist Missionary Society to write *Paradise Crushed*—essentially a theatre piece, albeit a rather physical one, which I performed with another actor.

Retrospect lends particular meaning to that period. Rob gave me the freedom and space I needed when I needed it. In later years, I would be looking after him and would have hardly any time at all to be my own person. But *Paradise Crushed* was very good for me. It was the first time I spoke properly on stage. I nearly didn't go on for the first performance; I was too terrified of opening my mouth in front of an audience. I could do anything with my body. Tell me to be a diplodocus, an amoeba, or a belligerent slug called Nigel – no problem. But using my voice was another matter entirely. I was still battling shyness from my school days back in Germany where we had compulsory public-speaking tests. They still haunted me. I'm grateful to Rob that he gave me the confidence to go for it and, naturally, that led to other things. The following year I devised a solo show called *MM*, based on Mary Magdalene. Rob and I had gone to the pub one day, had the idea, scribbled down some notes and then I produced a script. Rob helped to edit and direct the show, and I started performing, mainly on the Christian circuit. It was part dance, part theatre, and used projected images from films of my own childhood. Rob was my greatest fan; he also did a very good job as mentor. *MM* was my firstborn piece and planted me firmly on my feet.

In so very many ways, this wild-haired Welshman gave himself to me selflessly. The level of genuine delight he took in my achievements built me up. Clearly, that expression of nurturing and tending me, captured in his poem, had become his credo. Our marriage, as well as our professional relationship, was enriched greatly.

'Let's work together. Let's cross over and do a show together.' Rob's eyes were alight. 'What do you say?'

'Well ... I'm ...'

'Look, we've been touring apart and both been busy, so let's do a show together, and then we'll see a lot more of each other!'

'You know the biggest risk, though?'

'What?'

'Well ... you know, being on tour together all the time?'

'Aah, yes, I see what you mean ... you end up either adoring or loathing one another.' Rob squeezed the bridge of his nose in mock consternation. He sighed heavily. 'Well, we'll just have to learn to hate each other then. That's all there is to it.'

'Okay then.' I returned his faux sentiment as he stifled his amusement expertly. 'You are a hideous and hateful, heartless excuse for a human being.'

'And you are a conniving, two-faced, tight-lipped, selfish old sow.'

We stared, each daring the other to break into laughter first.

'Same time tomorrow?'

'It's a date.'

So in the latter part of 1998, Rob wrote *Grey Daze* for us to perform together the following year. It was an allegorical account of Jesus' life, set in a future world without colour. Into the mono-chrome pours the colour of this rebel leader – but, of course, people prefer to measure themselves against their less challenging, more familiar grey-scale values. Like *MM*, *Grey Daze* was physical the-atre that incorporated video. Rob and I found that we worked very well together and, although we were often tired, it was very positive spending time doing everything as a couple.

Grey Daze ran for about sixty shows, and it was responsible for us meeting Bill and Rachel Taylor-Beales. We were performing at Soul Survivor, which was one of the first showings of *Grey Daze*. Despite thinking we could cope with the technical aspects of the show, we soon recognised that having a technician would alleviate some of the pressure on us, so we advertised at the festival.

'We've just got back from Australia?' Rachel squinted at Rob and me in the bright sunlight, her Englishness mixing with her antipodean rising inflection. 'This is just the kind of thing we're looking for.'

'We can only afford to pay one person,' Rob said and looked from Rachel upwards to her tall husband.

'Well ...,' Bill muttered from behind his sunglasses and stub-ble, 'you'll get two for the price of one because we want to tour together.'

Standing in that field in Somerset, surrounded by marquees and music, the four of us agreed to work together. It was the start of a wonderful friendship.

Grey Daze toured for about a year, during which time Rob started working on another new idea. He got an appointment to see James Catford at HarperCollins to find out whether they might be vaguely interested in his paraphrase of Genesis 1, written in a streetwise style he had been experimenting with for a few months. An hour or so later, he walked out of their offices nonplussed, hardly believing what had just happened. They offered him a contract to write a streetwise version of the entire Bible.

To say Rob was pleased would be a huge understatement. He knew the creative possibilities this afforded, and I saw the light in his eyes. Immediately he started planning, thinking, musing, scheming, laughing. At last, here was a big meaty challenge for his writing skill to sink its teeth into. His appetite was undiminished throughout the long creative process that followed. Already a hard worker, this new project proved his capacity for the sort of commitment such a challenge brings. Rob had great expectations.

We human beings seem to constantly lay ourselves open to surprises. Is it because we are so used to accepting the status quo that anything else is unwelcome, or is it that we entertain hopes and fears only within the scope of what we know? Perhaps we cannot be anything but vulnerable because we believe totally in our own sense of indomitability. The unknown will always dismay or startle. Toward the end of 1999, there was talk of millennium bugs and computer systems crashing worldwide, with the collapse of financial systems too dependent upon new technologies. The looming millennium gave the tabloid press plenty of opportunities to play the prophets of doom, except they were armed only with flimsy evidence and the usual stock of headline puns. What was it that was lingering in the shadows ready to pounce? Armageddon, the horsemen of the Apocalypse followed by global annihilation? Or an alert window on the computer screen saying, 'Your date and time function cannot be verified'?

As the celebrations for the millennium drew near and *Grey Daze* continued apace, Rob became tired and picked up urinary infections again. A few tests revealed the possibility of some cancerous cells.

'Don't worry about it.' The consultant was cheerful. 'It can happen randomly. Unusual cells in the urine one day and then all clear the next.'

'But are they cancerous?'

'They might sometimes have the appearance of being cancerous, but they could very well be anomalies. We'll do more tests in February. Meanwhile, don't worry. Enjoy the millennium. Are you doing anything nice?'

'We're spending New Year in Vienna.'

'Sounds perfect to me. We'll see you in February, okay?'

We stayed with Rob's brother Derek, his wife, Janet, and their three children, who lived in Vienna at the time. The city was fabulous as the sky crackled with fireworks that new millennium's eve. We needed the break so much and were very grateful for our time together away from the pressures and tiredness of touring. The nonevent of the millennium bug, however, stood in marked contrast to the very real but hidden threat during those first two months of 2000. Friends and contacts were rallied in prayer, and our outlook remained positive. Subsequent biopsies revealed nothing, although the cancerous cells persisted. By the time we finished *Grey Daze* around Easter, it had been confirmed: cancer was indeed present, but its location was a mystery.

Rob's four-year reprieve had ended.

Chapter 5

Staying the Night

I once watched a large dragonfly struggling to emerge from its pupa. From the outside, what looked like a dead insect began to split slowly. Quarter of an hour or so passed while I watched the transformed life inside starting to penetrate the membrane. The struggle went on far beyond a nine-year-old's attention span, and when I returned later, it had still not emerged fully. Had the dragonfly been struggling all that time? How often did it rest to find new strength to carry on? It was obviously a very challenging task to accomplish, and yet it seemed nothing would stop it. The dragonfly finally kicked, wiggled and unfurled its iridescent body and wings into a new life of flight and liberation. Not that I saw it – I got bored waiting. I was much happier doing cartwheels and forward rolls on the grass.

Rob's and my life together felt different from other people's more predictable routines. Touring introduced us to new places and new audiences all over the UK, while the nature of our work – performing, writing, rehearsing and so on – generated a whirl of creative possibilities. Others would comment on our lifestyle at times. 'I wish I could do what you're doing.' 'It must be wonderful working together as a couple, doing what you love best.' 'Your work is so special. I can see God at work there, right in the core of it.' But, as human nature will always have it, we would sometimes succumb to a very slight envy over the more predictable lifestyles we saw around us. Friends of ours with their own houses started having babies, and at some point we would want a family and a place big enough for children. But like that dragonfly larva, we had no idea of the prolonged metamorphosis that was about to hit us.

'There's nothing to be seen in the bladder lining. The biopsies show a redness over the whole bladder, but that could be left over from the treatment four years ago. The best thing to do is to treat it again.' The consultant's books on the shelf behind his head stood neatly, sentinels keeping their keen cancer watch. One tatty volume leaned into the rest as if weary from a long tour of duty. Perhaps a new edition would soon supplant it, fresh faced and eager to communicate new findings from within its pristine pages – or simply regurgitating the same old information in a different font.

I held Rob's hand. Our fingers curled up together, comfortable, easy. The consultant pushed the bridge of his glasses to the top of his nose. 'So if you're thinking about having children, you probably should try and go for it now, maybe even before we start the treatment, because we don't know exactly where the cancer is . . . it's just a good idea, that's all.'

In my peripheral vision, I saw Rob look at me. I imagined him with a cheeky, playful look in his eye and a comment waiting in the wings to do its comic turn and draw laughs from its audience. But in that moment, I was a little shocked. I didn't return Rob's look. My eyes widened and I drew breath – I had always planned to be a mother at thirty and not before. I had been quite adamant with myself. This was a decision that had to be made on our own terms. I finally looked at Rob. Instead of cheekiness, his eyes held compassion. He smiled and squeezed my fingers lovingly.

'But I'm only twenty-eight,' I said.

Rob just raised his eyebrows, his smile broadening, as if to say, 'So what's a couple of years between friends?'

It was the consultant who broke our stare.

'I would like to start the treatment in two weeks.' He then chuckled as we looked back at him. 'So you'd better get a move on.'

After our nervous laughter had settled down, we agreed to treatment dates and shook his hand. 'Good luck!' he called as we left. And I imagined the bookshelf sentinels gossiping together at their master's unusual manner and how this was anything but a fertility clinic. You know ... perhaps even the dog-eared one was now *compos mentis*. The consultant probably grinned knowingly to himself.

I came off the pill immediately. It was just after Easter 2000. Amazingly, I fell pregnant straightaway, surprised and stunned. Suddenly life's complexion was beginning to alter. Rob's shock at the news he was to be a father was matched only by his nervousness at the treatment that lay ahead. At first he thought it would be another form of tackling early cancer, as before, and that it would soon be over and done with. Then life would carry on as usual. But the weeks that followed were debilitating, and our experience of the hospital in Camberwell was negative–except for Thelma, the urology sister. Rob had experienced her style of humour and comforting presence before. Most, if not all, of Thelma's comic routine revolved around catheters, and she couldn't help but compound the stereotype of Very Jolly Black Woman in her 40s.

'Now then, what you're looking at here is Thelma and Louise,' she would say, waving a catheter under Rob's nose. 'I am Thelma and this here is Louise, and she's going to ease you going to the loo. Hah! Loo Ease! Hah ha! But no one's driving off the edge of no cliff this afternoon ... though you might want to if you don't make friends with Louise. Hah!' Without the wonderful Thelma, memories of that hospital would be unmitigatingly awful.

'Now you may wonder why I sing songs when Louise here is being inserted. Well, that's because my other name is Urethra Franklin. Hah! Adds a whole new meaning to 'Taking the Tube' now, doesn't it? Hold still now–"I heard he sang a good song, I heard he had a style ... La la la la la ... telling my whole life with his soooong...." Just go with the flow now, Mr Robert! "I felt all flushed with fever, embarrassed by the crowd ..."'

She was the perfect accompaniment to undignified procedures, and Rob's gratitude for her grew from his deeply held belief in the vital importance of compassionate service. Besides which, Rob just loved to laugh – and at the most inappropriate time or place. There was very little laughter elsewhere in our experience of that hospital. While Rob was on the ward in late July, he wrote the following:

TWO DIFFERENT WARDS

WARD 1 - 'MORPHINE AND THE UNDERWORLD'

My thirty-eighth Birthday Party: Setting. Tied by tubes to my penis linking my kidneys and bladder to three bags of different vintage Rose Pee Wine.

Minimal movements make you want to confess the crime, before you fight off the morphine-induced hallucination of being tortured to breaking point.

Guest list:

Bed 5 next door: Unseen Glaswegian – an 8-pints-a-day challenge for the anaesthetist, in to realign his drooping lip, probably from a broken bottle brawl.

Bed 4 in the corner: Unknown Snoring Snorter. In for his broken arm, possibly snapped by the weight of his tattoos.

Bed 3 in the far corner: Possibly dead, 3 packets a day, 92 years old, voice coach of Reggie Kray, and his daughter (or granddaughter, or long past love child from the days of leather condoms) – Waynetta Slob and her five-year-old daughter Sarah who smiles nicely while recoiling from the 'f' & 'c' words echoing round her head.

Bed 2 across: Lean druggie-eyed lad, with Meccano set frame around open wounded lower leg, on phone to one of his girlfriends suggesting to her (and as many people as possible): 'Let's do it doggy style while watching the X-Files.'

Bed 1 opposite: Fat Late Fifties Man, fighting with his errant tubes from his eprdrill / epiduring / epijury / epijewel

/ etc. machine, and his Essex Girl daughter giggling at Filth
Boy's every line.

And they're all staying the night!

A snoring, snorting, farting, belching, fetching-up-
phlegm-and-swallowing-it-again assortment of men to help
me see my birthday in.

WARD 2 – 'AFTER THE CATHARTIC EXPERIENCE'

Two days later:

I was on a ward with Gordon, who I wanted to get voice-over
work for, if only they could fully repair his lisp.

In the corner was Steve, an ex-bike courier who loved
nothing better than being on, or working on someone's bike,
who, since losing his leg in the accident, has realised that
mechanical and computer skills are close cousins, and, once
he gets the use of his fingers back, is going to design web pages.

In the far corner was Alf, a dry old geezer who fell from
a stepladder when he tried to help his daughter decorate their
new council flat and she wouldn't let him.

Across from me is Paul, a minister's adopted (now, prodigal) son, who yesterday cried for the first time in ten years
of violence, fatherhood, prison and six weeks of not knowing
whether he'll get to keep his leg. Who, when I told him God
had plans for him, to give him a hope and a future, he even
knew it was Jeremiah 29 v 11, 'cos it has been prophesied over
him half his life ago.

And opposite is David, the Man from Everywhere, who
talks too loud in too many alternating regional accents and is
strangely keen to tell everyone in his combined Cornish and
Camberwell accent that he's diabetic, that he's had a bionic
knee installed and that he's from Aberdeen. In between his
running commentary on his regime of straight leg lifts, he risks
telling that before his op was the first time, in a whole life of
not being wanted, that he'd ever felt really frightened.

Two days later, it's a different ward.
But nobody moved me.
Or them.

Rob Lacey, July 2000

We were assigned a new consultant. After the first round of treatment, in which the lining of the bladder had been stripped away again, tests revealed that the cancer was still present.

'It must be somewhere in the urinary tract. It could be in the base of the kidneys or the prostate. We don't exactly know. The whole area has the same genetic makeup, like I said earlier ... so we don't know. We assumed, statistically speaking, that it was back in the bladder because that's where it had appeared before. That's what one expects.'

'You assumed?'

'Yes. We assumed.'

I was furious. The whole procedure had been for nothing. Poor Rob was left with a very tender bladder again, but this time we were no nearer knowing what was going on.

During this period, three months pregnant, I was still performing my solo show, trying to earn some money. I was also teaching an adult dance class in the evenings in Camberwell and at the Dance Attic in Fulham.

Throughout the summer, Rob was structuring ideas for *the street bible* whenever he could, carefully planning which parts of the Bible he would look at. I have a lasting image of him sitting on a hospital bed in September surrounded by books and his laptop. He had to spend two days occupying a vacant bed just waiting until the consultant's appointed day to fit some nephrostomy tubes directly into the kidneys. Rob was clearly inspired by the whole challenge of doing the Bible in street language. He shot me a gleeful look as I arrived, eager to share with me the possibilities for the book.

'Guess what I'm going to start with.'

'Genesis by any chance?'

'Job!'

'Job?'

'Think about it. It's perfect.'

'What, all your family dying, endless catastrophes and your friends saying, "Curse God and die"? That's got to be one of the most depressing books of the Bible.'

'Yes ... what I said. Perfect.'

I screwed my face up.

He carried on. 'It'll be a bit like method acting.' Rob could see I wasn't convinced. 'How else am I supposed to empathise with a man who has lost everything? My pain won't be half as bad as his must have been. It's perfect.'

Of course, he was right. The fact that he started writing from under the skin of one of the most famous victims in literature gave him a rock-solid confidence for the whole of the rest of the book. His pain became Job's pain and vice versa. One of the reasons for the success of *the street bible* was that people engaged with Rob as much as with the characters themselves. By the time the book was re-released later as *The Word on the Street*, the public were much more aware just how autobiographical some of it had become.

Later that day, as I returned from getting a cup of coffee, Rob played me a song he had just discovered. It was the classic James Taylor track of 'Something in the Way She Moves'.

'Listen to the words, Sandra. This is how I feel about you. It's about how good you are for me.' He handed me the headphones and hit 'play'.

'I feel fine anytime she's around me now ...' I looked at Rob looking at me. His eyes were shining as the clarity of the vocals impressed upon me the simple truth of the lyrics. *'If I'm well you can tell that she's been with me now.'* I couldn't help smiling back at him.

When the song had finished, he just put his arms around me, kissed me and whispered into my ear, 'You are so good for me.'

By the time I was five months pregnant, I had decided to stop performing. The stresses and strains of day-to-day life and living with
diagnostic uncertainty were enough of a burden. Besides, I wanted
us to enjoy the pregnancy as much as we could.

The tests in July had involved the collection of urine from different points in Rob's urinary tract. Tubes ran everywhere. Rob
could do nothing but lie on the hospital bed performing this poor
impression of the London Underground map. It revealed cancer in
the base of the right kidney and in the two ureters from the kidneys to the bladder, one more so than the other. Again, the cancer
appeared to be in its early stages – in the lining and not in the wall
of the organs. So once more, the BCG treatment was employed,
but this time through nephrostomy tubes directly into each kidney,
where it was dripped in very slowly due to its highly concentrated
form. The BCG would then be washed through the urinary system
with the urine flow. Rob was the first patient in Britain to experience this technique. It had been done before in Denmark, where
the consultant had previously practised, and he was very confident
it would work. The procedure was complicated and 'quite uncomfortable' – the usual medical euphemism for 'very painful'.

The nephrostomy treatment began in September. Even now
it feels difficult to write about this. That autumn, as the leaves
changed colour on the trees, Rob's plight became more and more
desperate. Any excitement over the new life that grew inside me
was tempered by Rob's condition, and there were times when the
encroaching winter seemed to offer more bleakness than usual. It
seemed as if life revolved only around the hospital visits. The tubes
had to be inserted while Rob was conscious because he needed to
be able to alter his position during the procedure, an almost impossible task for staff dealing with an inert body. So, unsedated, Rob
endured the agony of having tubes inserted through his back and
into his kidneys. Normally, nephrostomy tubes are used when the
kidneys are dilated, but this was not the case for Rob's kidneys.

The restricted insertion of each tube was very intricate and 'quite uncomfortable'. It also involved live X-ray to guide the tubes to their destination. Only one side could be done at a time, and Rob had to roll over so that the tube in the other side could be inserted. After experiencing the gruelling pain of the first one, it was the hardest thing for him to just let it happen all over again. I stayed just outside, helplessly praying, trying hard not to hear Rob crying out. There was nowhere to sit. I just hung around for an extremely long two hours. Finally, when my lovely husband emerged, his face was grey with trauma. He had never known pain like this. Rob found one crumb of comfort; at least he now felt he could empathise with those who suffered torture.

After a couple of days, he was released to come home. The tubes had to be sealed in with plaster to remain sterile and to act as a barrier to any infection that might enter through the wounds to attack the kidneys directly. Rob was quite immobile and still in pain. He could only lie on his back. Any movement threatened to dislodge the tubes. If he lay flat, it really hurt, but if he sat up, he couldn't sleep. All I could do was build a ramp of pillows to keep him semi-recumbent.

Once his body was accustomed to the nephrostomy tubes, the six-week BCG treatment could start. Over such a prolonged period, the medical staff worried that Rob would be susceptible to infections as his weakening body fought off the BCG cells. His immune system was working overtime and, as is the case with chemotherapy, he was rendered fragile and vulnerable. The BCG could always cause other problems to flare up; the fear was that he would get a fever. And so our frequent trips to and from the hospital started. Rob never wanted to go; he hated the place. I had to convince him to make the journey because I was terrified he was going to suffer kidney failure. It was my biggest worry. I would lie next to him in the night, monitoring his breathing—him with his tubes and me six, seven months pregnant.

The whole hospital experience throughout that autumn was a nightmare. I have nothing but terrible, dark memories. With every step I took towards the exit at the end of each visit, my weeping would intensify until I was sobbing audibly while walking to the car. I felt I was deserting Rob and allowing hopelessness to come crashing in. I would drive home, barely able to see the road ahead through my tears. My chest ached with wretchedness by the time I threw myself on the bed at home. The weekly treatments were repeated six times. Rob could come home each time, but if he was running a fever, they would keep him in. During my final trimester, I had to cope with everything: looking after Rob, cooking, cleaning, shopping. Because Rob needed to drink copious amounts of mineral water, I found myself having to lug the packs of heavy bottles from the supermarket up the stairs to our first-floor flat. During this time, it seemed as if there was nobody to talk to. Our friends lived quite a distance from us. There was a support network and people were praying, but there were very few friends close by. I was frustrated, tired and worried for the well-being of my husband, my baby and myself. I didn't say anything to Rob because I didn't want to make things seem worse. I think he knew, though, just how hard I found it. Such was his compassion. But he wasn't well enough to help even though he wanted to. I was angry at life and the far-from-pleasant circumstances. I thought, *This is my first child. I should be enjoying this.* And then the next thought was often, *Who knows what's going to happen to Rob.* I went to antenatal classes on my own. There were a couple of sessions for husbands, but Rob couldn't make them. Everything was difficult for the two of us. We both felt isolated, helpless, with only prayer to sustain us.

Rob's mum always entertained the number 38 as being significant. She and Rob would joke about it – if a random number was needed, it was always 38. Their house was number 38. Rob's thirty-eighth birthday had been on a hospital ward. And during this nephrostomy treatment, 38 degrees* was the body temperature threshold I had to look out for. If Rob exceeded this, I had to take him straight back into hospital. The two treatments in the spring and the autumn left him weakened, and his bladder lining was extremely tender. This meant that as the higher concentration of BCG made its way through his delicate system, Rob would know exactly when it hit the bladder and then his urethra. He was desperate to drink something in order to dilute it and minimise the pain, but he had to wait for the BCG to drip through before he could relieve its effect with more liquids. It was important that none of the treatment remained undiluted in his bladder.

Rob's body always reacted to the treatment. A couple of times, the treatment had to be delayed because he just wasn't strong enough, or his blood wasn't right, or his temperature was up. Twice nursing staff had to cool him down with a fan and paracetamol† before anything could be done. After a very long seven weeks or so, towards the end of November, the tubes were removed. The regular hospital visits ended. He could finally rest at home.

Around this time, we were amazed to be offered jobs as artistic directors for a brand-new arts centre in Cardiff, yet to be built, called The Gate. The prospect of having some security with a regular salary was nothing short of amazing. Rob would oversee theatre and I would oversee dance. It was an unmissable opportunity to help formulate an Arts initiative in a community with which Rob had connections. After a few meetings and some telephone calls, we went to Cardiff one Saturday to look at three potential houses. We picked the first one. I had to handle everything concerning the purchase and the sale of our flat while Rob was completing his treatment. I had never bought a house before! Things like that were always Rob's department. Finally we bought our current home on

---

* 100.4°F.
† Acetaminophen.

13th December. Our excitement could hardly be contained. The day the call of confirmation came through, we were in bed with the phone between us like two giggly children ready for a chocolate factory tour complete with endless free samples. We were leaving London and starting a family. With his treatment behind us, we could now perhaps get on with being the 'Couple Expecting a Baby'.

'Rob, I was thinking ... now that you're getting better and before the baby comes ...'

'We could climb Everest?' He eased himself up a little in the bed and waved his hand in the air. 'Just pass me my diary would you? I think tomorrow's good for me.' We both laughed. 'You know why they call it Everest don't you? Because if I climbed it, I'd need to rest forever when I got there. A bit like Ever Ready batteries ... when they're flat they're only ever ready for the bin. Do you suppose Ever Ready workers never sleep? Maybe they never have holidays ...'

'Shush, mister.' I placed my finger on his lips. It was good that he was exercising his creativity again. I loved him all the more for it. He widened his eyes and bit his lips, slipping into naughty boy role. I couldn't help laughing. 'No, stop it. Listen, maybe we can go to Paris for a little weekend. You know, really get away. And Germany for Christmas again. Or both! Because I'm not allowed to fly, I've been looking at Eurostar. What do you think?'

'Is a little weekend actually smaller than a normal weekend? Or have you found a hotel run by dwarves? With a small front door?'

With only six weeks to go before Lukas was due to be born and in the light of the horrendous seven months we had just endured, it was a brilliant idea. Of course, Rob agreed and we began to set our sights. But it never happened. No Paris. No Germany. And almost no Christmas either. Two and a half weeks after he came home, Rob started to get excruciating pain in his prostate. Severe shooting pains eventually brought agony, and Rob became very distressed. The bladder was still raw and he was weeing copiously ...

literally, all the time. At first we thought it was the after effects of the treatment and that it should get better, but it actually got much worse. Before Christmas, Rob was back in hospital. We weren't going anywhere.

A week and a half was spent analysing what the situation could be. The good news was that tests revealed a complete absence of cancer in the whole urinary tract. We were ecstatic! It felt like a wonderful Christmas present. But what about the pain? The bad news was that the consultant suspected TB in the bladder.

'It can happen. It's very unusual. But the best thing to do is to start treating for TB.'

It seemed obvious to me that the expert was as much in the dark as we were. Complications to this new treatment had not been fully explored. 'In order to determine whether it is TB, we'll need to grow a culture. This will take six weeks at the very least, and we can't wait that long for diagnosis in this case. The best thing is to assume that you have got it so we can treat you straightaway and get this under control.'

More assumptions. But at least this time we were being told *before* treatment started. Anyway, there seemed to be little or no choice. He carried on spelling out the conditions. 'You won't see the effect of it for a month or two, so even though you take the tablets, you'll still feel as bad.' My heart sank. A month or two coincided exactly with the birth. I knew deep down that Lukas's arrival into the world would be compromised, and in that moment I had to let go of my hope for a happy start to parenthood for the two of us.

'Okay, if that's what has to be done.' I held on to Rob, and he placed one hand on my large tummy. He realised too.

Just before Christmas, Rob came out of hospital. He was very weak and pummelled by pain. Christmas Day that year was awful, utterly awful. It was a catalogue of misery. We knew it was going to be a long haul; the treatment for TB was going to take three months, and the tablets Rob had to swallow were huge. Our flat was very cold with its old, ill-fitting single-glazed sash windows. Even with the heating on full blast, we still shivered. Outside temperatures dropped. We kept the curtains closed all day to try to preserve some heat. Rob had a bucket next to his bed continuously, and he had developed a rolling technique to empty his bladder without getting up. Sometimes he would need to wee twenty-eight times in a night ... perhaps I should say thirty-eight. Even during *Grey Daze*, dating back months and months, Rob had needed to relieve himself throughout the night. Lack of sleep had become the norm for us both. So it seemed while everyone else was celebrating the happiest day of the year, we were enduring our most miserable. I really missed my family. Christmas Day at home in Germany was always delightful. Rob loved it as much as I did. My family hadn't seen me pregnant since the third month, and I wanted to share my coming to full term with them.

Bill and Rachel came to spend New Year with us, and they did a great job trying to cheer us up, but we were quite depressed. It had truly been a long dark night for us between September and the end of that year.

Then it was my turn to be admitted to hospital. I found myself in St George's, in Tooting. The baby was due on 24th January, but my blood pressure had risen and there was protein leakage from the kidneys into my urine so, on 9th January, Rob became a hospital visitor while I suffered pre-eclampsia. The medical spotlight certainly focused upon both husband's and wife's urinary tracts that winter. Rob was just about well enough to make the two-mile trip to visit me when he could. Not that it was easy for him. As soon as urine hit his bladder, it was screaming to get out, so he would have to urinate every five or ten minutes: toilet at home, bottle in the car, toilet as soon as he got to St George's. Then more bad news—the labour suite was at the opposite end of a long corridor from where the toilets were situated. Rob was dispirited and worried as the implication hit him. He and I agreed that he would just have to bring his bottle in with him in order to see his son enter the world. I was induced on Sunday, 14th January, and Lukas was born at two o'clock on Monday afternoon.

At the twenty-week scan, we had learnt our baby's gender. We wanted to know. Perhaps we needed a sense of control over this aspect of our lives. We chose his name and, in the earlier part of my pregnancy, I wrote him a little book.

Hello, Lovely Lukas, welcome to this life. Your mummy is pregnant, that means you are hiding inside me. We saw you today on a scan. Your head, your arms, your legs ... Your daddy isn't feeling very well, but by the time you arrive, everything will be fine.

All that year I seemed to have set targets: by Easter Rob will be well, by Christmas Rob will be well, by the time Lukas is born Rob will be well. So many pinpoints of hope. But it didn't happen. When would the ugly dead-looking insect be transformed into something great and glorious that would take flight? Could the cancer be left behind? Could we hope to see God's great healing touch? Could there be a glimpse of heavenly hope? I held on to my huge belly as the baby shifted inside. At least this was one transformation that was bound to happen soon. But nothing was soon enough for me. I smiled. Cartwheels and forward rolls were definitely out of the question.

After being induced, nothing happened, so Rob went home. On Monday the midwife said it was going to take ages, so I waddled to a phone at ten o'clock that morning.

'Oh, Rob, don't worry, nothing's going to happen for a while. If you're here by twelve, it'll be fine.' I put the phone down and started to walk back to the ward. Suddenly I was hit by a huge contraction. I turned and waddled more urgently back to the phone. 'Rob! Rob! Come now! I need you! I ... oooooh!'

I wasn't prepared for the level of pain that soon overtook me completely. *Come on Sandra,* I thought, *you're a dancer, you can cope with pain.* My reassurances to myself fell on deaf ears. The midwife strapped me down and linked me to a monitor. I struggled. Instinctively, all I wanted to do was to move, to dance my way through it somehow.

'No, come on now, dear, you have to lie down.' The midwife obviously had coped with women like me hundreds of times. 'We have to look at how frequent the contractions are.'

'How frequent are they?'

'Not frequent enough at the moment.' She became dismissive. 'Oh, it's going to take ages yet.'

'What?'

'Pull yourself together. It's going to be a long time. This is just the start. It's going to get much worse. Relax.'

'Relax?... Oooooh!' Clearly this woman thought I was exaggerating. My body seemed to be yelling at me that it could be anytime soon, but who was I as a first-time mother to question her wisdom?

At that time, Rob and I were part of the Icthus Fellowship, the Camberwell Congregation. The pastor's wife, Julie Stokes, was my birth partner. I was grateful that she was willing and that I'd had the foresight to think of asking her. I had suspected that I wouldn't be able to rely on Rob being well enough and, in any case, despite all the different kinds of pain he had endured, giving birth wasn't one of them. Julie had two children and was wonderful, a real prayer warrior. If anything went badly wrong, I could rely on her to pray fervently and faithfully.

Rob arrived around eleven, and Julie came at midday. By then I was already a centimetre and a half dilated, and the midwife broke my waters. The pain then increased to a level I couldn't tolerate, and I demanded an epidural. The doctor arrived, and by the time she had injected my spine, I felt I needed to push.

'I need to poo! I need to poo!' I gasped. Meanwhile Rob was in the corner of the room weeing into a bottle.

'What the hell is he doing?' The midwife was outraged. 'What is he doing! You can't do that here!'

'He's just had cancer treatment.' I panted. 'The toilet's too far … oooooh! I need to poo!'

'That's usually the sign that the baby is coming out … let's see.' Once she had taken her admonishing eyes off Rob, she looked back to the more familiar sight found in a labour suite. 'Oh, yes, you're ready. That's the head. I can see him.'

At one point a little later, they warned me that I might need a caesarean section if I didn't push the baby out right then. They took a little blood sample from the crown of his head to monitor the oxygen level. It was fine. I was pleased that the epidural left me with sensation in my legs, that I was not paralysed and that it had reduced the pain. But then I wasn't in the correct bed. Everything had happened so quickly. I had to transfer myself onto the delivery bed, which I could still just about manage. My blood pressure was 160/140 by the time Lukas was delivered. My eyes felt like popping out; it was awful. I was weak and exhausted. Then my blood pressure dropped to 60/40 and I felt light-headed and floaty. I had started haemorrhaging quite badly.

Lukas was blue when he came out. They put him on my tummy, but he didn't cry. I was worried. He was spirited away quickly so they could get him breathing. I told Rob to go and be with Lukas, but he didn't know where to go. Then panic gripped me deep inside. Was Lukas never going to breathe? It wasn't that superficial screaming type of panic. It was deep-seated and quite terrifying. It robbed me of my positivity and threw the first real sense of hopelessness into my face. When I did speak, all I could manage was, 'Is he okay? Is he really okay?' Rob could see me almost fainting and, of course, he needed to wee again.

Throughout all this chaos, Julie was heroically encouraging me and praying at every turn. If the circumstances hadn't been so life threatening, it would have made a good comedy scene. The next chapter in the hilarious scrapes of the German Dancer and the Welsh Poet. But then the threshold between comedy and tragedy often seems so slight as to appear negligible – or piddling.

Lukas was having his nostrils cleared under a lamp in one corner of the room (while his father busied himself with a bottle in another). Then suddenly Lukas cried his first lungful of air, and everything was fine. He didn't have to be taken away. But as he was returned to me, it became clear that everything where I was concerned was far from fine.

With the removal of the placenta, I had lost a lot of blood, and it was now gushing out of me. The poor midwife had been so overstressed because I had given birth so quickly that, not only had I been in the wrong bed but there was no line into a vein. Now I was deteriorating, and Rob stared in bewilderment as my consciousness threatened to slip away. No one could stop the bleeding. I tried to hug Lukas, but I couldn't.

'Rob, you hold him. I want to hold him' – not only was my strength ebbing, but I was starting to panic – 'but I can't ... I'm going to drop him.' Suddenly the door flung open and six doctors gathered around me as I lay there exposed to the world. They were desperately trying to find a vein, but with no success. They said everything was fine, but their actions and their expressions told a different story.

Because Rob had been so unwell, in my mind there had not been even an iota of doubt that anything would go wrong with this birth. Lukas was going to be fine, I was going to be fine. I didn't even think about it because Rob was already ill. Julie was praying, and I know other people were praying for us too. I really believe God was there to say 'Stop!' And that's what happened. Finally, a line went in and I was provided with saline and blood and so on.

The haemorrhage ceased and my blood pressure returned to normal. The next day, some of the same doctors came to see me.

'We're really sorry about yesterday.' I had not experienced medical staff apologising to me before. Perhaps they were worried I might seek litigation. 'It was pretty hairy, and it shouldn't have happened.' It was only after, as I pondered upon the events, that I realised I could have very easily died.

Lukas and I came home after three more days in hospital. Rob was coping and doing quite well. He could enjoy changing nappies and helping a bit. He was also writing *the street bible* at the time. There was pain, but it was manageable. Then, around the end of January and the beginning of February, the pain became excruciating as the TB took hold. At that stage, it had moved to his prostate gland. He had sharp, shooting pains in his rectum and would scream in agony. Rob described it as 'someone pushing a spiky branch up my bottom.'

I felt deeply compromised. I would be breastfeeding Lukas while Rob was crying out. They both needed me so badly. Being my first baby, that feeling of divided loyalties was dreadful, betraying my own child's dependency and vulnerability. I either felt like a bad mother or a bad wife. Because the cancer had apparently gone, nobody in our support network seemed to be paying much attention anymore. But Rob was in much worse pain than ever before. When the C word dropped off the radar, people just assumed we could be happy and enjoy our new baby, that everything was fine. But it wasn't. The most acute phase was during February; after that, the antibiotics started to kick in and alleviate Rob's condition. But he carried on–in pain–all the way through until September, when he finally had surgery.

FLIP YOU CANCER

Flip you cancer
Flip you cancer

Flip, flip, flip, flip, flip you cancer
I four letter word you, you cancer you
Cancer–flip you.

Rob Lacey, 2001

But there was a lot to be thankful for. Our lovely son had made his appearance, sharing a birthday with French playwright Molière, Welsh actor and musician Ivor Novello and civil-rights campaigner Martin Luther King Jr. Not a bad pedigree of creative and inspirational birthday buddies. Oh, yes, Google also informs me that the online resource Wikipedia was launched on the very same day as Lukas.

During March, we moved to Cardiff. The spring equinox that year signalled a new life for us. The dark night of the previous one with its confusing mix of dreams, nightmares, torture and near death had passed, and we emerged, setting off westwards with vernal hope of new beginnings.

Chapter 6
Sold-Out Specialists

Cardiff always appeared to me to be a much brighter and friendlier place to live. Each time Rob and I went to meetings about setting up the Gate Arts Centre, the sun seemed to be shining. London with a baby did not appeal, not to mention the traffic and the cost of living there. Cardiff, on the other hand, was still a capital with an Arts scene and plenty going on, but there were also mountains nearby to remind me of Germany. And it was by the sea – always an added bonus. And, of course, Rob's roots were there. What could be better?

Before Rob and I met, he decided that it might be prudent to take out critical illness cover for himself, perhaps mindful of his father's medical history. The cover would provide a continued salary in the event of a debilitating illness. Later, after we got married and as part of his plan to help me pay for my studies at Laban, we decided to reduce our financial outgoings. So we cancelled the policy. It was Christmas 1995. Just over a couple of months later, Rob was diagnosed with cancer. Of course, not only did he lack the insurance cover to provide a salary but having now been diagnosed, he could no longer get critical illness cover. The irony was not lost on us, and Rob always felt a degree of regret, not unnaturally.

When I was a little over five months pregnant with Lukas, I stopped performing. I did a little translation work, which brought in a minimal amount, but clearly we needed more income. Rob still managed to perform his one-man shows or fulfil a performance poetry gig here and there. His last ever *People Like Me* was in May 2001, having done over three hundred performances over the years. He could 'shake it out of his sleeve', as we say in German. He knew it so well that each request required very little rehearsal. But he frequently collapsed after these shows, utterly exhausted. It would take days for him to find his feet again. His appetite to work was irrepressible. Rob knew how important it is to stay in your audience's consciousness, especially with a forthcoming book that would benefit from the exposure. Being freelance performers hardly ensures a salary, let alone any sick pay or maternity leave.

Rob did all he could to ensure we would survive. During the autumn of 2000, we had sent out a newsletter to friends and contacts explaining our situation and asking for prayer support. Some friends from Rob's student days at Canterbury sent a cheque for £10,000 out of the blue. It was a jaw-dropping moment. It was wonderful. Unbelievable . . . and it felt like sick pay. It was as if God was saying, 'See? I'm looking after you, okay? And, anyway, I can do a good line in irony as well.'

The money lasted us quite a while. Also, the equity from the sale of our two-bedroom flat in London more than paid for our three-bedroom Edwardian terraced house in Cardiff. So we had a chunk of money put aside, which really helped, especially with the new house needing a new roof. This proved to be a very humbling time. Other smaller contributions from concerned people came in from all over the country. Somehow we managed to live for two years with extremely little earned income. There was always enough money to buy life's essentials, and I even, once or twice, forsook my familiar Lidl and Aldi for Sainsbury's! To this day, I don't know precisely how that provision came about except as an answer to prayer. In any case, it meant we could concentrate on our priorities – nurturing our baby son and getting Rob better.

Our life together was entirely different from before. New house, new church (for me anyway), new friends, new work prospects and

... a new bladder. At least, that's what became the next hope, the next possibility to help Rob. Although his pain had diminished, it was still present. Every time urine hit the bladder, Rob became desperate to urinate. He couldn't go anywhere farther than a few metres from a toilet. An entry in Rob's journal from that time reads, *'Night sweats and stabbing pains, I wee a hundred times in the day and thirty times through the night ... not a lot of sleep.'* The farthest we dared venture as a family was to Rob's parents' house, just a mile or so from where we lived. Even so, we had to time it carefully in the car.

'The tests show that the bladder is now about the size of a tennis ball.' Our new consultant looked from Rob to me and back again. 'Normally when it is distended with urine, it can grow to the size of a volleyball. So, obviously, such a small space fills extremely quickly.'

'In fact, quite a wee space then,' Rob said. His quip didn't hit the mark with the consultant, and I realised we needed to start all over again with this new consultant-patient relationship.

'What are the options?'

'Well, we can remove the current bladder and have a look at creating a new one by using the intestine. It's called orthotopic bladder reconstruction. It's quite effective, although you have to press down on the new bladder in order to stimulate urination.'

'Are there side effects?'

'Well ...' – the consultant drew breath, a signal that bad news was to follow – 'neobladder surgery can result in impotency in men.'

Rob and I looked at each other. We had to think about this. A few minutes later, we were on our way home. We weren't going to rush into new bladder reconstruction without serious consideration.

'Apart from squeezing the new bladder, I have got another pressing question.' Rob focused into the distance pensively.

'What's that?'

'Do you think Job lost his libido?'

'Well, he lost everything else.'

'But because he'd lost his wealth, by definition he was hard up.'

I laughed. 'That's terrible ...'

'He certainly didn't have any soft options.' Rob was giggling too now. 'Seriously ... we all know sex wasn't invented until after the Bible had been written.'

'What about Song of Songs, eh?' I waggled my finger at him mockingly.

'Duh!' He struck his forehead with the heel of his hand and then tried to eat my finger.

Watching Rob at work on *the street bible* was a privilege. He immersed himself in biblical literature, wonderfully lost in a world of discovery. Sometimes, when Lukas was asleep, I would find myself tinkering with nearby papers or leafing through a book or two, just to be near Rob. It wasn't that I wanted to disturb him, I just wanted to be part of this wonderful world he had found. Characters and stories came alive in his imagination, and he became absorbed despite his physical discomfort.

We had worked so much together that sometimes I couldn't bear to be apart from Rob and this new project. Often he would read passages to me, testing the register, the cadences, the flow, the effect. I loved these times. I could hear a whole new world taking shape, a world with its own characters, phrases and references. There was a sense in which I could be a little girl again, glorying in fantastic adventures straight from a creative source on tap. Of course, I am sure there were moments he just wished I would stop bothering him, but for the most part he knew and understood my fascination.

Job stands up. His heart's ripped to pieces ... [he] rips his coat, so it looks like his heart feels: torn to shreds. His life's been stripped from him; so he shaves his hair to prove it. He falls

flat on his face in front of God and whispers, 'I was born with
nothing; I'll die with nothing. God gives; God takes back.
God is God and God is good, always.'

The Word on the Street by Rob Lacey, page 133

Sometimes, knowing I was watching, he would allow his fingers to increase their speed ridiculously on the laptop keyboard, his head lolling slowly forward, eyes closing as if he were a concert pianist abandoned to the music. Then the mock snoring would kick in. I'd try not to laugh. Rob the joker. Rob the buffoon. Suddenly his head would jolt up again with a manic gurgle, and I knew what was coming. Jack Nicholson in *The Shining*. His head would turn towards me as if possessed, his eyes wild and demented. Pulling back his fringe and flattening his hair to reveal his widow's peak, he would bare his teeth and snarl, 'Here's ... Johnny!' Then he would go back to typing again calmly, as if nothing had happened, while I giggled helplessly.

Other times, when I thought he needed a break, I would return the compliment by putting on some early 1980s Christian worship music and perform stilted movements in a pastiche of the most predictable and literal 'sacred' dance, which would also render him helpless with mirth.

For a while, Rob was prescribed steroids to help him through. And, of course, there were the incessant toilet visits. But unstintingly, as long as his body would allow, Rob created his quirky, streetwise paraphrase of biblical narrative ... day after week after month. With each new and innovative expression that percolated up from an ancient source, I witnessed Rob's skill as a writer grow. Naturally, he grew weary. Sometimes very weary. And I often found myself nursing both man and baby boy.

Inevitably, as new parents, we gloried in our gorgeous son. Sometimes we would hold him, simply staring at this little miracle, talking about his life and his future. We played our doting roles well, charmed by every little sign of Lukas's development.

Despite the sense of being stuck at home, we spent some great times together. For one thing, I didn't want to go out and meet friends.

'No, you must.' Rob wanted me to build a life of my own in Cardiff. 'Don't worry about me. I want you to go out.'

'But what if Lukas wakes up and is grouchy and you're not feeling up to it?'

'What if he doesn't? And what if I'm not? Go on . . .'

I would go sometimes, but it was hard, knowing that Rob couldn't go out and meet friends. A simple task such as food shopping could also prove tricky. Generally, though, I was still trying not to feel lost. Rob had attended Glenwood Church before, and we knew a few people already, so logically it wasn't like coming to an entirely new place. Emotionally, however, it was a different story. My own creative endeavours had vanished, and I was grappling with two new roles, motherhood and wife of a housebound husband. Looking outwards became important. I had found out about Welsh Independent Dance, an organisation in Wales supporting professional dancers through training events and the provision of grants for productions. Because I wasn't working at that point, though, I didn't contact them. But I did find a mums and toddlers group where I eventually made a few friends. Compared to our London life, it seemed an impoverished existence, and yet, in a strange way, it was one of our most precious times together.

'When you are better,' I said to Rob one day, 'we'll look back to this time and say it was actually a really good time even though it seems horrible now.' I think it was simply that we just had to spend so much time together. When Rob *was* much better later on and we jumped into all that life had to offer with both feet, we found ourselves more argumentative and stressed. I realise now that those first few months in our new home, frustrating though they seemed at the time, did turn out to be among our best. Being ill gives you so much time—you can't do anything else. All you want to do is get better. You can't bear being ill. Maybe you spend a day reading a book and sleeping, but then, after two days, you think, *Right, that's it. Enough now!* Facing a long illness can prove to be extremely difficult. We prayed for change, for healing, for anything other than what Rob faced physically. It was hard accepting our current lot and being patient. We were eager to see answers to prayer, to see healing. Although, as human beings, we always seem to be predictably addicted to the current status quo ...

BROADLY THE SAME

Lord, won't ya keep things broadly the same
Frankly, revival would drive me insane
I'm busy, I'm tired so I'll ask you again
Lord, won't ya keep things broadly the same.

Lord, keep us from the unknown
I know that I'm damaged, but I'll leave it alone
I'm busy, I'm tired and I'm injury prone
But Lord, please keep us from the unknown.

Lord, won't ya keep us quite uninspired
At least, please wait till we're all retired
I'm busy, I'm tired, to be quite so fired
So Lord, please keep us quite uninspired.

When we sang 'Lord'
We didn't mean it; it's just a catchy tune.
When we said, 'have your way'
We didn't mean every single day.
When we said, 'change us'
We meant 'more polite' not 'outrageous'.
When we said, 'follow'
We didn't say how far behind you'd find us.

When we said, 'Lord, have your way
and change us so we follow'
Can't you see it was irony

That's now gone rather hollow.

So, Lord, please keep things broadly the same
Frankly, revival would drive me insane
I'm busy, I'm tired, so I'll ask you again
Lord, please keep things broadly the same.

Rob Lacey, 2002

To help perk him up, steroids were prescribed by Rob's GP, Tony Parsons, who also happened to be married to ex-Trapdoor member Diana. For a whole year, Diana came to our house every day to pray with us for Rob's healing. We felt very supported by this selfless act of love, and Tony too was always on the end of a phone. To this day, I am still grateful for their wonderful support. Rob went on to respond well to the steroids and found more strength and resilience. By August, he was well enough to travel, and the three of us spent a holiday in St Ives, Cornwall, with my mum and dad, my brother, my sister and their families. Its picturesque cobbled streets and quirky cottages, almost enclosed by the Irish Sea, was a welcome destination. We still had to know where the nearest toilet was and when we might have to improvise. For example, following a short journey from our holiday cottage, the car park on the edge of St Ives didn't provide a facility, at least not a bricks-and-mortar one. Rob had to avail himself of the bushes nearby when nobody was around before we could walk into town.

Doing the 'Toilet Check' was a major feature in our lives, bladder spasm a constant threat. Once when we were walking in London, Rob needed to wee. We went into a nearby park. Thankfully, the place was deserted, and Rob went behind a tree. Out of nowhere, a policeman appeared and screamed at Rob. It was like an animal reaction and very shocking.

'Oi you! Are you a dog? ARE YOU A DOG!' Rob explained about the cancer, but the officer was unsympathetic and clearly didn't believe him. However, he let him go with a warning. But back to St Ives.

One day we stopped in a studio in an artist's house. I fell in love with an abstract painting straightaway.

'Wow, this is brilliant!' Rob saw my eyes light up. 'The reds and purple are so rich ... so vibrant ...' I could hardly tear myself away from it, and we fell into conversation with the artist. Rob understood what the painting seemed to mean to me. There was passion, certainly, but also so much depth and life encapsulated in its lavish pigment. Somewhere, it seemed, our life together was captured there.

Naturally, our minds were still occupied with the neobladder surgery, now scheduled for September. We decided to visit Germany to get a second opinion. But as we were preparing to go, Rob began suffering back pain. We thought at first it was a result of his having helped to lift a new sofa into place, but it persisted despite a couple of visits to an osteopath. Once we were at my mum and dad's, the conversation turned to alternative therapies for cancer and, in particular, the work of Dr Helmut Keller.

'He was our GP for many years. Do you remember him, Sandra?' My dad sat next to a weary-looking Rob while my mum played with Lukas. 'He specialises as an oncologist now and has become quite famous for his natural treatment of cancer. It's called Carnivora.'

'What's that?'

'Something eating meat,' Rob chimed in sleepily, never one to miss out on the derivation of a word.

My dad carried on. 'Yes, that's right ... Look, everybody knows chemotherapy is just the worst treatment. At the very time when you need your immune system most, you destroy it with toxic chemicals. And quite often the cancer is then free to go and spread over the whole body.'

I translated briefly for Rob, who eased himself up to take part in the conversation.

'What Dr Keller developed,' my dad continued, 'was a system to boost the immune system whilst at the same time attacking only the cancer cells, but using a natural substance. He first started this in the seventies.'

'What substance is it?'

'This sounds a little crazy, but it's from the Venus flytrap plant. You know?'

'Hence meat eater,' said Rob. 'Although there's not a lot of meat on a bluebottle ...'

'He noticed that the secretion the plant uses to kill the fly doesn't eat away at its own cells. He isolated the enzyme, or whatever it is, and found a way of eating the cancer cells and nothing else. Ronald Reagan took it regularly.'

'Ronald Reagan?'

'That's one of the reasons why he's famous.'

'Who, Dr Keller or Ronald Reagan?'

'Dr Keller!' My dad laughed. 'You should call and see him.'

'Who? Ronald Reagan?'

'Ha ha! No! Dr Keller ... he lives only about twenty-five kilometres from here, you know ... It's worth a try. Maybe he can just do a maintenance treatment with the alternative stuff just to keep your immune system boosted so the cancer doesn't come back.'

My mum looked after Lukas while Rob and I drove to Dr Keller's house. We later learned that he hardly ever sees anyone in his own home, but he made an exception in our case. The visit was an eye-opener, medically and politically.

'Don't ever do chemotherapy, it's the worst thing for your body. Shy away even from X-rays. The radiation from them just loads your body with toxins.' Dr Keller went on to outline the fact that multinational pharmaceutical companies maintain a monopoly on the chemotherapy business. Their multi-billion-pound industry, he said, is intolerant of alternative therapies despite the efficacy shown in treatments such as his.

It made for a very powerful argument. The active component of Carnivora, plumbagin, had shown signs of being a powerful immuno-stimulant. It is a phytonutrient, a naturally occurring plant chemical that strengthens the human immune system to help it kill invader cells, such as cancer. It has also been demonstrated that Carnivora is non-toxic, non-mutagenic (that is, it does not cause cellular mutations) and has absolutely no side effects. In some cases, complete remission had been reported.

It was a lot of information to assimilate. By the time we returned to the UK, Rob's back pain had become more severe, and we still weren't sure what was causing it. The idea of trying Dr Keller's treatment began to grow in our minds. Still, we decided not to cancel the suggested bladder surgery, which was scheduled for Thursday, 13th September. The year was 2001, and that particular week turned out to be a very dark one indeed.

By this time, Rob's first draft of *the street bible* manuscript had been completed and submitted. It had been a huge undertaking. It had challenged, uplifted, exhausted and delighted him. It was amazing and humbling to see what he had achieved, considering the pain and discomfort that threatened to sap his strength and swamp him. Rob's vision remained undimmed. His love of words and irrepressible creative energy drove him on. Then, as now, I read certain passages and felt the struggle he had to commit some of those sentences, paragraphs and chapters to the virtual pages on his laptop screen. It was as if actual words had to be drawn out of his flesh and wrestled into submission onto the page.

On Sunday, 9th September, the phone rang. Could we come into the hospital for a chat? The consultant wanted to talk through the results of a preliminary X-ray and CT scan. We had refused a bone scan based on Dr Keller's recommendation.

'We have found some abnormalities on the lymph nodes,' the

consultant explained. 'It could be cancerous, but we can't be sure without a biopsy.'

The year before, we were told the same thing when small nodules had formed in Rob's kidneys as a result of the tuberculosis brought on by his BCG treatment. It turned out to be a harmless side effect, so we were hoping it would be a repeat of this.

The consultant continued, 'We can't be sure. We will still go ahead with the procedure, but if it proves cancerous, then we can't do the neobladder surgery. There wouldn't be time to learn how to urinate again using the newly constructed bladder, not to mention the additional stress to the body as it recovers from the operation. You would then need to have chemotherapy as soon as possible.'

I looked down at Rob's hand, held by mine, wishing his health problems had been limited simply to the annoying eczema he'd had on his fingers for so many years. At least that was only irritating and not life threatening.

'And, of course, you would need to be as fit as possible in order for that to start. So, instead, we would have to do a shorter procedure to give you an external bag in place of the bladder, a urostomy bag. This collects the urine directly, diverting it out of the body, bypassing the bladder entirely.'

After a few more questions from us, Rob smiled slightly. 'So, in effect, a short operation is bad news and a long operation is good news?'

'Yes.' The consultant smiled back, and his humanity seemed to surface. 'Well, when you wake up, Rob, if you've got a urostomy bag, you'll know what happened.' He turned to me. 'But, of course, I'll let you know.' This vagueness was not what I wanted to hear.

'Can you please phone me the moment you know?' I made a point of fixing his gaze. 'I don't want to wait until the day after. I need to speak to you as soon as you've finished the operation.'

'Of course. I'll ring you.'

Good news or bad news? More doubt. More turmoil. More

shock. Especially as Rob had started to look quite well. Despite the intense activity in his waterworks and some back pain, he seemed fairly healthy. He even had some energy. All we could do was wait for the operation to find out. But we adopted a positive attitude in our thinking and praying.

'It's got to be the side effects, the nodules. Of course it is. Please let it be nodules!'

Thursday, 13th September. While the media were alive with graphic accounts of the world-shattering horrors of that Tuesday – the ending of the American Dream, the Mighty Nation stricken at its heart – our own world was about to quake from shock. Rob's surgery was the first of the day, so I expected to hear something quite soon. Despite household distractions and the need to attend to Lukas, my mind centred on the telephone. The answerphone was set so I could screen the calls. I didn't want to get caught up in unwanted conversations.

I can look back and see myself through a filmic lens, but then I was too absorbed. Images of crashing jet planes and fireballs. Buildings collapsing and my baby crying to be fed or cuddled. The telephone ringing, but it not being the call. Household chores calling out to be done. Talk of terrorism everywhere. The lone mother trying to focus on getting through ...

But when you are caught up in your own drama, that objective eye, the camera lens, is not your concern. Your own life-and-death issues are the focus, and I knew how important this phone call might be.

In reality, I was not on my own; my mum had come over to be with me. But it had been two days of nothing but unbelievable images on television and in the newspapers. Perhaps because the plane crashes and subsequent destruction of the World Trade Center had looked so unfortunately Hollywood, almost like staged special effects, a sense of heightened reality took hold. As I held our son and kissed him, I wondered what kind of a world he would experience in the future. And I hardly dared to think about Rob not being part of it. All day I kept chanting, *'He will not die but live to see the glory of the Lord'*, from Psalm 118. As if I hoped the constant repetition would brainwash me. *'He will not die … He will not die …'*

Eleven o'clock … the consultant had not rung. Twelve o'clock … I still hadn't heard. One o'clock … nothing. It was good news, surely? The long operation, the neobladder surgery, it had to be. Two o'clock … I still hadn't heard. My day seemed frozen like a DVD still image. Advancing too slowly, frame by frame. Fast-forward not an option. Then at three o'clock the phone rang, the answerphone beeped and the voice belonged to Mr Matthews, the consultant. I snapped up the receiver.

'Yes! Yes? Hello? Sandra speaking …'

'Hello, Mrs Lacey, er, Sandra … I really am very sorry, but we have found cancerous cells. And they might have spread.' His words hung in the air. Then they seemed to soak into my body. A creeping osmosis of unwanted understanding. Yet another unbelievable moment that week.

'You're sure?' I knew it was irrational, but I hoped that, just maybe, different words would leave his mouth this time, perhaps with an opposite meaning.

'Beyond doubt, I'm afraid.'

Our friend Rachel Taylor-Beales was at the house by five o'clock, following two desperate hours of me trying to occupy my mind. By six o'clock, Rob was moved onto the high-dependency ward. Rachel waited outside while I went in. There were endless tubes everywhere, and I was quite shocked even though staff had shown me the day before where my husband would be after the operation. Rob was waiting for me. He had woken up, and he knew what his situation was. He was very calm.

'Okay, we've been through this once, we'll get through it again.'

'We've got to keep positive.'

'At least I have a new accessory.' He patted the urostomy bag and smiled. 'Very Pee Saint Laurent, don't you think?' The translucent plastic was ugly and undignified.

'Very chic.'

There was a pause. Rob looked around the small room and then back at me. 'But there are bigger shocks ... and bigger suffering ...'

'Hmm?'

'The World Trade Center.'

I saw the sadness in his face. I must have looked at him quizzically. It wasn't that I couldn't understand what he was saying, it was my amazement that this man, conscious of his own spreading cancer, could find such compassion for others. It shocked me a little because I wasn't expecting it.

'They had no choice, no time to say good-bye.' There were tears in his eyes. 'No opportunity to try to turn it all around somehow. Life snuffed out in a split second.'

A day or so later, we had a long chat with the oncologist.

'How aggressive is the cancer? Can you give a prognosis?'

'Well, I don't like giving prognoses, and I usually don't ... but it will continue to spread.' He scratched his jaw, as if weighing up the odds of something far less weighty. Then, as if realising the gesture might be misunderstood, he looked at us more soberly. 'But, statistically speaking, if you have chemotherapy and the chemotherapy goes well ... you've got a year to live.'

The meaning of his words seemed, at first, a million miles away. Slowly, as we talked, listened, questioned and then after he had gone, the impact became more real.

The next day, when I brought Lukas to visit Rob, I noticed nurses talking behind their hands and looking at us. I imagined they were saying, 'Poor little woman and her baby. Her husband is going to die of cancer. And such a gorgeous little boy. Poor woman.'

Pity was the last thing any of us wanted. Perhaps they weren't saying that at all, but I felt angry. Determined. Resolved to fight. It was weird and saddening to walk away from Rob at the end of a visit, carrying away his beautiful baby son. As if I was taking away his future.

'We would be a lovely happy family without this death sentence hanging over us,' I whispered to my big-eyed, trusting nine-month-old. 'We'll get Daddy better, won't we? Pray and pray it goes away.' I kissed his head as an *amen*.

My birthday was on the following Monday, and Rob was still in hospital. I turned twenty-nine. The last thing I expected was a present from Rob, much less a big present. He had bought the painting by the artist in St Ives. Without me knowing, he had returned to the studio and made the arrangements for it to be delivered to his mum and dad, who brought it round for me. My clever, lovely husband. I was stunned. The abstract looked even more wonderful than the first moment I had set eyes on it. And now it meant so much more. It instantly signified hope and life in the light of the events of the preceding few days. The picture became, and remains, a symbol for Rob. I look at it even now at different times of day when the light changes and see so many colours. The longer I stare, the more I see and the better it becomes. I feel so keenly that tangible hope for healing or for heaven, which burgeoned in those ensuing months. Rob wrote this poem a few weeks later, as you will see by the date.

SO WONDERFULLY WRONG

Oh, oh, we're gonna be so wrong. So so so wonderfully wrong.
And that's fine by me. 'Cos we're going to see.
Heaven as it is—fully paid up front, to us no charge, for free.

The brochures are too 2D.
The photos miss the point completely.
It's wrong—to try to compact it all onto a promotional
    CD-ROM

The tour agents just can't talk for long enough,
Can't say strong enough about how it's going to be.
When we see heaven as it is for free.
Heaven as it is—fully paid up front, to us no charge, for free.

Look who's there! In which chair? Where are all the chairs
And why is it no one cares? What time did the singing start?
Since before time clocked on and still coming from the heart.
And everyone around gets given a voice?
To add to the perfect sound their own harmonic part.
I look around and see even
The Over Comers are overcome and hit the deck
They all bend their neck. Vulnerable, open.

We're going to leave our slimy hole and
See the full fourth dimension of WHOLE.
We'll be fully filled in on the story on the earth bound three.
When we see heaven as it is for free.
Heaven as it is—fully paid up front, to us no charge, for free.

What's missing? It's bugging me—no church services in heaven.
It's an all-day thing. A living it out as our souls sing.
And so many worship styles—classical to jazz, to rock and
*   gospel, to soul to*
solo, by sold-out specialists who inspire total excellence from
*   the non*
musicians for whom there's work to do, projects to do, places
*   to be.*
From being comes doing—the order right at last
And the job satisfaction gets total reaction.
The chance to travel, to learn more of the scale, the beauty,
*   the range of what*
He spoke into life.

And the meals, the food, the taste of a table where
*   misunderstandings are*

ironed out and where laughter and hugs from estranged
*   partners make earth*
seem so far away.
The time travel where memories are healed.

But then I could be wrong.
I could be so, so, so wonderfully wrong.

Rob Lacey, November 2001

I heard someone say the other day that after the Second World War, sermons used to dwell a great deal on the subject of heaven. Ordinary life at that time was a very poor existence, conditions were appalling and the hurt had been so great that heaven was more than a viable option. But these days, our world is full of acquisition, enjoyment, consumerism. It's about living in the moment ... cars, holidays, pleasure ... and little else matters. It's existentialism with knobs on ... or touch-sensitive screens. Once a terminal illness hits you, though, all these things become superfluous. Meaningless. It's only then, with questions about faith in God or no faith in God, that the reality or absurdity of heaven becomes pertinent. Meaningful. Vital. We found ourselves spending every day facing the relevance of such questions.

I have a good friend who works as a psychiatrist. She sees a lot of pain and mental anguish in people and, consequently, finds it hard to believe in God herself. Originally from a Greek Orthodox tradition, she now declares herself an agnostic. 'I just can't see how there can be a God of love. Because how can he let all this stuff happen? Especially what happened to you two?'

It's a question we all hear from time to time. Following our conversations, she finds it hard to accept that I can believe in God and the reality of heaven. Of course, there have been many times when I have doubted, times when both Rob and I doubted. But what would faith be without its grudging and negative friend Doubt? Faith can only be faith if we are not sure to start with. I have always been wary of unbendable assertions of absolutes.

What if it is all a fake story? Some kind of palliative to bring comfort? I would not wish terminal cancer on anybody, but once it sharpens your focus on life's utter essentials – the need to survive not just day to day but sometimes hour to hour – your thinking about God and heaven is tested to the ultimate degree. Faith really is thrown into a fire. It seems obvious now to say it, but the fact that there was no room in our lives for anything non-essential meant that our faith had to count. It's got to mean something. Rob and I doubted all we held dear and, not unlike Job himself, some very fundamental questions and challenges were thrown our way. But we clung on. Sometimes desperately. We clung onto all that we truly cherished as essential and, as it turned out, it centred around our faith in Christ. The hope of heaven, of Rob ultimately getting a new body, inspired us to pray all the more fervently for his healing. The mettle of our faith was stressed to the breaking point, resulting in a greater resilience. Its strength was made possible only by exposing its weakness. Heaven has now become my only comfort since Rob died. He has no more pain, he has a new body and I believe my life, with a capital *L*, will only truly begin when I get there myself. But, looking back, there was something else too.

During my gap year in Sweden, someone said to me that they thought God was saying, 'I will take you into ways you've never dreamt of before. You will do things you never thought you could.' No doubt on that score. For better or worse, I could not imagine the situations we found ourselves in. But Rob and I shared two qualities: determination and persistence. As a young gymnast, I quickly became accustomed to picking myself up whenever I fell with a bump. It was a necessity. Every gymnast has to manage their bloodied hands and knees, their pulled muscles. The same with dancers. Strained ligaments, blistered toes and heels are bound up, blood or no blood, and you get on with the dance. Time and again I have witnessed the strong spirit of competitors and artists demonstrating their acceptance that injury, exhaustion and physical duress come with the job. But then Rob did so much more. He was continually knocked down by cancer, and he kept getting back up, time and time again. I never saw gymnasts or dancers actually face death and walk straight back in there. Their risks are measured and managed carefully. But cancer throws the rule book out of the window. All it wants to do is kill you. Rob showed us all what a fine human being he could be by simply getting back up after each life-threatening crisis. I saw him get up so many times and go back to the beam or the rings or the relentless choreography that was his life. And he would carry on.

Chapter 7
Stakes Escalate

The strobing rhythm of palm tree shadows along East San Ysidro Boulevard flicked across our eyes and the minibus windows. It was a rude reminder of how little sleep we had managed to get since leaving the UK. I was grateful for my sunglasses. The driver swung right onto the on-ramp of the San Diego freeway, heading south towards the Mexican border. We passed scrub oak growing in sandy soil as the bright sun poured through the windscreen, bleaching our vision. The air-conditioning was rendered almost useless by the driver's open window, and the aromas from outside found their way to us. Despite my hope that these might consist of lemon trees, cinnamon, or even roasting coffee beans, all that met our senses were exhaust fumes, hot rubber and a dubious corn smell which seemed to emanate from one of our fellow passengers.

This was our first trip across the border into Tijuana for alternative cancer treatment. Rob sat in the front, the crutches that now aided his walking propped against the seat. Rachel Taylor-Beales had come with us to look after Lukas, and the three of us sat in the back with other cancer sufferers bound for a variety of clinics operating outside the jurisdiction of the United States medical system. The minibus was a daily pilgrimage of hope against the odds.

Lukas had stuffed my little finger into his mouth repeatedly that morning. He had hardly let go of it since we woke up. I smiled at his littleness, his dependency, and sighed. Up front, Rob scratched his head slowly and yawned. Jet lag and cancer. Not a good cocktail. It was hard to believe we had come this far and were only just starting. My armour of positivity against cancer's evil failed me for a few seconds as I thought again about the connecting flight from Chicago to San Diego thirty-six hours earlier. Unlike the trans-Atlantic flight when we had travelled business class, thanks to the generosity of friends with air miles to spare, this second flight was purely domestic, and we found ourselves in economy. By this time, Rob's pain had become significant. He had appreciated the relative comfort of the first flight, but this San Diego–bound aeroplane had narrow seats which did not recline enough for him. Sitting upright was the worst possible position. Added to that, he had used up all his painkillers. We had been travelling all day, and by the time we would land in San Diego, it would be the equivalent of eight o'clock the following morning for us. As soon as the seat-belt sign was turned off, many passengers stood up and remained in the aisle for most of the five-hour journey. I tried hard not to entertain uncharitable thoughts about indulgent, overweight Americans and the fast-food culture, but it was difficult not to do so as, clearly, these people were too large to fit comfortably into the narrow seats. Having already flown the seven hours from Heathrow to Chicago and then waited a few hours for this connecting flight, we were all very weary. Lukas had cried a great deal, and Rob now needed to lie down. Rachel and I stood up so he could have three seats. With no more tablets, Rob's pain got worse still. A stewardess helped by providing an oxygen mask, which calmed him down, and he eventually did sleep a little.

The only place I could find to stand was by the toilets at the back of the aircraft. There was a little table just the right height for me to rest my arms. I held Lukas who, having just been breastfed, was now sleeping … thankfully. I didn't want to put him down and risk him waking up again. I stared out of the door window and into the blackness beyond.

'What am I doing? Dear Lord, what am I doing?'

Tears drenched my cheeks. I felt wretched. 'What am I doing taking my ill husband and my ten-month-old baby halfway round the world?' I shifted the weight from one leg to the other yet again. 'And just not knowing, never having been there, not knowing what to expect on the other side …'

A sense of panic twisted inside me and sobs threatened to overwhelm me. 'What if all this is just … a wild goose chase? What if it's all rubbish?' Fear started to surface. I was also desperate to yawn but suppressed it, aware that the shuddering sensation in my torso might release my emotional floodgates. I focused on Lukas. I must keep hold of him. I couldn't just collapse in tears. But what *were* we doing? 'Shit, this is bad.'

The thought had the clarity of a chiming bell, but its resounding dissonance disturbed me. Fear gripped hold. We had only just started out, and Rob seemed more ill than ever. I bit my lips together, determined to stand fast and be strong. I stared resolutely at the nothingness outside, but I might as well have been seven years old again. I was lost, alone and very far away from home.

The minibus slowed as it approached the border, which was bedecked with Stars and Stripes in a patriotic display following the terrorist attacks on the Twin Towers the preceding month. It was October 2001. We joined a short queue, and our driver reached for the pile of passports. Rachel had pulled out her folder containing all the print-outs covering alternative cancer protocols, which she had gleaned from the Internet. A lot of it had made for interesting, and sometimes challenging, reading, alongside information on Dr Keller's Carnivora treatment.

Rachel flicked through a few pages looking for something. I glanced at some of the articles we had studied in detail before leaving Cardiff: there was Laetrile, or B17, a synthetic form of the natural substance Amygdalin found in raw nuts like almonds and also in apricot or peach kernels; then there was Graviola, a natural phytochemical found in the Brazilian paw paw growing in the Amazon rainforest and shown to be 10,000 times more effective than chemotherapy. So many theories, so many assertions, so many questions. So much cancer.

The bus edged forward. Rachel's auburn hair shone in the sun, and I was staggered all over again not only at her friendship and support but at her utter selflessness in putting her whole life on hold just to be here with us. Rob shifted in his seat, and I could tell that the pain was kicking in again. Even though I could only see the back of his head, I knew so well the strained and weary expression on his face. I closed my eyes briefly and saw his smile on our wedding photos. It seemed so long ago. *Mein Mann.*

Walking had become difficult recently and he tired easily, despite his determination. For the most part, he was eating well and hadn't lost weight, but the pain in his back persisted, which really worried me. Now his upper leg joints were also giving him problems. The doctors back home had strongly advised a bone scan before we left, but because of Dr Keller's warning that this scan in particular has very high levels of radiation, we thought it best not to have one.

So it had all come to this. Trailing halfway round the world. After Rob's operation, I had phoned Dr Keller to tell him what had happened. He recommended his clinic in Tijuana because the one in Germany had been closed due to some management issues.

'They are saying Rob must also have chemo straightaway.'

'You know the damage that can do.' Dr Keller's tone was kind but firm. 'If I were you, I wouldn't delay. The Tijuana clinic could accommodate Rob immediately. But it is your choice. You must do what you feel best.'

And so we had started looking at the viability of the trip. A whole world opened up about which we had no idea. Browsing the Internet compounded that sense that there are a lot of weirdos out there. A sense of helplessness set in. At least Dr Keller had been my family's doctor for years. It was bad enough having to go all the way to Mexico, but at least there was a personal connection. When we looked more closely, we discovered other clinics in Tijuana offering similar therapies. Some provided accommodation, but this option proved too expensive.

Naturally, the National Health Service consultants had been sceptical to the point of being dismissive.

'I think you need to exercise a great deal of caution here. I've seen people die very quickly because they don't receive the treatment they should be getting.'

'Some places just get you to drink tea all the time.'

'You can't know what you're really buying into.'

It felt as if they were saying, 'You say no to us now, and we'll say no to you when you come back.' It was not overt, but implied nonetheless. Rob and I talked it through and, in the end, sensed very strongly that we had to try. The consultants had not actually said they would refuse subsequent chemotherapy, so we concluded we could always cross that bridge upon our return if Dr Keller's treatment didn't work. It became a pilgrimage. Over a few days, our thinking clarified, all the time mindful of the poisoning effect that chemotherapy has on the immune system. Anyone eavesdropping on our conversations would have heard things like:

'Let's give God some space to try out something different.'

'Look, Revelation 22:2 says about the Tree of Life, "And the leaves of the tree are for the healing of the nations." It's God's earth and God's creation.'

'And ... I think we've forgotten how to use natural remedies that have been passed down through generations. Somewhere they got lost.'

'Also, Jesus is always on the side of the underdog. The pharmaceutical giants can't make money from naturally occurring remedies, and the alternative therapies struggle in the face of it.'

And so the discussions fed into our decision. We would go. David against Goliath ... stepping out, trusting our slingshot faith.

'We'll support you, Sandra, you know we will.' My mum's and dad's concern on the phone had been palpable. 'We've got some money and we want to help.'

'We've costed it all out and it's going to be quite expensive. Around ten thousand pounds in all.'

'Tsch ... who cares about the money? Your mother and I think you should go for this. We want to support you. All right?'

'Thank you ...' I heard mum's voice in the background. 'What did she say?'

'She said, "There can be no price on love."' Mum and Dad gave what they could. It wasn't the whole amount, but Rob and I were humbled and very grateful.

Friends of ours had also suggested we go to a healing conference at a church in Toronto, where healing miracles had been reported. Despite our feeling uncomfortable and a little sceptical about stories of people roaring like lions and other charismatic activities, we started considering it. Other friends talked it through with us too.

'Well, sometimes it just seems to be where there is faith, miracles happen.'

'But we don't need to go to Toronto. God can heal here.' I wanted to be certain, to have covered every angle. 'God can use anybody to heal Rob. Anybody can pray a prayer whether it's ... Lukas or ... an archbishop.'

'But seeing miracles happen doesn't mean that those people are any better, or any worse, as Christians. What have you got to lose?'

Rob and I started to sense that this visit could be included in our pilgrimage. If nothing else, there was a growing realisation that desperation might be only just around the corner.

'Let's go. Why not? Three weeks or so in Mexico and then on to Toronto.'

'On to Toronto Tonto pronto!' Rob had to have the final word. I failed to understand it, so he had to explain the reference.

'Darling, you've forgotten,' I teased him, flicking my hair coquettishly, 'I'm far too young to remember the Lone Ranger!' It was wonderful how we could still share a joke in the face of everything.

We made our plans for the trip known to Glenwood, our church in Cardiff, and the congregation was asked if any were willing to support us. That was where the air miles came from. A group of ten people had already planned to attend the same healing conference and arrangements were made to meet them there. By now, thanks to a great deal of love and concern, the full ten thousand was met and our tickets were booked. To this day, I am profoundly thankful for everyone's generosity.

The minibus was waved through without any passport check. Mexican tarmac featured more holes than its American counterpart, and the bus jostled us around in the back. I was grateful that Rob was in a more steady seat up front. Rich culture gave way to poor, and it was only a matter of a minute or two before we found ourselves edging slowly along crowded streets where car horns blared continually and forlorn beggars' faces became conspicuous among the crowds. I gulped at the contrast we found in Tijuana, compared to San Diego's quiet, ordered boulevards. Then there was the irony of us rich Westerners entering a poorer country to seek cancer treatments while so many suffered without the means to pay for their own medicines. It felt far from comfortable. Ill people with little or no clothes to wear could be seen sitting in doorways or slumped against lampposts, hands held out forlornly. Beggars with missing limbs also took their chances among the pedestrians. It soon became apparent just how aware the people were of this curative cross-border trade, playing on visitors' sympathies for handouts. Mexican pharmacies sell drugs that normally require a prescription for much less than in the US, so every day a steady flow of Americans find their way south to stock up. Mexican authorities are keen to encourage their visitors, but the same cannot be said of American immigration officials. Very few Mexicans gain entry into the United States to find better-paid work to support their families, although hundreds of them try. Our minibus passed long lines of traffic heading for the US border as dozens of shops advertising medical services, dentistry and plastic surgery assaulted the eyes. Our driver found the first clinic and dropped off the relevant passenger. We set off again through the hectic, noisy streets.

We had flown west on 21st October. We'd had to wait for Rob's operation incision on his tummy to heal before we could fly, and on the way to Heathrow I'd been very positive. I drove us out of Cardiff.

'This is so right. So right. You know, God's going to do so much. I just know it.'

Rob sat beside me in the front while Lukas was in the back with Rachel. Rob smiled, but I knew he was in pain. So many times recently I'd seen his furrowed expression as he winced, and I had thought, what is this pain? I talked about it with Rachel but not with Rob – I wanted above all else to keep things positive for him. But the questions blighted my outwardly sunny disposition. Could it be the cancer? It can't be. It mustn't be, but why would it hurt so much?

'I'm so glad we're going to stop at San Francisco between Tijuana and Toronto. A short holiday ... well, a little sightseeing. It'll be wonderful, especially after the treatment. You'll see.'

On and on I went as the car ate up the motorway miles from Cardiff to London. Unknown to me and away from my rearview mirror, Rachel sat in the back, weeping silently most of the way. I just couldn't see my own desperation. I wanted to concentrate on Rob getting better. Nothing else mattered. We stayed the night with friends in Hounslow who took us on to Heathrow the following day. Dale said he would look after our car for us while we

were away. Progress to the airport was very slow because Fathers
for Justice had staged a kidnapping and the M4 motorway was
closed. Rob closed his eyes as we sat in a traffic queue, and I wondered whether our heavenly Father's justice extended to Rob's healing. His situation seemed so unfair. I couldn't think about other
people's suffering, just my husband's. That was the extent of my
positive determination. I had to be utterly focused. And now that I
reflect on it, there could have been no other choice at the time. We
were putting everything on the line during this trip. For the sake
of Rob, for the sake of Lukas, it had to work. It must not fail. Rob
would be healed. It soon became my only expectation. I stared at
my husband and my baby. Life. This was our life. Our only one.
Our only chance. And then I remembered a poem Rob had written
the year before.

HEAVY CROSS

How can carrying a heavy, rough-hewn cross
   Help me look up more?
How can carrying a heavy, rough-hewn cross
   Help me stand taller?
How can carrying a heavy, rough-hewn cross
   Help me run the race better?
How can carrying a heavy, rough-hewn cross
   Help me keep the pace longer?
How can carrying a heavy, rough-hewn cross
   Help me carry others stronger?
It's bizarre
But I believe it.
So I pick up my heavy, rough-hewn cross
   And put it on my back:
My spirit soars,
My rage against injustice roars,
As I carry the cross for the cause.

                                    Rob Lacey, 2000

At Heathrow, I asked for a wheelchair for Rob. I couldn't think of him struggling all the way to the departure gates on crutches. Again, at Chicago, we got a wheelchair and discovered the benefits of travelling 'disabled class'. Despite the increased security, we always zoomed to the front of queues, and security staff seemed very happy to wave us through. Rob, however, always harboured a naughty joker inside. He loved to find the worst possible joke to make in a given situation – the more serious the situation, the better. He would then censor himself not to say it so as to avoid causing offence or creating unnecessary problems, but he would always tell it to me, or to whomever, after the event. It was one of Rob's naughty qualities that endeared him to close friends and family.

On this occasion, though, he did not censor himself. Security following the recently declared 'War on Terrorism' had tightened, and the awareness of US immigration officers went well beyond their already stringent standards. Rob was drowsy with painkillers as I wheeled him towards the officer who quizzed us closely. I was already feeling nervous because we had been advised to state that we were on holiday.

'And what is the purpose of your visit?' The man studied our passports, his face set in stone. I shouldn't have stared at his epaulettes; it only unnerved me further.

'Holiday . . . erm, vacation.' I fumbled for the right words, aware that explanations involving cancer treatment in Mexican clinics and daily trips from San Diego across the border could so easily queer the pitch. I was not comfortable with this compromise but, seeing the wisdom of it, I concentrated on the holiday part of our itinerary. 'We're hoping to stop off in San Francisco to see the sights . . .'

Suddenly Rob opened his eyes and turned towards the man.

'And we've got a bomb.' He chuckled to himself and closed his eyes again.

'What?' The officer's intense eyes quickly scanned mine and Rachel's.

'He's joking! Erm … er …' All my nervousness surfaced, and I had visions of being taken into interrogation cells and strip-searched. In my head I was screaming, *Rob! What are you doing? Are you crazy?*

'It's the drugs.' Rachel seemed a lot calmer, and I was instantly grateful for her presence.

'Yes, he's taking drugs for … quite a few things. Medical …' I had to hold this together. 'He is not fully aware of what he is saying out loud. He has a wicked sense of humour. Sorry.' I tried smiling. It wasn't reciprocated.

Thankfully, Rob appeared to have fallen asleep, and the immigration officer gave us the benefit of the doubt and waved us through, his grimace as unchanged as Mount Rushmore.

The minibus dropped off another couple of patients at the next clinic, and it occurred to me that none of the other passengers seemed as ill as Rob. For a moment I saw my husband through their eyes. Pain torn. Weary. Scarred by suffering. Again I asserted my positive attitude and told my head and my heart to cling to God's promises. I stared out into the ramshackle streets of Tijuana passing across my vision. *Rob will be well. He will be well.* Eventually we arrived at our clinic. It did not look typical. It looked more like a standard type of apartment block six or seven storeys high. There was no sign over the entrance. We checked with the driver, who assured us it was the right place.

'You go look … Santa Cruz … Dr Santa Cruz. Second floor, third door right. You look, okay?'

When we found the door, there was nothing on it, no name of the clinic or the doctor. Rachel and I glanced quizzically at each other and knocked. Someone peeped through the blinds at us before opening the door. This was not the reassuring experience I wanted it to be.

'Welcome, welcome, I'm Doctor Santa Cruz.' Warm eyes

twinkled and a smile broke through his dark beard. 'Please, come in, come in. Have a seat through here.' I was struck by the clean white marble floors and walls, but the place was deserted, apart from him and a nurse. I spotted other doctors' names on a sign, but not his. It was clearly a surgery, but it felt as though he had just borrowed it. Other factors unsettled me further when we went through to another room. There was a pile of furniture in one corner covered with a sheet as if someone was in the process of moving in – or out. Or perhaps it was somebody's attempt at clearing up the place hurriedly, as if there was something to hide. In one corner, large reclining armchairs were arranged on Astroturf. There was an aquarium and a goldfish bowl as well as a parachute, which was draped around the ceiling. Rachel took Lukas over to stare at the fish.

'Dr Keller has been my family's GP for many years, back in Germany,' I told Dr Santa Cruz, thinking it best to establish the link that had started our quest. Maybe it was the fake grass that put me out of kilter. What if this was a scam? What if it was all a fake setup to extort money? It did seem a very strange place. But Dr Santa Cruz soon banished my suspicions as he talked about Dr Keller and the clinic's practice and so on. I warmed to him quickly and my trust was restored. Rob and I listened carefully as he outlined the schedule of treatment.

'We would like you to attend the clinic every day, Rob. We will put you on a drip for about five hours a day altogether. If we start at nine in the morning and have a break for lunch, then you will be finished by three o'clock. We will provide food for lunch.'

Rachel came over to join us, and Dr Santa Cruz jiggled Lukas's foot affectionately. 'And this little fellow is always welcome whenever you want. It's up to you.'

'Sounds good.'

'Thank you.'

'Every day I will test the blood also. So that is where we will start right now.' After running some tests, Dr Santa Cruz gave us print-outs of the blood analysis, tracking Rob's calcium levels. The information not only proved fascinating, it empowered us.

The name *Tijuana* is popularly believed to have originated from a mythical matriarch, Tia Juana or Aunt Jane, who traditionally provided travellers with good food and rest. This was certainly the case for us. As the days progressed, we appreciated the good fresh food that was readily available in the city and at the clinic. Fresh papaya, melon, mangoes and freshly squeezed orange juice. By contrast, the food available within walking distance of our Best Western motel in San Diego was scant. We had few choices because we had no car. The little that was on offer comprised fried chicken, burgers, fries and sugary drinks. It wasn't long before we found our north-of-the-border diet most unpleasant, to the point of being nauseating, and couldn't wait to do our ten-minute journey south to better nutrition. The contrast of the rich country and the poor country side by side, with opposite food values, was ironic to the point of absurdity. It was weird. It was harder for Rachel on the days we left her at the motel with Lukas. Often the food we brought back for them was consumed eagerly.

But another phenomenon that struck us was the vast numbers of Mexicans trying to gain entry to the US. The northbound border queues on our return journeys were very long, and we would often find ourselves inching forward, surrounded by migrating hopefuls outside the minibus and, of course, the cancer sufferers within. Added to that were the American shoppers returning home with their pharmaceutical bargains and bottles of tequila, while the US immigration officials continued their vigilance during that heightened state of tension after 9/11. We were obviously displaced aliens, and a creeping sense of surrealism started to colour our days in that strange world.

And then Lukas wanted to walk. Almost every waking hour, Rachel found herself bending over continually, holding his hands so that he could find his feet. One afternoon at the clinic it got to be too much.

'This is doing my back in. It's all he wants to do. Walk walk walk ... We've been at it all day.'

'Oh, dear.' I could see Rachel had a problem. 'We'll have to teach him to crawl.'

'I certainly can't keep this up. Come on, Lukas.'

'Lukas! Look at Mummy and Rachel.' The two of us got down on our tummies on the fake grass alongside him and started encouraging him to use his arms and legs.

Rob was lying on one of the fold-out armchairs with a drip attached to him, peering down at us. 'When you've finished the crawl, turn over and teach him the backstroke, could you?'

We laughed and instantly regretted it, due to the fact that our diaphragms were pressed into the floor. But clearly, we looked stupid.

'Oh, and by the way, you've forgotten the water.' Rob closed his eyes, gratified to be surrounded by a little silliness as he coped with his physical discomfort.

So the campaign to get Lukas crawling kicked off, and within a couple of days or so he got the idea. But by the end of the trip, he had started walking anyway.

Rachel's presence was a huge boon, especially when Lukas would wake at five in the morning to be breastfed. The knowledge that I didn't have sole responsibility for him throughout the rest of the day was very reassuring. A part of me could relax. But not for long.

Throughout the first week, Dr Santa Cruz was careful to explain everything clearly. The treatment would be gradual and cumulative. We were very well looked after and heartened by what seemed to be turning into a good relationship. But there was concern about Rob's back pain, so the doctor applied heat to his muscles and carried out some rudimentary examinations. On Friday night at the end of the first week, Rob ran a very high temperature. We were in our motel north of the border, and I rang Dr Santa Cruz to tell him what Rob and I knew, from experience, was wrong.

'He's got a kidney infection,' I said.

'Okay, try to get the fever down. Give him paracetamol. Now, you have the antibiotics?' Thankfully, the doctor had anticipated something like this and made sure we were equipped. 'Good ... start him on those right away, and I will see you on Monday morning. And Sandra ...'

'Yes?'

'Don't worry.'

Rob's temperature had dropped a little by the time I received a telephone call from Olivia, the sister of a friend with whom I had studied at Laban. She lived in San Diego and had welcomed us at the airport and taken us to the motel.

'Why don't you guys come and spend some time with us?' she offered. 'We'll show you around San Diego.' Naturally, we were keen to see something of the sights, but it all hinged on Rob's health.

'Well, Rob was running a high temperature last night, but it's calmed down a bit now.' I looked at him and he gave a thumbs-up. I knew he wanted us to have as good a time as we could. 'So ... that would be great. Thanks, Olivia.'

'I'll come over and pick you up.'

Following a Starbucks coffee, we saw dolphins and sea lions on the coast. We enjoyed a tour of the neighbourhood, complete with Stars and Stripes in almost every yard.

Rob had improved by the time we returned to the clinic on Monday, but the pain in his back persisted. It was so bad that the strong painkillers couldn't suppress it. As the week progressed, Rob would wake each night in agony. He had taken all that he could. I would sit up with him, unable to do anything except offer comfort and prayer.

A combination of Rob needing me and my constant vigilance didn't allow for a great deal of sleep. I was beginning to feel extremely tired. When you know your husband is in such pain, though, your own condition naturally takes a back seat. Rob had also started to lose all feeling in one leg; it was numb with tingling sensations. This meant he wasn't able to put on his own shoes or his socks anymore, so I had to help him get dressed. I sensed these degrees of change, but was too tired to allow the significance of them to impact me immediately.

'You need to inject him every night to help control the pain.' Dr Santa Cruz saw my worry. 'It's quite easy, really.'

'But I'm not a nurse,' I countered. 'How can I? I don't think I can ...'

'Don't worry, it's quite safe. Just push it together at the bottom, like this ... and then just whack it in ... like that.'

'Oh, I can't do this.'

'The faster you are, the quicker and less painful it is for him.'

Then Rob looked up at me. 'Don't worry about it, Sandra, it's me who gets the point.'

Under the doctor's expert gaze, I practised on a polystyrene sandwich box. Slowly, I got the hang of it and that night, the second Monday, the CV of my unplanned nursing career was augmented. It was a painkiller, Voltarol, that I learnt how to administer. Poor Rob. He knew only too well when I got it wrong. That first night he had one at midnight, then another at four o'clock. I was almost elated how well the first one went, but the second one was a disaster. Rob screamed.

'I'm sorry, I'm sorry, I'm sorry!' I couldn't bear the irony of inflicting pain in an attempt to relieve it, quite apart from adding to Rob's suffering.

For the rest of the two weeks in San Diego, I was his night-shift nurse and, more often than not, thankfully, the injections were painless ... although Rob would have been quite justified in describing his wife as a pain in the arse from time to time.

Part-way through the second week, Dr Santa Cruz looked worried. 'Sandra, the calcium and iron levels are extremely low.'

I looked over the blood test results as he continued. 'Also Rob is anaemic. I think there's more going on here. We could do with a bone scan and check to see if the cancer has spread into the bones.'

A few hours later, Rob's body on the image immediately reminded me of the white outline of a murder victim on the ground. I tried shrugging off the negative thoughts, but they didn't go far enough away.

The doctor explained the areas in red. I hadn't expected a colour scan, just a standard X-ray monochrome. Cancer. The red was the cancer. It burned like flames, and I felt myself stop breathing as I stared. All I could see was fire burning Rob up from the inside. There was so much of it. I forgot to move. I almost forgot to speak. There was too much fire. My eyes darted to every piece of red, backwards and forwards. Almost all of the pelvis and the lower part of the back, mainly on the left-hand side, with a small dot of red on the front. I tried breathing again, but the intake was too sharp, too quick, and my body shuddered. In slow motion, the walls of our life loosened and fell. I was staring at my husband's death consuming him inexorably from within. 'Once it's in the bones …' I had heard this incantation of hopelessness so many times regarding cancer. I didn't even search for another explanation. It made perfect sense. The logic was irrefutable. I held the evidence. The jury had returned its verdict. And it was hateful in its cool simplicity. Rob would die. And there, in a small and inaccessible clinic in hectic Tijuana, I saw our life fall apart and crumble. Nothing but dust.

'That's it.' Only I felt the words form in my mouth. They weren't even whispered, just my tongue gently connecting with my teeth.

'There's really nothing we can do. The alternative treatment won't work at all now.' Dr Santa Cruz had warned me before the scan. Now it was beyond doubt. 'It's slow, like building a house, you lay brick on brick on brick. And eventually the house will withstand the storm, but if the cancer's advanced, each time you build the wall up, *boom* – it's all gone again. That's what's happening here. The cancer is too strong for Rob's body to withhold. I am very sorry.'

I placed the scan on the table, aware that, given this news, I should, perhaps, be shaking now. But I was numbed by the shock of it all, and my body seemed to drift.

Although he saw the bone scan, we didn't share with Rob the implications of it. Rachel, Dr Santa Cruz and I kept the information from him. This is the one chapter he couldn't have written. For the most part, Rob was disengaged from everyday life anyway. His focus had to be on pain management as he drifted in and out of disturbed sleep. I walked out onto a balcony overlooking concrete, rusty railings, succulent green leaves and blue sky. City clamour filled my ears. The heat enveloped me. But it all faded to nothing as I allowed the sobbing to rise from within. The presence of such a powerful fear and the worry that followed in its wake twisted me into a withering heap. My fingers pressed hard against the concrete wall, their fingernails scraping up its tiny particles. Then they held my head and my body shook.

The earthquake's aftershock.

'Bill, you've got to come. Please.'

I had no idea Rachel had telephoned her husband.

'The cancer is more widespread than we thought. It's in his pelvis. In the bones. They can't do the treatment.'

'That would explain the difficulty walking.'

'Bill . . .' A pause. 'He's dying.'

A longer pause. Rachel's voice faltered as she tried not to cry. 'I need you here. This is too much for me. I can't do another week and a half on my own.'

Poor Rachel was as exhausted and worried as I was. Back home, Bill approached Glenwood Church to meet the travel costs and, within forty-eight hours, had joined us at the motel. But Rob's kidney infection returned. Olivia invited us to stay with her family over the second weekend. But by the time we arrived at her house, Rob's temperature had gone up again and he had to take to the sofa immediately. Throughout the day it kept rising and falling. We managed to enjoy a live jazz band when we did get out, and then we returned to the motel on Sunday. It had been a welcome break, but I knew Rob was suffering. It would have been better for him to have stayed at the motel.

The next week he became very sick just as we were about to go to the clinic. He vomited by the side of the minibus, then we picked him up and loaded him in for the cross-border drive once again. He was too weak to travel even just the ten minutes to and from, but we felt we had to keep going. By now we were approaching the end of October and with it Halloween and All Saints' Day – the struggle between good and evil, life and death. In Mexico the festival is somewhat different. *Día de los Muertos*, or Day of the Dead, lasts three days and involves vigils in cemeteries, feasting and singing, street parades, garlands of flowers and the brandishing of skeletons and skulls everywhere you look. Of course, we had no time or inclination to take in these celebrations. We had our own life-and-death struggle to cope with.

The infection hit Rob harder than usual, and the doctor said that because of his anaemia, he would need a blood transfusion. Clearly, Rob was getting weaker and weaker.

'But because his blood type is B negative, it is quite rare and has to be ordered. This will take two days.'

I stared at Dr Santa Cruz's eyes, trying to detect any sign of desperation. If there was any, he didn't show it. 'Rob needs to go to a hospital and have it done there because it will be administered over twenty-four hours.'

My mind started racing. Blood transfusions in Mexico? Do they have the same screening for AIDS? Is it the same legislation as we have in Britain or Germany? I felt panic bubbling up. My instinct was to refuse it, but the doctor continued.

'His body is desperate for it. If he doesn't have the transfusion, he's not even going to fly back to Britain.'

I didn't stop to question his implication. I agreed to the transfusion. The painkillers had rendered Rob semi-conscious, so there seemed little point involving him in the decision.

'Rob will have to stay in Mexico overnight.'

'Can I stay with him?'

'Yes, of course. But they do not allow children, so Lukas will need to be looked after.'

The next day I told Bill and Rachel to have a day off together. Bill had arrived the day before, and I took Lukas with Rob and me onto the minibus. Once we arrived at the clinic, however, Dr Santa Cruz announced that the blood had arrived at the hospital a day early, so the transfusion could start right away.

'I've booked it for you today.' He smiled.

I returned the smile uncertainly. 'Okay ... er, thanks.'

'I think Rob should have it as soon as possible. They've got a bed. You should go.'

The helplessness of wanting to be in two places at once hit me. I needed to say good-bye to Rob, take Lukas straight back to Rachel and Bill and then return and meet Rob at the hospital. The doctor told me its Spanish name, but I had no idea where it was. He also said he would get Rob to the hospital while I returned to the States. My mind was racing. Of course I wanted to be with Rob, but I had to get Lukas back. It was around midday by the time Lukas and I got the minibus for the journey back to the motel. But would Bill and Rachel have gone off somewhere? What if they had decided to take a taxi to the beach or gone for some food in San Diego?

What would I do? We only had one mobile phone between us, and I didn't have it.

'Are you going back into Mexico at all today?' The driver cocked his head towards me without taking his eyes off the traffic ahead. 'Are you going back?'

'Maybe.'

He scratched his chin. 'There is possibility I pick up more patients.'

A possibility. A maybe.

'I need to get back later, please ... Please?'

'I will knock on door. Okay?' He smiled and, reaching over, took hold of Lukas's fingers to waggle them.

I stepped into the motel car park and half jogged to Bill and Rachel's door. *Please, dear Lord, please let them be in.* No answer. I waited. Lukas suddenly felt much heavier. The air was hot. I calmed my breathing. I knocked again. Still no answer. I started a long, deep controlled sigh.

'Hi, Sandra!' Bill and Rachel came across the car park behind me. 'Want a pecan swirl?' Bill held up a brown bag.

After explaining everything, I gave them Lukas, all the baby gear and my wallet so they could buy some food for us.

'I have to get back. I don't want Rob to be on his own, especially all night.'

'That's okay. Look, why don't we take Lukas for a walk and you get some sleep?' They were both wonderfully calm. 'There's nothing you can do until the bus gets back, so just get some rest.'

So off they went, and I laid down for a while. Suddenly the driver was banging on the door.

'I'm going back now, yes? You want to come?'

'Okay, okay ... great, I'll come.' I must have drifted off. Hurriedly, I grabbed my passport and clambered into an empty minibus. I told the driver what I could remember of the hospital name, and he seemed to know which one it was. It wasn't until we were going across the border that I realised I had been so focused on getting back to be with Rob that I had overlooked some critical details. I had no wallet. No money. Any addresses and phone numbers were also in the wallet. I didn't have my mobile phone. It was just me and my passport. No way of contacting Bill and Rachel, Dr Santa Cruz, Olivia ... no one. Now we were driving down streets I didn't recognise. What was I doing? I wasn't thinking straight. Was I crazy? I don't know this man. I've no idea where I'm going. I don't know where he's taking me. Had I remembered the name of the hospital correctly? What if he takes me to the wrong one? What if he pulls over somewhere remote to rape me? This is really stupid. Stupid. *Lord, please don't let it be the wrong hospital. Please, Lord, let it be the right one.* I knew how impulsive and foolish I had been, but I couldn't bear the thought of deserting Rob, as ill as he was, to an unfamiliar Spanish-speaking hospital. What kind of idiot was I? No cash, no address, no mobile. No sense in my head. It had been driven out by desperation. I clung to my German passport, the only semblance of reassurance. I had made myself utterly vulnerable. For all I knew, maybe there was a black market for foreign passports. What was I doing? For a while I felt I had lost everything. Worse, I felt I had lost myself.

'Here it is ... okay?' The driver stopped the minibus abruptly.

I climbed out and tried to read the sign to verify the name of the hospital, but in the time it took for me to make sense of the words, the minibus had gone. And I hadn't even thought about asking him to wait while I checked to see if Rob was actually there. What was I going to do if he wasn't? It was idiotic. My pulse raced.

'Excuse me, do you have somebody called Rob Lacey here?' The receptionist looked at a list. In those few seconds, waiting for an answer, I was the most lost I had ever felt in my life. Sense was abandoned. I was abandoned.

'Robert Lacey? Yes, room 14.'

Thank you, Lord ... Really, really ... thank you.

Rob was sleeping, the blood dripping slowly. Tubes in, tubes out. I couldn't tell him what I'd done. I kissed his hand gently so as not to wake him, just so glad and relieved to be there. I sat in a chair next to him, talking when he woke and whispering when I wasn't sure if he was awake. Of course, I hadn't brought anything with me – no book, nothing to help fill the time. I just sat next to him for hours on end, praying and simply staring into the corner. I too sank into sleep periodically, shifting my position regularly to find a more comfortable arrangement for my limbs.

Whether what I experienced was a vision or a dream, I cannot be sure. I saw a very healthy-looking Rob performing onstage in a kind of church. For some reason he was wearing a white and blue striped top. He smiled at his audience. 'I'm healed, I'm healed,' and they applauded loudly. I thought consciously, *Okay, let's just get to Toronto … we have to make sure we get there.*

Dr Santa Cruz came the next morning when the transfusion was complete. With fresh blood, Rob felt quite a bit better, and we returned to the clinic with Dr Santa Cruz for more treatment.

It was important to keep Rob's attitude positive by continuing with the treatment, despite the latest prognosis. But then another kidney infection struck, a really bad one this time. His temperature was very high and the paracetamol didn't touch it. It surged past 38 degrees[*]; in fact it was 40[†]. In the middle of the night, I rang Dr Santa Cruz.

'You need to get the fever down again, it's really important, strip him down, sit him in a cold bath.'

'What?' It seemed counter-intuitive to me, cold water and bladder infections never went together in my mind. 'A cold bath with a kidney infection?'

'That is correct. Sit him a cold bath.'

Bill and I helped Rob into the bathroom.

---

[*] 100.4°F.
[†] 104°F.

'Darling, we've got to sit you in a cold bath, okay?'

'Okay, if it gets the temperature down.' Rob was burning up. Bill and I stripped him and he put his right foot in. 'Brrr ... that's cold. That's really cold.'

'I know my love, sorry.'

Then he put his left foot in.

'Aarh! It's boiling hot! Boiling hot!' Rob nearly freaked out. The nerve damage caused by the cancer in his left leg caused an exact opposite sensation. His brain couldn't cope with the conflicting information. After a few tense minutes, Bill and I gradually soothed him into the water. Rob had nearly fainted, and his emotions swung to and fro. Bill and I stayed by his side as we talked, prayed, read a few psalms, laughed and cried. It was quite bizarre. Added to which, we discussed Americans and their throwaway culture. It was a surreal episode, but then we were beginning to realise that our whole time there was increasingly made up of surreal episodes. And there were many more as the days went by.

There was Francisco, the quirky assistant at the clinic, who was keen to expound his conspiracy theory regarding the September 11th attacks. He had a ponytail, a little moustache, regularly used avocado as hair conditioner and gave us some CDs of U2 B sides. Bill couldn't work out if all these factors were supposed to be connected in some way.

Rachel did communion Anglican style on the motel bed with her own improvised version of the liturgy – using soup and crackers.

We were overcharged for everything in the Tijuana shops, but were too tired to care. Rachel and I bought some nail polish just to cheer ourselves up. Another time we bought a talking toy for Lukas, but it only spoke Spanish, and we couldn't turn it off. By the time we set off to go back to the border, we knew it would drive us mad, so Rachel jumped out of the minibus at some traffic lights and dumped the thing on a wall. The driver was so appalled that he got out and rescued it for his own children.

There were people from all over the world with whom we shared the bus–the cowboy with lung cancer; the young Australian woman who, tragically, was extremely ill; the woman who was a mayor and whose husband, a classics lecturer, had the most enormous beard. All the time there was talk of treatments. On one occasion, the mayor had a panic attack when her husband was absent. Bill spent a long time talking her through it and calming her despite the fact that she smelt heavily of corn chips, which almost made Bill retch. Each day the selection of minibus patients shuffled. Though it was often an emotional journey, Lukas always had a positive influence on the passengers.

'Hello, little Lukas.' A chirpy-looking American woman chucked his cheeks.

'Hello.' Rachel noticed the woman's makeup and smiled at her. 'You look good today.'

'Aah, that's what two pints of blood can do for you, honey.'

They fell into a conversation.

'So what do you do?' Rachel was always good at engaging with people.

'Oh, I work in a pawn shop. You know, usual thing . . . most of the time I'm selling guns and videos.'

Rachel's eyes widened. 'Really? Gosh . . . so, how did you get into that . . . er, I mean . . . did you, you know . . .'

It wasn't often Rachel seemed flummoxed and now she was blushing. 'Sorry, you don't look like . . . I mean . . .'

I could tell what had happened and started sniggering. The woman said 'pawn', but Rachel had assumed 'porn'. Perhaps the woman's makeup had been a little too enthusiastic.

Things always looked their bleakest whenever Rob deteriorated. Dr Santa Cruz told me that if he had known about the cancer in the bones, he wouldn't have recommended we come. He was adamant that we get back to Britain as soon as possible to have chemotherapy and radiotherapy to attack the cancer. On one occasion, he took Bill to one side to say that we needed to think about the options for getting a coffin to transport Rob's body back to Britain.

Then there was the time Rachel discovered a family of illegal immigrants hiding in a room at the motel. She had Lukas with her, and since they were gone a long time, I panicked, not knowing their whereabouts.

And, of course, there was the constant presence of the armed guards at the border crossing and the mayhem of the Tijuana streets, which included, bizarrely, a begging clown with one leg. At all times we were surrounded by both celebrations of death and the threat of death. Bill compared the border crossings to the River Styx scenario: always on the threshold between life and death, going backwards and forwards. I hated and feared crossing a border so many times; it reminded me of all the tense crossings between West and East Germany when I was younger. And one time, because of my nationality, a Mexican guard pulled me out of the minibus.

'You are a German while all of the others are American or British. You need a visa for Mexico.'

American immigration had said that Mexican officials weren't bothered about visas, but this Mexican immigration agent was insistent.

'You have been in Mexico, but you haven't got a visa. You should have had a visa for Mexico.'

He made me walk to the pedestrian exit. I couldn't sit in the bus with my husband or my baby. The guard at the other exit said it was fine and not to worry. I didn't need a visa because I was only going in and out and not staying overnight in Mexico. Apparently, the first officer just wanted to flex his authority to feel powerful. Every day we felt sorry for the tide of migrant workers who crossed to do the undervalued, menial and poorly paid jobs in the States and who returned to be treated like second-class citizens.

Another time a border guard wanted everyone off the bus. This hadn't happened before, and it was very unfair, especially for those who were ill. Most of them simply treated the minibus as an ambulance. Despite his condition, Rob stood up for justice yet again and insisted that they take the passports for inspection but allow. everyone to stay in the bus. Thankfully, an older guard who had a relative with cancer sanctioned our passage without fuss.

On top of all this, add the mounting desperation about Rob's condition and our urgent prayers, which often included strong expletives demanding God do something—not to mention the jokes and banter with Rob in between such sessions—and you end up with a pretty weird set of circumstances. But that is how it was.

SOMEONE REWROTE MY LIFE
Some Hollywood script doctor rewrote my life.
It was always meant to be a small town romantic comedy.
A feel-good movie,
Harmless escapism that you might just want to see twice.
If it caught something for you.
It was scheduled for limited release in some art house cinemas.
And then expected to be available in the remote section of
    some of the bigger video rental stores.
That's all.
So what's all these explosions?

Suddenly there's Special FX, the budget's ballooned out of all
    proportions
And I'm sucked into this race of conspiracy theories about
    the suppression of the natural cures for cancer by the
    all-powerful Pharmaceutical Companies. The obstacles
    become more sinister as the plot develops. The stakes
    escalate, the enemy figures appear more ruthless, better
    armed. The whole thing is an adrenaline rush from
    start to finish.
Is that how my life's meant to be?

What ending will be decided on?
Do I still have any say, as the subject?
Or am I irrelevant?

Rob Lacey, November 2001

Rob's latest fever came down eventually and, together with the antibiotics and the pain-relief injections, he slept well. At this stage, however, Rob was in agony all of his waking hours. At the clinic on a Friday, another medic saw Rob and suggested inserting a small tube directly into his spine for pain relief, not unlike an epidural. The procedure would render him immobile, but it would help the pain. So we went to his clinic in another part of town just for that procedure. It worked quite well. The next day, Rob was doing okay, having some pain but mostly feeling okay. Then on Sunday morning, because of wriggling and manoeuvring himself overnight, the tube had come out of his back.

'Oh, great ...' I was not pleased. 'We spent four hundred dollars having this little operation done, and it was all for nothing.'

But I was to be proved wrong.

Every seventh day, Rob seemed much better. Of course, it was a combination of factors, but we couldn't help kidding him that he was just being too demanding for the other six days. In fact, at this time we had been praying for guidance about whether we risked the trip to Toronto, considering Rob's worsening condition. We didn't know what to do. We phoned friends back home who, despite us telling them how bad Rob was, held out for us to go to Toronto. On the one hand we saw Rob in total agony, but on the other hand we had to return in that direction anyway, and there was a healing conference going on. We were also aware that our desperation would make us cling to anything. So we made our position plain to God: if Rob had just one day free of pain, we would take that as a sign that we should go. Otherwise we would cut our losses and return home, even though it would be a bitter pill to swallow.

That very Sunday, amazingly, Rob woke up completely pain free, despite the loose tube. Clearly, the blood transfusion had also helped enormously. In fact he was in good spirits. The weather was fine, so we took a car that Olivia had loaned us and headed due west to the Pacific Ocean. The fresh sea air and the azure sky welcomed us as we unloaded the car and got Rob into a wheelchair that we had borrowed. The beach was deserted, being off season, but the temperature was around 22 or 23 degrees*.

Just as we were about to wheel Rob onto the sand, a beach guard came to speak to us. We were impressed that there was someone on duty even at that time of year.

'Hey, guys, there's no way you'll get that wheelchair through the sand. I'll give you a beach one, okay?'

'A beach wheelchair?'

'Sure.' He opened a small shed and pulled out what appeared to be a kind of plastic sedan chair on four big, fat, rigid bright orange tyres.

'Here's the beastie baby. It's all yours.'

It was clear we had quite fortuitously chosen the right section of beach. At that time of year, there aren't many beach guards present along the San Diego coastline, perhaps only the one.

Sure enough, the beastie was perfect, and we were soon down in the surf with shoes and socks off. Lukas loved the sand. I did cartwheels and back flips. We had a wonderful, stress-free time. Then we all pushed Rob towards the ocean. Suddenly a huge wave came in and, before we realised what we were doing, the rest of us ran back onto the sand to keep our clothes dry, leaving Rob completely stranded with waves slapping at the seat of his chair. Everybody collapsed with laughter. So much for caring for the terminally ill ... throw them into the sea! We imagined him sailing off helplessly towards China, and I thought our laughing would

---

* 72˚ or 73˚F.

never end. It was fabulous to see Rob enjoying himself. The sense
of freedom from all his suffering was so tangible, and for a moment,
there he was, as carefree as he could be. My tears of laughter mixed
with those of gratitude and poignancy.

October 2001, Rob attempts a sea trip to China
from Imperial Beach San Diego

A little later we all walked along the empty beach. After a few
minutes, a couple appeared, heading towards us. It was as if they
had come from nowhere. They just walked straight towards us and,
without delay, the guy went up to Rob and looked him in the eyes.

'Oh, you're going to be fine. You're going to be well.'

He was in his early sixties, with piercing blue eyes and quite
weathered skin. He didn't ask what was wrong. There were no
greetings or small talk. And having delivered his message, he and
the woman walked off as quickly as they had come.

We were somewhat stunned and joked that they were angels.
And part of us believed that maybe they were. It was another weird
occurrence to add to our ever-growing list. That and the pain-free

day sealed our decision to go to Toronto, and we phoned our friends back home to tell them.

Rob's pain reasserted itself, and we prayed around the clock. Our perception of life intensified as the stress failed to diminish and a hyper-reality kicked in once more.

Dr Keller phoned the clinic from Germany to talk to me. 'Sandra, I cannot emphasise enough how seriously ill Rob is.'

I remembered stories about Dr Keller treating my uncle so many years before, how he had saved him from severe skin cancer by surgically removing a huge affected area in his chest and then treating him, resulting in a full recovery.

'There's nothing anybody can do. It's incurable, Sandra. It's gone too far. The Carnivora won't work. That is it.'

It felt like a stab to my chest. A cold, lacerating betrayal. Hearing him say it was very hard indeed. But we were convinced we should try for healing at Toronto; none of us was intending to take Rob home in a coffin.

There was another trans-Atlantic phone call, this time with Phil Stokes, our pastor from the Ichthus Church in Camberwell and husband to Julie, who had been present at Lukas's birth. Because he was part of our prayer chain, he had a good grasp on our situation and was already scheduled to go to the conference in Toronto.

'I'm coming out to San Diego right away.'

'But if you're already going to Toronto, we can meet up with you there. We'll be there in two days time anyway.'

'No, no, the thing is, I believe God has told me to come to you now.'

'Oh … right …'

'So that's what I am going to do. I'm getting a plane right away.'

And he did, spending our last twenty-four hours in San Diego with us. His support was wonderful, and it was heartening having such a faithful and loving man to care not just for Rob but for all of us, his prayerful presence boosting ours. Each day we were desperate for a miracle healing to happen. And each day it didn't.

Quite late on our final night in San Diego, Rob was drifting in and out of sleep, moaning. I was breastfeeding Lukas, so Rachel went to have a lie down in her room. Later, she described the experience she had as a kind of astral projection. As she drifted towards sleep, she had the sensation of floating on a cloud with a tremendous feeling of peace. Suddenly, as if there was a bang, she realised that Lukas was about to fall off the shelf on the other side of the room, and she leapt out of bed to catch him, only to find that she had imagined it. Slightly spooked, she went outside to find Bill, who was praying. At exactly the same time this had happened to Rachel, both Bill and Phil had sensed a sudden urgency to pray. Bill has since told me that although he considers himself much more liberal than charismatic, he felt compelled that night to fight in prayer against a looming darkness – all the time with an imagined sword in his hand. Exhaustion, stress and tightly focused vision can, of course, lead to weird behaviour, but, even so, this was something different and very tangible. And Phil, fresh to the situation, experienced it as well. Bill and Phil paced up and down in the car park petitioning God for healing, asking him to break through like day, eradicating night, good overcoming evil.

'I understand you have decided to go ahead with the Toronto visit.'

Dr Santa Cruz was gentle but firm. 'Please reconsider. Go straight home. Rob needs to be able to survive the flight because it will be very hard for him. He will need to lie down. Sitting up will be very uncomfortable. And the longer you leave it, the worse it will be.'

'But we have to try Toronto,' I explained. 'Having come all this way, we want Rob to have the best chance possible.'

He knew we would not be moved, and I respected his expertise and concern for Rob. His head nodded and he sighed slightly. When he looked up again, his manner was less insistent and more gracious.

'He needs to have the spinal tube inserted again before you leave tomorrow. We can give him a syringe for the pain control so he can administer it himself. All right? We'll get Rob to the clinic this afternoon.'

'Thank you.'

So the day before we were supposed to fly, we returned to the other clinic. But there was a problem. The wait at the clinic was extremely long, and, as the minibus driver was due to return at five, it soon became apparent that we would be cutting it fine. By five o'clock, the driver had returned – and Rob still hadn't been seen.

'We must go. Yes?'

'I'm sorry, but we haven't been seen yet. We're still waiting.'

'Okay, well I'll go and pick up the other patients and then come back. But you need to be ready when I come back.'

'When will that be?'

'As long as it takes. The border closes at seven. We have to be there.'

He drove off, and we turned our attention to the clinic staff, imploring them to see Rob as soon as possible. Our flight was very early the next morning. We couldn't afford to be stuck in Mexico overnight. It was not an option. Despite our urgent pleas, the staff simply told us not to worry. They did not appear to quicken their pace. We worked out that we had about half an hour. Our eyes darted from the clock to the staff to the car park and back again. This was not good. Flying without the pain relief would prove agonising and intolerable for Rob; he simply had to have the procedure. Clock, staff, car park. Still nothing. Minutes ticked by. Our heart rates quickened, breathing became more shallow. More minutes slipped through our fingers. Would we be stranded in Mexico?

Finally, it was Rob's turn to be seen. He had been in for just a few minutes when the minibus appeared. When the driver learnt we weren't ready, he was agitated and stomped up and down, the engine running.

'We have to go back! Come on! The border will close!'

'I'm sorry, please just wait one more minute, please, please!'

'I have all the other patients in there, everyone is ready. Come on! You put everybody at risk.' He looked at his watch for the tenth time. We had delayed him five minutes already.

Just at the point when it seemed likely he would get back in and drive off, Rob came out. Bill pushed him in his wheelchair down the corridor far quicker than was safe, Rachel and I bundled Lukas and his car seat into the minibus, Rob was loaded on, and off we all zoomed, making it to the border with just minutes to spare. Our final experience in Tijuana more than conformed to the highly stressful, almost paranoic set of circumstances surrounding our whole stay. If any of us had been able to take stock then, we might have realised that we would look back on this as one of the weirdest and most life-changing episodes we have lived through.

Chapter 8

The Sinking
of the Sun

Whenever we went through the official channels at an airport, Rob would employ all his acting skills. A smile would transform his war-torn face in order to impress upon his audience of one – whether it was the airline employee at the check-in, or security staff, or a flight crew member at the departure gate – that he was really quite well and simply wheelchair bound. This was critical because it was all too possible that he would be refused passage if there was a concern that he might cause the flight to be diverted – as would be the case in the event of a serious illness or death. On one occasion, in fact, while we were waiting in departures, Bill overheard an airport official worrying that Rob might die en route and suggesting that he be removed from the flight. But, what with the effect of the drugs and Rob's impish expressions, his solo performances often resulted in most people assuming that he had learning disabilities along with physical ones. This made him laugh all the more, when he was able, which was not often. The pain had increased substantially since our last flight, but Rob always knew he had to pull a good act out of the bag.

So we worked our way onto the plane bound for San Francisco, a part of our consciousness taken up with the minor fraudulence required by circumstance. It was literally a sick masquerade and felt quite horrible, belying our usual honesty. And yet, somehow, it didn't seem to matter. We were all exhausted, fraught and very preoccupied. I wouldn't have been surprised if the rest of us looked as though we might have caused the flight to be diverted. Lukas, of course, was the exception, and his sweet innocence sustained a life-giving hope as always. The short flight to San Francisco proved bearable, although it was still tense. Rob tried to be quite chirpy, despite needing to lean to one side to alleviate the pain.

'There's a Best Western here and another there, but I guess you guys want the nearest, huh? You look all done in.'

The woman at the help desk at the San Francisco airport flashed her best PR smile in Rob's direction as she pointed to some options on a map. 'Okay, now, there are taxis out front or a shuttle bus to your right. You have a good time now, you hear?'

She turned away from us, dispatching us into her mental out tray, but I wanted to press my nose into her pristine face and say, loud enough for more people to hear, 'That's my lovely, clever, talented husband sitting in that wheelchair, and he's dying from cancer. This is our life you've just cast to one side. Our life! How can you just throw us aside like that?'

Of course, all I did was whisper a thank-you and head for the door. Most of the time, being completely focused on keeping someone alive and pain free from one minute to the next coloured our perception of the rest of the world. It often seemed distant, unconnected. Sometimes pale or translucent. Insubstantial, even.

We decided on a Best Western hotel again because that was all we knew, and it was a reasonable cost. Wanting to save money, we took the shuttle bus instead of a taxi. Big mistake. The driver seemed intent on breaking some land speed record to get to all the hotels on his round. Two factors made it even worse for us. First, the only available seats were at the back of the bus, and second, our hotel was last on the driver's itinerary. We bounced over speed bumps and lurched around corners, all the time Rob shouting out in pain. Jostling up and down, I tried my best to hold on to Lukas and our luggage while Bill and Rachel fought the same battle. By the time we were disgorged into our hotel reception, our levels of resilience had sunk even further – a result, no doubt, of being bruised and shaken. Any sightseeing options fell off the end of our to-do list.

Inevitably, Rob wasn't well, and I tried to pump the spinal medication into him via the tube. It didn't work. Initially I thought I must be doing it wrong. I got Rachel and Bill to have a look, but nothing would go in. It was blocked. It seemed, upon inspection, that the solution had crystallised. Again, our money had been wasted. It hadn't even lasted a full day. Frustrated, we had to pull out the tube and rely solely on the Voltarol from nurse Sandra's needle. Rob's continuous pain kept him from decent sleep, but it was rest that we all needed. We were due to fly to Toronto within twenty-four hours.

The next morning before checking out, which was too early for breakfast, Bill used the toilet in their room and blocked it solid.

'Don't use the toilet, Rach,' he said as he left their room for a minute or two. Thinking he was referring merely to an unpleasant odour, Rachel did use it. Her flushing caused the whole thing to overflow in volcanic fashion. Semi-solid waste matter rolled and bobbed around in a never-ending sea of foul water that swamped the floor. Panicking, Rachel grabbed what she could to soak up the deluge – every towel, face cloth, bath mat and blanket. She was even eyeing up the curtains when she managed to stem the flow and slam the bathroom door shut. Bill heard the commotion when he returned.

'Quick! Bill, let's get out of here!' They grabbed their luggage and dashed towards reception, both incredulous, shocked and very amused. Feeling like naughty children, they contained their mirth as long as possible in order to check out.

'Everything all right for you?' The young woman chimed her ubiquitous incantation unthinkingly and smiled the required

American smile. Noting the unexpected pause, she looked back up at Bill, who raised himself to his full six feet, three inches.

'No.' Bill is a master of the deadpan expression. 'Actually, I'm a little disappointed with your plumbing.'

Rachel had to turn her red face away, the pressure cooker of her amusement almost ready to explode. Bill remained his understated self. 'The toilet is blocked.'

'Oh, brother ...' The clerk rolled her eyes.

'And there are one or two foreign bodies currently residing on the floor.'

We made for the exit, leaving behind a now fixed but uncertain smile beneath the receptionist's anxious gaze.

Toronto was not optional. I knew it was our last hope. I knew Rob might die and, even though I had not yet fully allowed myself to embrace the certainty of it, I knew that we had nothing left to lose. We had to keep trying. My steely determination drove us forward. Rob would be healed in Toronto. That was all there was to it. He had grown more disengaged from life's practical implications, commensurate with his increased suffering. So I had decided. Toronto was our hope.

The flight was horrible, but we made it. A couple of friends from our church picked us up at the airport and drove us directly to the home of an English family with whom we were staying. We unloaded our luggage and went straight to the church. As soon as we met up with the larger group of Glenwood people, I simply collapsed. I sobbed and sobbed and sobbed. Partly, it was an expression of handing over responsibility, but it was also the overwhelming gratitude at being among a small cross section of our church and community again. People who knew us. It was as if all could now be well, but exhaustion rendered me helpless for a while. It was heartening to know these people had come to support and to pray for Rob as well as to experience something of the remnants of the 'Toronto Blessing' phenomenon of the 1990s, famously held in awe by charismatic churches all over the world.

Our Ichthus pastor and friend, Phil Stokes, was brilliant. During the daytime he prayed continuously with Rob. That enabled me to let go a bit more and not have to be with Rob all the time. Phil and Rob did some deep soul-searching together and laid out everything through prayer. The focus was primarily worship and then about healing. And that seemed to be the 'Toronto' approach.

Being in the church meetings brought a sense of vulnerability, though. There were all these ill people, too many to count at times, desperate for healing. But nothing happened for Rob. The type of worship was alien to us, and quite mad things seemed to be happening. It was hard to accept the integrity of it at times.

There was one preacher who exclaimed, 'Think of the Holy Spirit as a big barrel like this.' He raised his hands as if encompassing a huge round object. 'Get hold of it, come on. That's it, pick it up. You got it. And all we have to do is take this big barrel and drink it all up! Yeah! Come on, drink up the Holy Spirit!'

Suddenly thousands of people were gulping together and laughing.

'Come on, people, swallow the Holy Spirit! The whole lot! Amen!'

Inevitably, the cynic in me reacted against it, but Rob and I had talked before we arrived there.

'Whatever God is doing, let's just be part of it. We're here, we've spent the money, let's just go with it.'

'Let's not let our cynicism stop God doing something if there is something to be done.'

So I was able to simply go with it and smile. I liked the fact that these people were being like children, unencumbered, playful. It occurred to me that this is what actors and dancers do. This is what we have to be good at – playfulness. I saw otherwise sensible and staid adults doing silly things, and it was quite liberating. I thought about all the sensible jobs these people had to do, day in and day out, and started to see that, maybe, the Holy Spirit's work here was as much about being playful and childlike as it was about anything else, and I was happy with that. So was Rob. After all, Rob always did do a great line in messing around. Perhaps the whole 'Toronto Blessing' was about discovering your inner child again and not being so overly serious to the point of being po-faced. After all, wasn't there a famous occasion when Jesus focused on a small child as an exemplar of faith, much to the annoyance of a few argumentative (and possibly po-faced) disciples? Anything that encouraged religious people to explore their humanness surely had to be a good thing.

But we were desperate for God to do something for Rob. We did see people getting out of wheelchairs after being prayed for and I thought, *It's fake! It's fake!* I was sure that they weren't real wheelchair users. But then I remembered them being pushed around normally before the meeting and realised it hadn't been set up at all.

Sometimes, though, the showmanship on the stage just wasn't palatable to our cultural sensibilities. And so it went on, the cynical and the faithful aspects of our personalities vied with each other the whole time. Rachel experienced a very good example of this. One evening she was so taken up with praying for Rob that she found herself on her own kneeling on the bathroom floor in an intense session of supplication. There had been lots of talk at that time about God changing people's teeth into gold as a sign of his power. It seemed absurd and far-fetched – yet, after quite some time in fervent prayer, Rachel found that her hands were covered in a silver sheen. Nonplussed and almost speechless, she stared at the undeniable evidence. She chided herself for not believing the golden teeth stories, but at the same time wondered whether her faith was somehow a little lacklustre, given the second-rate precious metal that now adorned her. Still a little stunned, she prepared to come and show us – only to realise that the silver had come from her tube of toothpaste.

Rob's pain did not diminish. In fact, it was so intense at times that his groaning and screaming were both disturbing and heart-rending. A Canadian doctor prescribed morphine tablets, which helped a great deal, and still we went to healing meetings at the church. Once, on the way back in the car, Rob became sick because he had overdosed on the morphine.

There were other things that annoyed us – things that we tried hard to put on one side. Lots of empty spaces were always reserved for the worship leaders in the church car park near the entrance. This made it difficult to find another space to park nearby in order to easily get Rob inside. It also seemed illogical that people, including us, of course, should fly thousands of miles to an airport church to get healing. Wasn't that a little crazy? Isn't God omnipresent? And on top of all that, the church building was nothing like a church. It felt more like a conference centre with too many corridors. There was little craft in the architecture to inspire or to reassure. But it felt petty to quibble over such considerations when there were other priorities. It was Bill who expressed how we were feeling.

'I'm willing for God to meet me in all this rubbish if it works for Rob. If someone says I've got to sacrifice a sheep for him to get healed, then I'll do it.'

We nodded.

'And bear in mind, I'm a vegetarian.'

We decided to just go with the flow and keep focused on our aim. Even Bill, a non-charismatic, found himself praying in tongues for Rob and having a go at the laying on of hands which, incidentally, did provide some relief for Rob at one point.

Canada in November is cold. It even snowed slightly while we were there. The contrast with Tijuana was great; it really felt as though we were in a different world. Staff at the church often had people like us staying with them. They offered rooms in their own homes, some of which had extra apartments attached. The couple we stayed with had an outdoor spa. It was exhilarating sitting in the steaming bubbles with snow falling on us. Even though Rob wasn't well, we persuaded him to come in, pointing out, not completely facetiously, that it would be like the pool at Bethesda, and perhaps he would be healed. The waters were certainly agitated with help from us, and he sank into its warm effervescence with a smile. Normally it would seem inadvisable to subject someone in Rob's condition to brave that cold, especially when the time came to get him out. But given all we had gone through, all we had seen and experienced, we entertained any possibility, it seemed, to find health and restoration for this beautiful, lovely man. And as our departure day drew near, behind every idea, every hope, every prayer, one question hung over us. Might Rob be dying – is he going to make it back home? I tried not to think about the seven-hour flight and how pain ridden, weak and weary Rob seemed now compared to almost five weeks previously. Our time was running out. Rob was willing to put aside all responses, reactions and feelings about what confronted us. He kept his focus clear. He spent many hours listening to Bible passages about healing on his Walkman and spoke of wanting to throw his crutches away.

Lukas took his first steps in the house where we were staying. It was such a joyful moment to see him find new freedom to move. Rob was thrilled.

'Oh … my son is walking! I want to walk again, without these crutches.' It was a strange moment, but I could sense faith rising inside him. 'I'm throwing the crutches away and walking!' He walked slowly around the living room, and we could see it was painful. But Rob thought, *I just want to make that step of faith,* and he did. He suffered afterwards, but it was very emotional. I cried. Then we all seemed to be crying and praying and whooping and laughing. Towards the end of that week, with such intense spiritual stuff going on and the absurdity of some of the things we did, I came to realise that, for us, having fun and our silly exhuberances did actually sit side by side with the serious. And I thought, *Why not?*

Also, while we were in Toronto, Rob had a dream. He was performing on a stage, everything going well, and the curtain came down suddenly. *Oh,* he thought, *that was the last one – that's it, I'm going to die. That was my last performance.* But then the curtain came up again and he thought, *Oh, it was just the interval!* When he told us this, we found it extremely poignant, and Rachel, Bill and I all thought, *Yes, yes … it's not the end.*

We all decided to go to Niagara Falls for the day. How could we be so close to one of the natural wonders of the world and not see it? The two-hour round trip required a car, so we hired one. Off we went, but Rob was really poorly, so we turned back. We helped him out of the car and went back to the house. He stopped.

'No! No. I do want to go … Let's go! I don't care.' He swallowed some more painkillers and we set off again. I had never driven an automatic before, and I kept hitting the brake accidentally, so we kangarooed a fair bit. I kept shouting apologies to everyone, especially poor Rob, who felt every bump as we skirted around Lake Ontario. Eventually I got the hang of it, and Rob even managed to sleep on the way. As soon as we opened the car doors in Niagara, the icy blast hit us. It was freezing. Bitterly cold. We all togged up as best we could, and I had managed to find a little grey knitted hat for Rob, with a bobble on. It only just fit him. He woke up and pulled the hat down to just above his eyes and bent the tops of his ears over. He stuck his head out of the door, looked around briefly at the sights and adopted a weak and breathy comedy voice.

'What's all that about then?' It was such a lovely, funny moment. Just like the normal Rob. All three of us creased up with laughter, and he kept up his act a little longer to please his audience still further. 'Hmm? I say … what's all that about then?' The moment became the funniest on our whole trip and the most memorable. It remains, even now, one of those iconic Rob moments for Bill, Rachel and me.

So we went down to take a look at the Niagara Falls. The roar was astounding. Everywhere was wet with spray, and there were three rainbows. I had never seen three in one go. I was amazed. I stood and stared, lost in the power of it all. After a while, Rob lay down on some chairs in the restaurant nearby, and I stood with Lukas bundled up warmly in a sling on the front of me. I was right up close to the barrier with the vast frightening drop into the waters far below. Lukas, technically, was suspended in the air with nothing below except the void. But he was safe. I was safe. Rob was safe. We were all safe. Safe in God's hands. My heart filled with gratitude. The rainbows shone. Their solidity seemed so real and yet they moved when I moved. Just a trick of the light and yet so real. A living promise of God. Three times over. I glanced back at Rob with his silly hat and I smiled. There and then I knew what was going to happen. Rob would be healed. It may not be in Toronto, it may be in months to come. But it would happen. Of that I was certain. The three rainbows signified so many things. Rob, Lukas and me. God the Father, Son and Spirit. Faith, hope and love. I was moved all over again. The massive power all around me was overwhelming, and I thought, *How big is God if this is so huge?* It began to snow, and I treasured my 'God moment' deep in the warmth between my baby and me.

SILVER LININGS

Someone shut the power down on the sun
It dimmed and dived and drowned.
Blackhole darkness sucked me down.
As I thrashed around the prison of my soul.
Fists flew in fury at the self-appointed Judge and Jury
He'll fry on my 'Why?' after 'Why?' after 'Why?'

Finally the cataracts of my blind anger acts cracked
And crumbled, fell to the floor.
And I watched as my eyes accustomised to the emerging
*   wreckage*
Retinas sucked the last light out of the grey and dull and I
*   strained to find the broken shapes.*
The wreckage of my question marks, exclamation marks,
*   bold expletives flung around my soul and now strewn*
*   across its cold uneven floor.*
Unanswered.
Broken.
More heavy-handed question marks than my memory said
*   I'd spoken.*
Bent, twisted by the strength with which they were propelled.
In the night light I froze with fright
As every abstract shape took on a fatalistic form
And every random line predicted a far more damaging storm.
And I begged for total, utter darkness
So I could be blind again to the accusing shapes
And dead to the damage I'd done, since the sinking of the sun.

Seconds scraped past me, slugging along
And the darkness makes like it's beginning to belong.
But I remembered rumours of day.
The light which might just come again.
Maybe by then, or by then.
But then 'then' becomes 'now' and then 'then' again—past
*   tense.*
I'm way past tense.
Is there no sense in this?
Is there no other sense?
My eyes betrayed me, my skin, my nose, my tongue,
But my ears heard something from outside the cell.

The key hole, like a double mirrored question mark whispers
  its query:
'*Do the stars still light up the night sky*
When it seems like the clouds have won?
Does every cloud have a silver lining
Or just the ones in line with the sun?'

Rob Lacey, August 2001

Twice Rob went forward for healing during the church meetings in Toronto. The first time somebody prayed for Rob, he felt
something like electricity tingling through his body. But afterwards
he didn't feel any better. He maybe felt a bit of relief from pain for
a couple of hours, but that was all. It was so stressful every time
these things happened, I often found myself praying, 'Please, do
something, God. Please.'

The next occurrence came when the preacher on the stage said
that he had a sensation in his leg.

'I've got a twitch in my right leg …' but he indicated his left
leg. He continued confusing left with right. 'Perhaps someone here
has a pain in their right leg …'

'No! You've got it wrong!' a voice shouted from the audience.
It was Rob. 'That's your left leg. You're pointing to your left leg.'

'What? … Oh, yeah … left leg! If you've got a pain in your left
leg, come forward.'

This suited Rob just fine. It *was* his left leg that was giving him
so many problems, so he hobbled forwards. Rachel and I accompanied him, and we were praying and begging, pleading with God.
But the overall situation had become insidious. It was easy for
people to assert that the priority was about worshipping God and
not the healing *per se*, but if you are so desperate and you love the
sick person deeply, then of course healing becomes the priority. We
felt trapped by this. It was not liberating. We had been through so
much, embarking on what had turned out to be such a nightmarish

pilgrimage. The last thing we wanted was to be told that we should think solely about worship. We had stepped out in faith, we had risked everything already. Anyway, the time had come to leave, and we had witnessed nothing that convinced us that Rob was being healed. Perhaps he wasn't in quite as much pain, from time to time, but that was it.

'Bill, I can't cope.'

It was the day of our homeward flight.

'You know, being next to Rob for the long flight. Please, could you go with him in business class?'

Rob had sunk into some severe pain again, and I had hit my own limit. Every night listening to Rob groaning, every night lying there wondering how long the pain would go on. Every night praying he would sleep again. And still the groaning would continue.

'Anyway, you've got long legs; it would be better for you. Rachel and I can look after Lukas back in economy. Sorry, I really can't cope with Rob for seven or eight hours.'

Bill was wonderful. Especially as that flight turned out to be the most horrendous one of all. Once more we behaved as if everything was normal as we made our way to our flight. There was no smile from Rob this time, though. He looked disfigured and dribbled periodically. You could see from the reactions of others, their less-than-subtle glances, that they regarded him as mentally ill or brain damaged. Rob was prescribed only four morphine tablets for each day, but he had taken five already – that was the measure of the severity of his pain. Nine morphine tablets in total were allocated to last him all the way to the UK. By the time our connecting flight to Chicago touched down, he had taken eight of them. It was very frightening. Bill hadn't witnessed Rob in so much pain, and he got very close to not coping, but he hung in there.

The cabin staff in business class for the trans-Atlantic flight became very stressed. Obviously, regulations stipulate that seats have to be in an upright position for takeoff and landing. But this was the one position Rob could not endure. Sitting him upright caused him to shout out and complain in great distress. The staff insisted the seat be returned to its upright position. But every time, Bill put it back down when they weren't looking. Cabin staff also feared that the flight might have to be diverted. They could see how ill-advisable this situation was. Bill had to mask his own fears in order to reassure them.

'It's really all right. It's cancer, he's in pain, but he's not going to die on this flight. Relax.' And as soon as they turned away from him, down went the seat again, and Bill prayed fervently that Rob would not die.

There were so many problems for Bill to cope with, including the ludicrous situation of having to empty Rob's urostomy bag little by little into a small drinking glass and convey it to the toilet and back many times until the bag was empty. The whole situation was almost impossible for Bill. I went forward to try to help, but I couldn't take it. I had expected I would return to the UK with a healed husband. Instead, the exact opposite was the case. Despite clinging to all the positives, the unpalatable truth was that the cancer was eating away at him fast—his hip bones were crumbling, the cancer was growing, his bladder was useless, his kidneys were ravaged by infection. Rob was lost in a nightmare of pain. I went back to my seat and sobbed inconsolably almost all of the way home.

'It didn't work … it didn't work … it didn't work …'

Home did not embrace us in its welcome. I had put an extra mattress on the futon in our playroom because Rob just couldn't manage the stairs. At four in the morning, he was in absolute agony, screaming. Poor Bill and Rachel. I phoned them. They'd only just got home.

'What shall I do? He's in agony. I think he needs to go to hospital.'

'Ring for an ambulance.' So Rob was taken to Velindre Hospital in Cardiff, which specialises in treating cancer. It felt like such a defeat. Despite all our efforts to escape from chemotherapy and radiotherapy, we went straight to the place that supplied it ... big time. We hadn't even been home a whole night.

The next day, Rob's consultant, Mr Barber, explained to a group of student doctors how the cancer had progressed.

'Look here, on the neck ... this nodule. You can see how the cancer is progressing.'

There were tiny knots on his neck by the lymph glands. Rob was sedated; he didn't hear anything. I looked and there was a lump on his neck I hadn't noticed before.

Mr Barber lowered his voice to a whisper. 'The cancer is progressing. You can see little signs of it everywhere on the body.'

I raged inside, trying to shut it out. 'No no no no!' It was awful. Unbearably awful.

'Okay now, Sandra.' The consultant smiled gently. 'We'll do some tests and then start chemo as soon as possible.'

Our battle was lost.

The very next day, the staff got him ready for chemotherapy. Rob and I both prayed for a last-minute miracle before the treatment started. I thought that he couldn't survive it. *It's going to kill him.* I simply didn't want those chemicals in his body; we were so anti-chemo. It was a complete defeat, as if we did our whole trip for nothing whatsoever. DEFEAT DEFEAT DEFEAT. All that God had promised collapsed like a house of cards. Why did we do it? What was it all for? What had been the point? Rob could have had chemo six weeks before.

We watched the chemicals start to drip. No miracle. And so began the bleak Velindre time. Rob's mum and dad looked after Lukas while I visited him. He also had radiotherapy. The rationale was to blast the cancer because of the degeneration in the bones. Two weeks after his admission, and our submission, he was extremely poorly with terrible diarrhoea. Then he got a severe infection, septicaemia, and although the doctors got it under control, Rob's body suffered huge punishments. He lost a great deal of weight and was very weak. He no longer talked, just whispered. Everybody who visited him could see that it was near the end. The head of the Palliative Care team at Velindre at that time was Professor Finlay. She was by far the best oncologist we had dealings with. She was understanding, humane and quite lovely. Rob and I talked with her for two hours, addressing all the issues surrounding the possibility of death. It was a week before Christmas.

There were long discussions about more chemo, but Rob touched my hand with a gentle finger. I looked into his devastated face.

'I don't want anymore,' he whispered slowly. His eyes held mine. 'I just want to go home.'

The consultants didn't tell us at the time, but they expected Rob to die whilst at home. None of them thought he would see Christmas.

Despite all the evidence to the contrary, when Rob got home, my conscious thought was, *Okay, he's getting better again now.* I don't know where it came from. Perhaps my Niagara moment still resounded in me. Perhaps I had nowhere else to go, and I wasn't accepting death as an option. Whatever the explanation, life in our house focused on Rob's needs while other households put up their lights and Christmas trees. A community palliative care nurse called in, complete with endless drugs. A district nurse attended. A commode arrived. Had we not been so fixated upon Rob's health and survival, we might have paused to reflect on how different our Christmas gifts were compared to those arriving at other people's houses. Very weak and hardly eating anything, Rob lost more weight. Having been twelve stone originally, he now weighed only seven.* This emaciated man that was my husband could no longer get out of bed. He rolled out slowly to use the commode and then he rolled back again.

My mum and dad came over to support me. But Christmas day was a very sad occasion. Rob was so unwell and had become very depressed. I had lost my loving, witty, impish Rob. All that was left was a shadow. Bill and Rachel popped in to spend some time with him, but Rob seemed to be experiencing something almost primal. The gutteral noises he made were disturbing. He was angry with God. There were too many unanswered questions, unfulfilled dreams, unrealised potential. Even more saddening was the fact that he didn't have the energy to engage with Lukas. He found it very difficult to connect with him. This was a Rob none of us had ever seen before – so much so that it didn't seem like him at all. And to a great extent, I don't think it was him. Instead of heralding peace, goodwill and hope for humankind, that Christmas day brought us hopelessness, fear and a sense of wretchedness. The day of our Saviour's birth turned out to be our most bleak. It really was the deepest pit of despair. An exceptional darkness closed in upon us.

* Rob had weighed 168 pounds and was down to only 98 pounds.

Chapter 9

To Play for Grace

I awoke on Boxing Day, not that I had slept particularly well. There was a silence. I had stayed with Rob in the playroom downstairs. There was no noise. I propped myself up carefully to look at him. The weak winter light was just beginning to illuminate the curtains. Rob was breathing. So. I was not a widow then ...

His eyes opened slowly and I stroked his face. He smiled. I kissed his forehead. He was alive. I really had prepared myself for Rob to die, and I knew that the grieving process had already started. Over the few days before Christmas, we had talked together, in those rare moments of lucidity for Rob, about his death and how I wanted to be there to hold him. We had talked in some detail about the event, and his acceptance and gentleness left me a little breathless. Though I could have easily raged at the injustice of his life ending so early, instead I was filled with love for him all over again. I looked up towards the window. The morning light grew stronger. A new day was dawning–a slow, gentle dawning that would grow as a metaphor over the months ahead. We didn't know it, but it would grow to such a great intensity as to become dazzling.

I think something must have happened on that Christmas day. Even now I cannot fathom exactly what it was, and I don't think Rob ever could either. The mystery of that overwhelming darkness and depression will remain, and I sense that, for the rest of my days on this planet, I will never know what changed–or how. I suspect the explanation lies well beyond this world.

On Boxing Day, Rob was feeling a bit better. It seemed incredible, but he was a little better. I like to think that his eyes reflected the light of that new day dawning.

'Come on, let's try and get you out of bed a bit' – I helped him up slowly – 'even if it's just sitting up, just a bit each day.' Then slowly, the next day, he actually got up and walked through into the living room. It was a big occasion.

'I think he's got a bit of hope and a bit of strength and drive again.' I was sitting on the step in our kitchen, my mother crouching on the other side of the room with Lukas toddling between us. 'I've no idea where from ... or how.'

Then Bono from U2 gave Rob a hand. It was amazing, one of Rob's heroes right there in our own living room. The fact that he was singing on the television made no difference. For Rob it was a very significant and personally relevant moment. It was New Year's Eve and U2 were on a TV programme singing a single from the album 'All That You Can't Leave Behind'. Bono's delivery seemed directed at Rob: *You've got stuck in a moment / And now you can't get out of it* ... Bono was singing to him, giving him instructions and advice. Rob realised that his life was faltering. And, as in the song, he was trapped on a rocky pathway going nowhere, with no daylight, only night's blackness hemming him in on all sides. But the moment wouldn't, mustn't and couldn't last any longer. It was almost as if this came from heaven's perspective. Rob's respect for Bono had always been rock solid and it seemed no coincidence to him that Bono should be there for him with something relevant to say.

"Bono looked straight at me and sang 'this time will pass' and then I knew ... I am going to get better." Rob got out the CD and listened to the track over and over again. Every word found its place within him until he was not afraid. There seemed nothing that the world could throw at Rob that he hadn't heard or met before. The confidence this instilled was inspiring. If Bono was the inspiration Rob needed at that time, then mine was Lukas. He was almost one year old. His toddling was very endearing, each step seemed to delight him. Life was opening up for our boy and every time he smiled it was as if the light intensified the hope in me. I shouldn't have been surprised, the name Lukas means light. Bono had something to say about it too, when I stopped to listen. The lyrics showed me that the light Lukas had brought into our lives was enchanting and I started to see things differently. We began seeing the light and warmth of God's love shining upon us. It wasn't that God's love had disappeared, it's just that we were too overcome by cancer to see it.

The pain from Rob's bones was getting better, and his leg wasn't hurting anymore. Day by day saw tiny improvements. Each day a little more strength, a degree more positivity. By now he was on steroids and, because he hardly ate anything, he was given nourishment drinks that provided energy. After spending so much time on crutches or in a wheelchair, it seemed incredible that he wanted to try going upstairs one day. He was shaky, but he did it. On 13th January we actually went to the cinema. The first *Lord of the Rings* film was released, and Rob wanted to see it with a determination that convinced me we ought to try. Bill and Rachel went with us and drove right up to the cinema entrance so that all we had to do was go through the front door, ride up the escalator and straight into the cinema. Considering Rob nearly died at Christmas, this was unbelievable. The seats were very comfortable, thankfully, because it was a three-hour film. He did grow weary, but managed to see it all. The significant scene for us both was at the underground bridge in the mountains at Khazad-dûm where Gandalf stands against the enormous demon Balrog, complete with its whip of fire.

'Go back to the Shadow ... You shall not pass!' demands the

old wizard, bearing his magic staff. We both felt that it was as if God was saying to Satan, 'Up to this point for Rob, but no further!' Evil, death and cancer had reached its limit for now. That was it. No more. We looked at each other afterwards, tears in our eyes, recalling the scene.

'YEAH!' we chorused. It was as positive an 'amen' as any we had uttered. Rob and I derived a great deal of inspiration from that particular scene in Tolkien's fantasy adventure. We were spurred on, rejuvenated.

Rob's health improved further. After Lukas's first birthday, Rob's friend from university days, Cliff Guthrie, came over from America to spend time with Rob. They took a trip out to Cardiff Bay with Rob able to drive once again. He was still very tired and weak, but he had one or two hours each day when he found some energy. Cliff's presence inspired him, and by that time he was able to walk a bit more, which included going upstairs. So by the end of January, he was sleeping in our bedroom again. Rob was advised to carry on with the chemotherapy. After much discussion and uncertainty, we decided that we might as well.

Another four courses of chemo followed. We grew to hate Velindre Hospital. The big waiting room held about eighty people, all cancer victims together with a family member or a friend. It was easy to pick out the suffering wife or husband. Inevitably, I reflected on their stories and couldn't help imagining how tough it was for each of them. Each visit felt as though you had walked into a place of death and suffering. There was so much heartache, so many lives blighted. Then there was Hunt the Blood Vessel, a gruelling game involving six or seven tries to get the needle into a vein. If it was unsuccessful, it meant waiting another week before you could go back for another attempt.

By March, after Rob's third course of chemo, a scan was taken that brought good news: the tumour had shrunk quite significantly.

The pain in his back had been gone since before Christmas. But any optimism was tempered by the oncologist.

'It could simply be a result of the radiotherapy. It holds the bone cancer at bay for a while, but once it reasserts itself, we essentially can do very little. Radiotherapy suffices as effective pain relief. Initially it stops it, but then the cancer continues to spread.'

Friends as well as family rallied to support us. Rob's friend Dale Kirk came to stay and was a wonderful support. He kept our life flowing by giving lots of practical help as well as encouragement for Rob. Ex-Trapdoor member Diana Parsons prayed faithfully for us every day, often popping round to help out. Living close by allowed for frequent visits. Rob's mum and dad often had Lukas and helped with picking up prescriptions and so on. Meanwhile, Rob went back to working on the second draft of *the street bible*, doing revisions and liaising with his editor, Amy Boucher Pye. Because of the nature of the book, he could do chunks here and there, cope with the chemo and then do a bit more. If he felt he had two good hours, he could edit or write and then leave it again. Amy was very understanding and, because he had no other commitments or demands upon his time, Rob really enjoyed the work. Also, what had seemed like priorities before didn't seem like them now. We were very relaxed about money, so long as we had enough to cover bills and buy food. After what we had been through, we were grateful simply to be us. Well-being was slowly becoming a reality.

WELLOSITY

My soul, such strengthity.
Just look at the wellosity of the real me.
So settledified.
My vitaleousness is prosperousing
My vibrantosity is blossomousing.
As your Spirit shoots through

And my soul seems more like You
Than this illnessesque me.

My soul, such gracitude.
Just look at the healthity of the real me.
So fiteous.
My flourishinity factor is off the scalyness
My abundanlish score is completelyness itself.
As your Spirit shines through
And my soul seems more like You
Than this diseasementfull me.

My soul, such depthity.
Just look at the stablosity of the real me.
So completelyment.
My haleity is so heartious
My fettleity is so finitous.
As your Spirit soars through
And my soul seems more like You
Than this disablemous me.

Rob Lacey, January 2002

After the fourth course of chemo in April, we decided to go to Germany for a short stay. By now Rob had set himself small challenges: walking to the television or CD player instead of using a remote control, going to the corner shop and so on. Checkout and departures seemed a breeze compared to five months before. This was good. Very good. As if the ghosts of the past had been laid to rest.

One afternoon, as we went for a walk in the Bavarian sunshine, part-way up a steep hill, Rob experienced a very sharp pain in his back. He was instantly worried.

'It's okay, Rob, maybe you've just pulled a muscle. The hill is very steep.' Outwardly I remained calm while inside my reaction and language were strong. *No no no! I can't believe the cancer's back!* Or words to that effect.

Rob too tried to be positive as we went to the homeopath who lived around the corner from my parents.

'I don't think the swelling is the cancer. It would look different,' the homeopath said. 'I'll give you an injection for the pain.' Rob's back was swollen, angry and red. 'The positivity of the mind can make a big difference to your body. Think positive.'

But being positive about Velindre was a big ask. Back in Britain, there were more explanations after an X-ray.

'It shows a 99 percent likelihood that the cancer's back. But it's only the bone cancer that is holding out.'

'Ninety-nine percent?' I said, indignant. 'That doesn't mean 100 percent! I want to know 138 percent that the cancer's back. Twice doctors have assumed something and treated Rob, and it was all for nothing. I'm not going to base all our future on your assumptions.'

There was a pause. Rob gave me a look which said, 'Whoa! Who's the feisty one today?' followed by a little smile. I was adamant; I wasn't going to put up with any ifs and maybes.

May 2002. We talked to Professor Finlay once more, this time about the instructions that had been given to Rob's care team: 'Pain control only from now on. We can't do anything more.' Rob and I had been shocked by this, and we wanted a more thorough approach.

'All we ask is for 100 percent certainty, not guesswork.'

'You are absolutely right.' Her smile and concern were reassuring. 'We'll do a bone biopsy, and that will tell us exactly what's happening.'

'Thank you, that's brilliant.'

'It will take a while though, at least four weeks, because we need to grow a culture.'

'Don't worry,' Rob chimed in, 'it's taken nearly forty years and I'm still not cultured.'

Professor Finlay appreciated the joke. 'All right. Just don't hold your breath, that's all.'

My feistiness found its voice again. 'Could you ring us as soon as you know? We don't want to wait until the appointment in six weeks' time, so can you please let us know as soon as you get the results?' It was reassuring to realise that she knew we would not be trifled with. 'Can you put a note on our file to that effect?'

'Of course.'

I was washing a few things in the sink when the phone rang. It was a morning in the middle of June.

A man's voice. 'The results are back from the biopsy, and there's no cancer there.' He was almost matter-of-fact. The whole of me stopped for a second, my hands still damp from a cursory wipe on the towel and then on my jeans.

'Pardon?' I was incredulous.

'Yes, it's very unusual. I've never seen anything like it. We took several biopsies from different parts of the bone. Some from the areas where the cancer was obvious, and some from other parts' – his words were entering my head and I hardly knew what to do with them – 'six samples all together. None of them show any cancer at all. It even reveals that the calcium levels are very high, which shows signs of repair.'

Part of my brain knew this was the news we had prayed for so desperately and for so long, but the reality of the moment seemed thousands of miles off somewhere.

'What this demonstrates is that the bones are growing back. The body is repairing itself.'

Rob was asleep in bed. I ran upstairs and jumped up and down in the bedroom.

'Rob! Rob! Rob! The cancer's gone! The cancer's gone! The doctor just rang, the cancer's gone!'

'What? What!' The poor man's head was still fuzzy. 'The cancer's ... gone?'

'It's gone it's gone it's gone!' I threw myself into bed. We cried, we hugged, we kissed. Neither of us could believe it. Then, suddenly, I thought that maybe I had misunderstood. I was the only one who had heard it. I was worried, maybe I had got it wrong. Maybe it wasn't true.

'Honestly, I can't believe it, this is really stupid. I mean, we've been praying for this miracle endlessly, and then when I hear it, I don't believe it!' I told just a few other people about the phone call, and their response was wholly positive. We still had two weeks until the consultation, though, so we decided not to make the news public knowledge just yet. But then, of course, I was worried all over again that I might have got hold of the wrong end of the stick.

The appointment confirmed everything. They had never witnessed such a thing before.

'It is remarkable.' The doctor had not encountered such an occurrence in his career.

'So is it a miracle?' Rob leaned towards him.

'Well, I wouldn't call it a miracle ...'

I could see Rob biting his lips as if he wanted to taunt him playfully.

'Would you call anything a miracle?' We pushed the doctor gently to see if he would admit it was God's doing. All our thoughts urged him, *Go on, go on, say it was God!*

'Well it is ... erm, remarkable.' He smiled broadly.

We were so over the moon, we could hardly believe it all over again. More X-rays were carried out to check the lymph nodes, and on Rob's fortieth birthday, 25th July, we threw a big party. By the beginning of September, we heard that everything cancerous had gone. It was unprecedented. How can I begin to express what it is like to have your mind well and truly boggled? The shock kept setting in. One moment it was, 'It's not happening,' and the next, 'Rob's getting better! Rob is better!' It was a very weird phenomenon and constantly startling. I had to keep reminding myself, *I've been praying for this and now it's happened. I've seen a miracle.* Rob was the same. He used to keep his medication and herbal treatments in a paper carrier bag which said on it, *'Eau de Toilette, Miracle Homme.'* He would sometimes parade this for the benefit of friends and proclaim, 'I'm a miracle man ... smell me!' It was wonderful to see him slowly getting stronger. The only sign of the effects of the illness was some nerve damage to his left foot, but otherwise he was very healthy. Soon he was swimming again. By Christmas that year, his upper body strength returned, and he achieved eighty lengths of the pool. Life was ... well, we didn't know what the limits were. We were genuinely amazed and very thankful to God.

The four years that followed proved extremely exciting and rewarding. They brought with them huge challenges, of course, and not everything was rosy. But it was exhilarating, with a very real sense of creative potential discovered, fulfilled and extended. Christmas 2002 was superb, the exact opposite to the one before. Rob wrote a very special poem for me (see page 12) and presented me with two eternity rings. We had gone to choose one, and I couldn't decide between two, so Rob gave me both! Hence the 'two eternities' line at the end of the poem. Our German Christmas was superb. Bill and Rachel joined us. After all we had been through together, it was simply wonderful to relax and enjoy life. The four of us went on a memorable midnight adventure among the pine trees. The snow was very thick and we sledged down the forest slopes. It was magical and truly seemed as if we had broken through into Narnia. The following day we went for a walk in the snow with all my family, including my brother, Frank. Bill and Rachel came along. Lukas was sitting on my shoulders. It was beautiful, again thick snow in the quiet forest. Suddenly Rob leapt onto my brother's back just for fun. I was so shocked that I let go of Lukas in order to catch Rob; all I could think of was Rob breaking his bones. Lukas fell headfirst behind me into the soft snow. I couldn't believe what I had done. I was horrified that I had let my toddler fall. But Lukas was fine, just a little shocked. Nevertheless, it was a measure of how protective I had become towards Rob. It had become my whole way of life.

All Rob's work on *the street bible* was finished, and the book was launched the following March at Spring Harvest. He was immensely proud of it. I remember him waving a copy in the air.

'Look, this is my book! It's my book!'

He decided that he didn't want to simply read extracts in front of large audiences, he wanted to perform it. So he spoke to theatre director Jenny Boot, who had directed *Grey Daze* for us, and she agreed to help him prepare a short performance. While they were working on it, he took on more and more challenges. So when I saw the first show, I was staggered to discover just how physical it was. At one point, he stood on top of a high stool, and all I wanted to do was to go and catch hold of him. I was reluctant for him to go to Spring Harvest. I didn't feel he was well enough.

But there was more to it than that. It was as if Rob tried for fifteen years to promote the Arts within the church. He struggled to be heard. Sometimes, it seemed, his performances were classed as peripheral and 'merely entertainment', as if he was not communicating anything. Many times I wondered whether these frustrations, along with the other negative tensions from his early adult life, contributed to Rob's health issues. He embodied so much. So many times I witnessed him throwing up with the stress of it all or saw the bleeding eczema breaking out on his skin. Rob cared so deeply that he took everything to heart. He was so passionate, so committed.

And so we argued about him going to Spring Harvest. Vehemently. It was a very big difference of opinion. I wanted him to spend time with me and Lukas, to enjoy being a good dad and husband. For me, I felt there was a backlog of issues left over from when he was very ill and depressed. I felt that throughout it all, I had to be his bottomless pit of resources. I was his cook, his cleaner, his nurse, his counsellor, the main carer for our baby ... and I had to put my career on hold. I feared he would get sucked back in to a roller-coaster lifestyle with excessive working hours. We both knew what a workaholic he was. To give him credit, he was aware of this and did try to change, but it always pulled at him. There was also some history about the relationships between Spring Harvest and performing artists. Over the years, Rob and many others had experienced at first-hand how their work could be so quickly marginalised by conventional Bible teaching and seminars. Artistic expression was considered peripheral. It had been the case for a long time, but Rob wasn't ready to give up yet. His concerted efforts to pave a way ahead for artists had already been set in motion.

His arguments were powerful and, of course, I agreed with some of them: the need for the church to understand the provocative role of the artist, the prophetic voice of the artist, providing unique insights into the story and characters of the Bible, helping to effect cultural change and so on. But still our argument raged. Bill and Rachel were involved too, all of us trying to persuade Rob not to take on this big promotional commitment. But the row escalated, and Rob stormed out of the house. He didn't return. We ended up phoning friends and searching for him. Eventually Bill found him in the last place we thought he would be. A pub. And Rob was a little tipsy. This was his expression of ultimate rebellion. Find a pub and drink ... one pint of beer. He couldn't manage any more. Alcohol was never something Rob lived with easily, especially considering the huge amounts of medication he'd been forced to take. I couldn't believe I had let this man who had been so gravely ill and was so precious to me take to the streets ... and to drink! Ever since that event, we have all laughed in the retelling of it, Rob always feigning a much larger measure of innocence than the measure of alcohol. Where feigned innocence was concerned, Rob could be a ten-pint storyteller.

So we disagreed about the promotion of the book. I maintained it would sell itself because it was so good, but Rob didn't see it that way. He reasoned that the book needed him there. Anyway, he did decide to go, and he was proved right. The book sold out within the first six days of Spring Harvest. Everyone was amazed, including the publisher, Zondervan. The impact of Rob's presence not only as a performer but also as a walking miracle created a focus upon God's great work in Rob's life. Suddenly he found a new status as a celebrated author. Afterwards we joked that to make it as an artist in the Christian sector, you need two major pre-requisites: you've got to write a book *and* come back from the dead. He was no longer perceived as just another arty weirdo banging his head against a brick wall in a lonely corner.

Lukas and I did go to be with Rob at Spring Harvest. If he was going, then I wanted to be there with him. But I found it very hard because we met lots of Christians, many of them leaders, who were only too eager to greet us.

'Oh, it's such a miracle you're healed! We always believed it was going to happen!'

Some, whom Rob had once regarded as friends, had failed to ask after him over all those preceding months. I felt very hurt and my thoughts were not altogether charitable. *You weren't there for all the pain and suffering and everything we've been through.* I wanted the whole world to know how bad it had been. For both of us. Inevitably, the carer of the one who suffers so often feels that they lack appreciation, support and understanding. Sickness eclipses such needs so effortlessly. This was a tension that was not easily resolved for me, but Rob was able to move on more positively. I felt overlooked and, coupled with that perceived attitude of those who don't want to embrace the importance of the Arts, my sense of marginalisation intensified. In terms of the book, though, it was a very good experience. Rob began to find a voice that was being heard at last.

WHY ME?

Thanks, Emmanuel. Thank God with us. I'm well!

But why me? Not him? Why me? Not them?

It's not 'cos I memorised the whole of Job.
Or wore an anointed prayer shawl.
Or a special hospital robe.
It's not 'cos we cried 'Mercy!' a million times.
It's not 'cos I wrote a hundred prayers with rhymes.
It's not 'cos my wife deserves me.
Puts the sign 'reserved' on me.
It's not 'cos my son needs me.
Twin tower workers were parents too.
It's not 'cos we've hung on.
It's just that God pulled us through.

So is it 'because I'm worth it'?
Well I am, I'm worth everything to God.
But so was Jacqueline du Pré,
So was Eva Cassidy.

So why? And when?
Was it already planned right back then?
Or did God shuffle and shift?
And watch all our prayers lift up past his eyes?
And did he hear our cries?
And did they all add up to Abraham- or Moses-size?
When they dared to do diplomacy with God?
Did we, together, negotiate with God?
We'll never see the subplots,
The alternative scenes,
Until we get to heaven, read the script
And work out what it means.
There's no recipe for what God gives free.

There's no ace to play for grace.

It's not that I toughed it out with cameras up my nether
    regions,
Tubes pushed through my back,
Needles in my failing veins,
Platinum pumped through every track.
It's none of that.
It's not that I kept a certain attitude,
When interviewed.
I'm no more clued than you.
I could've been a saint and still got stoned.
I could've interceded for the lion with my name on it,
Been compliant with my giant.
I could've driven into Jerusalem on a clapped-out Robin
    Reliant.
And still, it might have been,
That I would die.
And we might have no idea why.
Would that have been God's will?
Or is it God's plan never to fill an empty grave?
Or does He save each one of us?
So how come some still die?
And why this?
Why that?
And with answers so shy
What's the point in asking 'why'?

So I won't try to work out why.
I won't sweat to work it through.
For now, Rob, just face it,
God's mercy is focused down on you.
So leave your questions lying there
You might pick them up again.

Leave your lopsided, left heavy, rational, rigorous brain
Just give God his fame.
The always different, ever the same.
Lift up your voice and yell . . .
Thank Emmanuel, thank God with us. I'm well.

Rob Lacey, October 2002

I had started dancing again too. Once we heard that Rob's results were good, I applied for a commission from Welsh Independence Dance and actually did the show just before Rob's fortieth as a work in progress. It was called *More Than Just a Jelly Baby* and was about freedom. Then in September I did the final version because Rob was well enough to look after Lukas. I really enjoyed dancing and choreography again. A good friend of mine from my Laban days performed it with me. I knew her really well and we gelled perfectly. Audiences loved it, the first professional thing I'd done in Cardiff, and it went with a real bang. Later, in March 2003, I got a phone call to say that Welsh Independent Dance wanted to use my piece to represent Wales in a forthcoming international tour starting in January 2004.

Things started taking off for Rob too. With ever-increasing sales of *the street bible*, the publishers were thrilled and the phone started ringing. Rob appeared on television and radio interviews and, whenever he could persuade them, which was almost all the time, he did short performances as well. The public response was palpable, and still the sales increased. It hit the bestseller threshold quite quickly. The public realised that *the street bible* had huge potential for all types of usage. It became an ideal book to put into the hands of unchurched people because its language was anything but religious. For both of us, the experience was a little overwhelming, but it felt like God was saying, 'Look, this is life coming back. This is abundant life after not having any for a few years. Enjoy it!'

It was thrilling, and we were very proud of, and happy for,

each other. The only downside was that we didn't have as much time together. There was talk of book number two, and Rob collaborated with writer Nick Page to produce a small piece called *Street Life*, which was more like book number one and a half. It was a witty, fun study guide, and Rob and Nick had lots of fun writing it together. Then book number two proper was finalised. *The Liberator* was to be an amalgamation of the three Synoptic Gospels, and Amy was to be the editor again. Rob started work on it in late 2004.

Zondervan, meanwhile, wanted Rob to go over to America to talk about the possibility of releasing *the street bible* over there. There was further excitement.

'They want to release a new edition in the States – in a hardback cover. They want to promote it at national conventions and music festivals and, as well as doing interviews and appearances, they want me to tour with the show of the book.'

It was a jaw-dropping moment. Suddenly our lives accelerated into a fast lane that only other people seemed to travel, certainly not us. We were always the struggling artists with just about two pennies to rub whichever way seemed the most artistic. But now we felt empowered. We had looked death in the eye, overcome it, and it seemed we could take on anything. The sensation was strange but immensely gratifying. We felt limitless. Some mornings after a rushed breakfast, we would stare open-mouthed at the latest invitation or punch the air with excitement. All that hard, marginalised and often underpaid work over the long years seemed vindicated. Rob's talent was valued. But, of course, it was a two-edged sword. This high-octane promotion and endorsement, flattering though it was, would not last. We knew that. But at the same time, we were determined to make the most of it.

There isn't room here to lay out all the details of what happened in the ensuing three years. Much of it seemed to pass us in a blur of frenetic activity anyway, compared to the long drawn-out days of suffering. It would take another book to truly do it justice, so we will have to satisfy ourselves with headlines for the time being.

October 2003. After some organisational changes at Spring Harvest, Rob was invited to become the Arts consultant for the leadership team. At last he was heard and respected. He had a voice and he used it well.

Christmas 2003. Ludwigsstadt. Despite my worries about heavy workloads, we found new focus and reassurance. Rob and I talked and prayed about what to do if *the street bible* continued to sell well. We would be faced with the unusual situation of having significant money coming in, and both of us agreed we wanted it to buy us time. Where possible, Rob would work a four-day week, and we would have longer weekends together. Also, at long last, we could make dreams come true by putting money into Arts projects to generate new work. We were excited but still cautious because both our careers had received unexpected boosts at the same time.

January 2004. I went on a six-week tour of Europe and Canada representing Wales with my *Jelly Baby* show. It was extremely hard leaving Rob and Lukas but, amid some stressful touring circumstances, I loved having time to dance again and also to visit art galleries, soak up different cultures, relax and be free from responsibilities at home. Meanwhile, with America in mind, Rob worked with theatre director Steve Stickley to restructure his solo show based on *the street bible*. They focused more on the role of Job, linking into the significance and suffering of the Liberator figure in the New Testament. Bill and Rachel also extended and developed the live music for the seventy-five-minute performance.

We auditioned Elin Kelly (née Jeynes) with a view to her coming on board as a solo performer to do the show alongside Rob, thereby fulfilling more bookings and relieving the pressure on him. But Elin surprised us.

'Why don't you have three people? It would be much more dynamic.' She bubbled over with more ideas. It was clear that we were going to get on very well, and it was also wonderful to employ someone younger with so much to give. So plans were put in place to find two more actors.

February 2004. While Rob was in Germany with Lukas for a two-week break, BBC 1 contacted him to appear on the *Heaven and Earth* programme with just twelve hours' notice. My mum looked after Lukas while my dad drove Rob to Nuremberg Airport, where he waited all day for Rob's return. Unfortunately, there was a delay and Rob ended up staying overnight in a London hotel after the filming, requiring Dad to drive all the way home again and then return to get Rob the following day. Despite the stress it caused, we later laughed at Rob's new-found 'stardom' at the BBC's expense. I returned and we had a party for Lukas's third birthday, delayed one month because of my absence. Of course, it felt fabulous to see them both.

'Mummy! I found you again! I thought I'd lost you!' Lukas was so sweet, jumping up and down. 'I missed you so much!'

March 2004. Rob realised that his body weight had doubled from that of two years before, and it was muscle tone rather than fat! He was swimming regularly again. And *the street bible* was voted the UK's 'Christian Book of the Year'.

April 2004. Rob, Bill, Rachel and Steve went to Nashville for a week to launch *the street bible*, now rebranded as *The Word on the Street* in hardback. While they were at a gospel music convention, Steve directed Rob as he started recording an audio version of *The Word on the Street* as well as a series of two-minute pieces to be syndicated on radio stations all over the States.

May 2004. Rob, Bill, Rachel and Steve returned to Nashville to perform at the National Pastors' Convention and to continue the audio recordings. This time, though, Lukas and I joined them. It was good to be with Rob, though I did find myself walking the streets of Nashville with Lukas in his pushchair at eight most mornings so that Rob could rest. He was always tired with aches and pains. Zondervan hosted the trip, and they called a strategic meeting about promoting *The Word on the Street* in the US. Rob was brilliant.

'First of all, before we get started, I just want to say something. God has brought me back from the dead, and my priority is my family, and then work. I have the tendency to overwork, and I will do everything that I can to make this book happen, but I don't want to get ill again because I'm doing too much.' My heart thumped with gratitude. I was so proud of him saying that publicly. His real passion was for us, for family. And of course for God, but work had to follow, not lead the whole time. For me this moment was a healing of all the times when I felt that I'd given out so much and got back so little. But even as he said this, we were aware that he was experiencing kidney infections which had already caused one recording session to be cancelled.

June 2004. Elin had invited a number of actors to audition, including Lucy Thampi and Abby Guinness, both of whom proved excellent choices to complete the trio that became Lacey Theatre Company. Rob adapted the performance script of *The Word on the Street* for three and rehearsals were scheduled for September – just in time for an autumn tour, the bookings for which had already started multiplying.

July 2004. A six-week tour of music festivals all over the States, profiling *The Word on the Street*. Rob, Bill and Rachel devised a mini-version of the show that would fit into the five or ten minutes allocated between acts. It was a big challenge to do something both eye- and ear-catching for crowds of up to 100,000 at a time. I joined Rob for the second part of the tour and saw how difficult it was for them to succeed in such a setting. One particular festival worked very well because they performed in a tent rather than on a huge outdoor stage. The nature of these Christian music festivals varied enormously from an 'edgy arts' expression to a more right-wing 'vote Bush' campaign, complete with 'turn or burn' T-shirts.

Our level of discomfort and culture shock was noticeable, although Lukas enjoyed the festivals.

'Mummy, can we go back to that fun fair again?'

With great excitement, we explored Los Angeles during an allocated holiday period: the Hollywood sign, Sunset Boulevard and, of course, Disneyland – for three days! We bought Norah Jones' *Come Away with Me* album, which became our holiday soundtrack as we did the tourist thing in our hire car. We had no plan, no structured itinerary. We just drove where we wanted and one day found ourselves in Santa Barbara.

'Wow, this looks really nice . . .'

'Shall we stay here for a couple of nights?'

'Yeah, okay. That hotel over there looks good.' We stayed for ten days. Ten wonderful days. It became obvious that Rob's plea to put his family first had been heard. To be able to take a holiday within the schedule of that busy summer was testament to Zondervan's compassion and commitment to us. But it wasn't without illness. Back pain and night sweats kicked in again during the last two days, and Rob knew another kidney infection was upon him. We were driving up to Monterey at the time with strong doses of the antibiotic and the usual stock of painkillers, Rob's familiar companions. The next day, his birthday, we flew to Boston, along with Bill and Rachel, to continue with rehearsals before the next festival stint on the East Coast. But Rob was really unwell. Sitting on that plane with him in pain was an unpleasant kickback to almost three years before, and I hardly dared to entertain the memories. Upon our arrival, we thumbed a phonebook for a doctor, but the bed-and-breakfast place where we were staying recommended one to us.

'Given what you've told me of your history, I think a high dose of Ciprofloxacin will zap the infection. These are 1000 mg, remember.' The doctor scribbled a prescription. 'The infection came back with a vengeance because you didn't rest sufficiently. So now don't do anything. Just rest and let the antibiotics do their work.'

But another performance at another festival was imminent. Plus, Cliff Guthrie and his family were visiting, and it was hard for Rob to just go and sleep despite being so unwell. Rob's long track record of living with pain and illness but still carrying on with life meant that he wanted to make the most of seeing his good friend, rather than lying in bed.

August 2004. Return to the UK. Some of the US festival performances had not gone so well, and reaction had been mixed, from 'That was really awesome!' to 'Why is this Welsh guy from England rewriting the Bible in a weird way?' and 'Who are you to tell us what we should think about God?' Some were more supportive. 'America is just not ready for you,' they would say.

September 2004. While Rob was back in America, in New York for interviews, I watched the very first performance of *The Word on the Street* by the newly formed Lacey Theatre Company. Steve had also directed this version and had worked with Rob on adapting the three-person show. The performance was wonderful. And so very different from Rob's version. The company of three grew from strength to strength as they started their tour. A dream had come true. Rob and I had been able to launch new artistic work that others could take forward. Elin, Lucy and Abby joked that they were like *Charlie's Angels*, never actually seeing 'the boss', but always talking to him on the phone. Rob loved this and played up to it constantly. In their repartee with their audiences, the theatre company made the most of 'Charlie', who had recently been interviewed on *Fox News* in New York and featured in *Newsweek*.

The Gate Arts Centre opened with Rob and me, together with Kelvin Thomas, as artistic directors. A large grant from the Heritage Lottery Fund had enabled an old church to find new life as a performance, exhibition, workshop and meeting place, complete with café. Members of the community had access to its facilities, alongside visiting professional artists. For a year leading up to this, I had run a children's theatre school on Saturdays as well as a small project in a local school – all as part of The Gate being born. The resulting performance, with me also dancing, was a brilliant celebration to help launch this invaluable resource for the community. As artistic directors, we managed to walk a fine line that enabled both the artistic and Christian communities to appreciate the value and importance of the facility. It worked, and a rich mix of people began to pass through its doors. The long wait and all the work had been worth it.

October 2004. *The Word on the Street* was promoted on special displays in Walmart stores throughout much of the States. The audio book studio sessions continued – but now in Cardiff with Rob, Steve and sometimes Bill making numerous visits to the studio to record with Terry Lewis of Tinderbox Productions. The idea was to make the book available as a series of downloads on iTunes. Meanwhile, a previous CD version of the stage show with Bill and Rachel's music was chosen as a finalist in the Audie Publisher's Association Award.

November 2004. Rob rewrote *Prodigal Grandson* as *Extravagance*, which was designed for four actors. He then directed a well-received production of it at The Gate. Also, Rob set up an *Open Mic* evening, which saw a variety of storytellers, comedians and performers from both the professional and amateur scene sharing acts and ideas. In the meantime, I got two separate commissions from Welsh Independent Dance to choreograph new solo pieces. Working with another dancer, I put these together to form *Final Cut*, which was also performed at The Gate. Rob was overjoyed with the show and extremely proud of me. People had often asked whether I had a whole evening of dance to offer, so I took the opportunity to create one. By the following January, I employed Donna Marie Morris-Lee as administrator to help consolidate Harnisch-Lacey Dance Theatre.

Rob and I had always talked about having two children, ideally quite close together, and because he had been so well, we were trying our best to conceive – when we had the energy! But it made planning for a dance tour very tricky. As a freelance artist-performer, you are promoting yourself six months to a year in advance, and I had no idea whether I would be pregnant come the next month. Thank goodness Donna proved so understanding.

December 2004. Rob was exhausted. One night we wrote down a realistic assessment of his time allocation per week. He read it back to me.

'I use half a day for administration, about half a day for publicising and interviews, a day a week for The Gate ...' By the time he'd finished listing his writing, editing, meetings, travelling and so on, the total came to seven and a half days. I looked at him. He shrugged. 'Well, the Beatles reckon there's eight days a week, so I've still got half a day in hand.' It was no wonder he was spent and drained. Any fully healthy person would be hard-pressed to keep up this pace, let alone someone whose body needed good rest and recuperation.

In consultation with Kelvin and the board, Rob took a sabbatical from The Gate despite it being so early in its existence. He no longer ran *Open Mic*, but stayed involved for board meetings and any vision shaping that took place. Kidney infections still threatened, but we did manage to enjoy our traditional German Christmas with my parents.

January 2005. Rob focused on writing *The Liberator*. He rented a little flat down in Cardiff Bay for three months. This arrangement turned out to be ideal. Rob really enjoyed leaving the house at nine in the morning and coming back at five, having had a little break in the afternoon to walk round the bay. His working hours were under control, and the routine suited us all, especially Lukas, who saw more of his daddy.

November 2005. The new Spring Harvest leadership team came to Cardiff to pray for Rob. We were both very moved by this gesture. It was a testament of their commitment to Rob. Despite myself, I couldn't help remembering the times I had been angry watching Rob throwing up after stressful differences of opinion with some of the former Spring Harvest leadership. I wasn't angry anymore, but sensed that perhaps there was a broader spiritual dimension to the issue. 'Perhaps they should apologise on behalf of the church for the way all artists have been treated.'

Thankfully, Gerard and Chrissy Kelly arrived a little before the others. Gerard and Chrissy are friends and co-founders of the Bless Network and, at that time, Gerard was pastor of the Crossroads Church in Amsterdam. I expressed my thoughts to them in order to measure their reaction. Gerard and Chrissy were great.

'No, you've got something there.' They thought carefully. 'You're right. Perhaps we should see it as a bigger picture.'

During the full meeting, Rob was fantastic. Utterly brilliant. He spoke passionately about the skills and the unique voice of prophecy that an artist can embody, how during the Reformation, the Arts were simply thrown out of church. He outlined the church's subsequent marginalisation of the Arts and artists – along with its conservative traditions and doctrinal agenda. It affected Rob deeply and he wept as he talked. He referred to the puritanical attitude that arose out of the Welsh revival – that the Arts were crushed by a lack of creativity and a lack of an appreciation of the Bible as a creative book – and it frowned upon what it saw as irreverence and irrelevance, especially if people were having fun. In his own culture, Rob traced the heart-breaking extinguishing of joyful expression. And artists in droves had turned away from the church.

Some time before this, Rob had commissioned Rachel Taylor-Beales to work her way through the entire Bible systematically, noting the general style of literature for every chapter and verse. The result was: 51% story, 29% poetry, 20% exposition. This became one of Rob's favourite facts. A huge 80% of the Bible was made up of narratives, plots, characters, lyrics, metaphorical musings, meditations and fun. How could such a wonderful collection of sixty-six books be rendered so culturally dull? Why did churches concentrate almost all their time and effort upon exposition when there appeared to be a massive creative manifesto right in front of them? Wasn't it time to redress the balance?

Rob also had much to say about the left brain, right brain dichotomy. The left side of our brain is often said to be logical, sequential and analytical, while the right side is intuitive, random and subjective. No prize for guessing which side Rob saw the church as tending to favour. He was passionate about getting the church to laugh at itself, he was evangelistic for respect for the Arts within the church and also for spirituality within the Arts. He also believed in evangelising the Arts in the spiritual. And, anyway, aren't we all part of one body in Christ? Shouldn't we be open to accepting every type of person and to respect their views? Then, on top of all this, wasn't the credo that all the Arts were God given in the first place?

Everything Rob said that day was very moving and left me, and I'm sure many others, with a sense of healing. Later, after Rob's death, Jeff Lucas (a member of the Spring Harvest team), wrote an article about Rob in *Christianity* magazine. It was a beautiful tribute to him.

> *I remember the day that he came to his first meeting as an advisor to the Spring Harvest Leadership Team, and he plunged in with both feet, letting us know that spring is not the time for harvest, a fact that had quite escaped us all before. We kept the name, but realised that having Lacey around was going to be warm, stimulating and fun.*

Jeff noted that the only time he saw Rob cry was not when he had talked about cancer or dying – it was when he talked about the Arts and artists being hurt by the church. The article finishes:

He insisted that we liberate the artists, sculptors, poets, actors and dancers to proclaim, prod, enlighten and inspire us with more than words. This was not a revolution to overthrow preaching, but a call to empower and include those who have often been left stranded in the wings. We must surely heed Rob's call: action is the best way to honour his memory.

Chapter 10
The Lagoon of Hope

It's time now to let Rob himself tell this part of the story. A good friend, Diana parsons, has kept and now printed out for me all of the prayer emails that Rob and I sent out to the hundreds of friends, supporters and prayer partners all over the world during the last year of his life. This wodge of paper in my hand feels weighty enough before I attempt to take on board once more the weightier matters that are contained within them. But, wonderfully, here is Rob's voice and his spirit too. I know there will be laughter mingled with the pain; how could there not be? I know Rob's faith and determination will only be matched by his irrepressible creativity in the face of such physical abuse. Because that's how he was. I expect to relive scenes from this grainy true-to-life drama-documentary that follows. I fully anticipate that there will be lots of handheld shots and quirky jump-cut editing. An unfinished feel. It was a very rough ride at times but, in the distance and perhaps surrounding everything, you might sense the warmth of a golden glow of family life, quality time and eager anticipation of God's great goodness settling upon us and sustaining us throughout. I have left all the spellings and punctuation as they appeared.

From: Rob Lacey
Sent: 10 May 2005 09:48
To: Prayer Shield
Subject: Prayer update

Lacey Prayers a bit rusty? Need some Info Oil?

Yes, sorry it's been a while but I had a double whammy virus—flu then gastric stuff, so wasn't functioning. Ironically, could've done with some direct inject prayer—but you were probably sending some up anyway. It's as if you have a direct line!

So, I'm back at the laptop and due to get back the editors comments on The Liberator 2nd draft I completed in March—pray for wisdom and inspiration as we (me, two editors and two theologians) tweak and nudge and cajole the manuscript as near as we can get it to great.

Having said that I'm exploring the best way for me to be on stage given my general weariness and other priorities—one thing that's clear is that I'm to space it out (maybe a gig a fortnight, say), but I'm evolving a sort of perform/chat/poem/chat/perform structure that allows me to avoid exertion while still connecting with an audience. I'm particularly buzzing about presenting ideas about the need for all of us to be creative—to reflect the way we're made by creator God i.e. in his image. This isn't about only the arts, it's about all of life! On the triangle of Mind, Body and Spirit—God's made it clear that I've been stuck in the Mind corner, pushing my brain to distraction while not spending enough time praying and exercising. So please pray (and nag me) that I'll implement my new regime of clocking off the brain stuff at 3pm each day and focusing on the other two parts of me. If I can crack this, I feel the brain will probably be less clogged with short circuiting stress headaches, so it's a biggie!

Thanks so much for standing/kneeling/hovering with me on this. God keep you smiling.

Rob

From: Rob Lacey
Sent: 06 June 2005 11:00
To: Prayer Shield
Subject: Prayer update

Prayer injections needed!

I've just come back from a morning at the hospital clinic (not my favourite place in the world) and they're going to give me some tests to get why I've been so exhausted lately–possible culprits include anaemia, high blood pressure and, of course, the ol' fav: urinary tract infection. They're planning to give me a general anaesthetic in a couple of weeks to collect more film footage of my, now legendary, bladder. Please pray that they suss the causes of why I've been swimming up stream lately. Much appreciated!

Also, Lacey Theatre Co. are due to go back out on the road with a 5 week national tour–so please pray for renewed energy (physical, emotional and spiritual) for this. Pray particularly for Elin as she plans her move to Cardiff to take on more of the management of the Theatre Co projects–she needs to find a flat, church, shoe shop(s) etc. Exciting times as things continue to develop.

Pray also that I have wisdom as I renew my role at The Gate Arts and Training Centre here in Cardiff. A wonderful project bringing creative Arts to the

community. Pray we get the Christian ethos right
and that we learn what it means to apply both Jesus'
parables of Matthew chapter 25 – (look 'em up!).

Thanks so much

Rob

From: Rob Lacey
Sent: 07 June 2005 09:35
To: Prayer Shield
Subject: Prayer update

Prayers focused on Mon 13th please!

I've just heard that the in location bladder
footage is to be shot on Monday aft. 13th June. Pray
that my performance is calmness itself – which should
be the case since I'll be under general anaesthetic!
Please pray for the Director and Producer as they
view the rushes (technical term, meaning film footage,
but having a particularly ironic resonance here!) and
that they stick to the truth when they write their
reviews of what they see.

Please pray for the host of the bladder in
question: that I'll be calm and assured that all is in the
hands of the Ultimate Creative Executive Producer!
Also for those who have to put up with the mood
swings of the Host of the bladder i.e. Sandra and
Lukas.

What we know is this: From last week's oncology
tests – I'm not anaemic and I have good levels of
blood and improving kidney function. What we want
to know is this: Do I have an infection my sad excuse
for a bladder? How best to treat this?

For once I can honestly tell you that the current
weariness is not from overwork – I've been a good boy

this last six months. But it would be good to know what's happening.

Please pray that I recover quickly from the general anaesthetic and that the results are conclusive and suggest non-invasive treatment(s).

Thanks for much

Rob

From: Rob Lacey
Sent: 07 July 2005 10:45
To: Prayer Shield
Subject: Prayer update

Dear aching kneed people

Thanks so much for all your prayers. The clinic results yesterday were good: a) No sign of cancer—not a comment on my zodiac positioning (with my birthday coming up on 25th July—sooooon—that makes me a Leo, and Leos don't believe in all that rubbish). b) No sign of infection—so no need for draining antibiotics, good! c) Still got an MRI scan next Tuesday 12th July and will have a follow up clinic on 27th July (two days after my birthday, note) to discuss results.

Current theories being grasped at is that my symptoms are a delayed reaction to the radiotherapy I had 3 years ago combined with all the chemo the bladder had to entertain. If so, not sure what they can do about the aching. Once they've ruled out the obvious suspects then they can start treating my symptoms, so not out of the wood yet, but as the 11th Commandment states: 'Thou shalt plod on'.

Ploddingly yours

Rob

From: Rob Lacey
Sent: 08 August 2005 12:10
To: Prayer Shield
Subject: Prayer update and your address please!

Hey, how are your knees? You might need to get praying! You can invoice us for the knee pads.

I'm due to be having my bladder biopsy this Tuesday and not looking forward to it. The last two weeks I've been in quite a lot of pain most of the day (especially the evenings/nights) and this 'doctor invasion' is only going to make things worse. Pray they find no cancer but also that they come up with some plan for sorting out a fried and grilled old bag of a bladder.

As ever, the working on Scripture has been a lifeline—creatively, emotionally, spiritually. I'm just at the end of this stage of the polishing of The Liberator and am really excited by how amazing the story is and how this could affect so many. Please pray that I get some 'a-ha' moments (not the 1980s Norwegian pop combo) and really express what it's about for both the loyal church goer and the anti-church cynic—both of which, I believe, are intrigued by what Jesus is about.

My hope here is to be 'prophetic' in challenging the church and also 'pastoral' in not knocking the church unfairly (since it's a lifeline for many). I'm not anti-church at all—it's been great to me—but I also know we don't get it right all the time and non-Christians appreciate us admitting that—which is the main aim of the book. So I've got the tricky challenge of speaking to different audiences as the same time—something the Master Communicator Jesus did so brilliantly. So help me God!

Pray for Sandra and Lukas as I'm off the scene (or on it and just grumpy/vague/depressed). Pray that it becomes clear where and when we can have some sort of holiday to replace the one we had to cancel in Greece. I'm sure God's got ideas on this and he's got a pretty amazing track record on being 'no man's debtor'!

Also, thanks for your prayers for Elin finding a flat—she moved into a great place last weekend. Pray for her as she settles in Cardiff and manages Lacey Theatre Company—bookings, profile, new cast members etc. It's great to have her more on board and taking the pressure off my aching body.

Thanks so much for sticking with us.

Rob

From: Rob Lacey
Sent: 19 August 2005 15:37
To: Prayer Shield
Subject: Prayer update

A quickie:

Just to say, this next Wednesday (24th Aug.) at 11am I've got my clinic where I should get the results of the recent bladder exams—please pray that I don't get a C grade!

We're holding out for an all clear in terms of cancer and some wisdom from the consultant as to what to do with the chronic pain. I don't want to just plod on in this survival mode much longer. What's the point in coming back from death if you don't have a life?!

Meanwhile it's a huge week for the Liberator book too—I'm making my final tweaks and responding to the comments from the theological advisors. So please pray for concentration and wisdom as I make the last changes. It's such an amazing story and I'm desperate to get it as great as I'm capable of. So help me God!

Thanks so much.

Rob

From: Rob Lacey
Sent: 30 August 2005 10:57
To: Prayer Shield
Subject: Prayer shield–test results

D'you want the good news or the bad news?!

The bad news is that my test results came through last Wednesday and they have found cancer in the bladder. I'm due to have one more test to check that it's not spread any where else, but assuming it's just located in the back of the bladder wall then they'll remove my bleeding bladder. Good riddance, I say.

I'll find out the results of the scan and if, and when, I'm having the operation on 13th Sept. Please pray for us that morning (9am-ish) if you can! The doctors have hinted that the actual operation would be a week or two after that–end of September-ish. One slight comfort is that my deadline for the copy edited penultimate stage of The Liberator book is the 20th Sept, so at least I'll be able to sign that off pretty much. Quite how soon I'll be up to reading through the final version after proof reading I honestly don't know–it's a big operation!

How weird is it to be working through the final chapters of Christ's passion with this hanging over us? But, despite the pain, I'm enjoying the process of completing two years' work and drawing strength from it (probably on levels I'm not even aware of).

Pray we keep on 'taking God at his word' that he's healed me and has plans for us as a family.

That's the bad news—the good news is that Sandra's pregnant and we're expecting in April. When we knew (back 2 weeks ago) we took this as God hinting at plans he's got for me to be well, and we're still holding onto that, and it's slipping out of our hands, and we're picking it up again, and it's slipping out of our hands, etc. Please pray we don't lose the plot altogether.

Sorry to lay such a heavy email on you. Thanks for standing with us—it's going to get bumpy!

Halle-blinkin'-lujah anyway.

Rob

From: Rob Lacey
Sent: 27 September 2005 16:25
To: Prayer Shield
Subject: Prayer update

Frustration!

Things still aren't conclusive with my test results. The report faxed through from the Pet scan last Friday says there are some enlarged lymph nodes, which would be consistent with cancer in the lymph nodes, but doesn't prove that they are cancerous. So my Cardiff doctors have asked for the actual images to be sent down so that they can compare them with previous scans (where my lymph nodes were also enlarged at times). I'll have another clinic on the 11th Oct to find out what the radiologist has deduced from these images. All very frustrating.

At the moment they're still expecting to operate to remove my bladder, and are booking me in for an op. sometime around the end of October. This willingness to operate indicates that they are not 100% sure the cancer is elsewhere apart from the bladder, since if it was <u>known</u> to be elsewhere they'd probably not recommend operating on the bladder.

The good news here is that the Pet scan didn't show any major tumour(s) anywhere else, but with my history they can't be sure.

All very frustrating and confusing. Please pray that clarity will come on what to push for and what to agree to. The deeper we go into this saga the more we realise that medicine is simply intelligent guess work and the more we're grateful that we're under God's care.

Please ask God to help us through and out of this—I so want to be able to take the weight off Sandra as she approaches her time of roundness! And certainly when she's got a brand new Lacey to mother.

One thing that happened, which we took as likely downloaded script from On High, was the admin. guy at the clinic recognised me and asked how I was. I came back, 'we'll see what they say', and his reply was 'It's never depended on what they said in the past—you've always done your own thing!'

Do pray

Thanks

Rob

From: Rob Lacey
Sent: 29 September 2005 09:20
To: Prayer Shield
Subject: Prayer update

This is somfing wot I wrote the night before the results. I think it speaks of mental battles and the wide spectrum of possibilities in all this:

The Eve of the Results:

Did God really say he'd be with me in the furnace?* Undeniably. Yes! Did God really say the waters will not harm me? Repeatedly. Yes! Did God really say you would not die but live to see the glory of the Lord? Incredibly. Yes! Did God really say he would satisfy me with long life? Poetically. Yes! Did God really say no other would take his glory? Fiercely. Yes! Did God really say that all things work together for my good because I love him and am called to his purpose? Emphatically. Yes! Did God really say he will give abundantly more than I can ask or imagine? Amazingly. Yes! Did God really say he has plans to give me a hope and a future? Famously. Yes! Did God really say his strength is made perfect in my weakness? Annoyingly. Yes!

Thanks for praying.

Rob

From: Rob Lacey
Sent: 30 September 2005 16:52
To: Prayer Shield
Subject: Prayer update

More news—more conclusive; more annoying:

The consultant rang me yesterday to say the radiographer had compared my recent Pet scan

---

* See page 242.

with previous scans and, yes, the lymph nodes were larger than before indicating that the cancer has almost certainly spread from the bladder to two of the lymph nodes in the pelvis and abdomen. This was a blow below (and above) the belt—literally and metaphorically. As a result they are not recommending the removal of the bladder now but offering chemotherapy instead. Mixed feelings!

One of our overriding reactions is that of anger but we're so far succeeding in directing it downwards, and not up toward God. But we want to state, for the record, that my recovery nearly four years ago wasn't as a result of me 'responding well to chemotherapy' as the medics annoyingly keep saying, but simply because God stepped in.

This is not just about Lukas (and his new brother/sister) growing up to know what an earthly father is like; it's not just about Sandra being able to dance and choreograph again because she has a husband to share the load with; it's also about whether God's name is going to get famed or defamed. It's about all of us going up a gear in what we believe God is capable of or, alternatively, slipping back into accepting second best—that God can help people through hard times, but not actually change the situation for them!

Having heard the doctor's news, I went for a walk around the local lake in defiance. I was trying to get my head round stuff and sort of praying when I saw three 12 year old boys coming the other way. When I was about a yard away the one boy turned to his two mates and announced to them, 'God has called you to be a warrior!' I have no idea what they were talking about and I was too stunned to do anything but scramble around in the bin for a scrap of paper and write the line down. Weird!

So please pray for wisdom as to what we tell the medics at the next clinic on Tues 11th October. We have to decide whether we accept their offer of chemotherapy given that it might well destroy my immune system at the time when I need it most. This can then prove counter productive by actually making way for the cancer to progress. It's a big decision. Our only other options are to pray like crazy or to pursue alternative therapies – or both. Ultimately only God's going to do the business but our current leaning is to follow the alternative approach (coupled with loads of strident prayers) since God created the healing properties of natural therapies in the first place and, even if they don't work, at least they don't run the risk of killing you.

Thanks for adding your Amens – do feel free to pass this on to any people you know who do that praying thing!

Thanks, as ever

Rob

From: Rob Lacey
Sent: 14 October 2005 15:39
To: Prayer Shield
Subject: Prayer update

Please distribute this through any channels you have at your fingertips ...

Here beginneth the next chapter of 'adventures with a rebellious bladder'. Let's pray for God to inspire an exciting read and ... please ... a happy ending involving full health, vitality and wholeness in body, mind and spirit.

Thanks to all of you for your prayers. Sandra and I have chosen to decline the offer of surgery and chemotherapy for the bladder and lymph node cancer. We feel that given that since the doctors have made it quite clear that they are not promising a cure and given our current family situation we have told them 'thanks, but no thanks'.

Basically, my previous heavy dose of radiotherapy makes the removal of the bladder an even bigger operation since they don't know what internal damage the radiation caused and what's now stuck to what. Cutting the bladder out could lead to other complications or serious bleeding. Not to mention weeks on end in a hospital recovering from such a big op.

The chemo option is also not offering a cure, merely a <u>possible</u> slowing of progress of the tumour with likely debilitating side effects. But, again, the doctors admit that they don't expect to cure what is a very aggressive cancer. Along with this possible benefit is the significant chance of the chemo knocking out my immune system when I need it most. The oncologist said he always hopes 'the chemo shrinks the tumour quicker than it shrinks the person'.

Of course, we'd agree to both surgery and chemo if the doctors were promising a cure, but their prognosis is similar to last time – which was, quote, 'a year if things go well', unquote – and I'm still here four years later. We see that as down to prayer and God stepping in. We need God to turn up with sleeves rolled up for action again. This is God's clear opportunity to prove his merciful intervention and lots of people (Christian/nonChristian/notsure) know this!

Amen?

Rob

Attachment:

SCHIZOID (EXCERPTS)

... Then I'm switching role, like I'm the old man John

An apostle in prison with no parole

peering through a prism and scribbling on a scroll

About the final resting/wrestling place of every soul

And the One who'll surf in on the clouds and take control ...

... Then I'm the psalmist disarming alarm

Schitzo enough to talk straight to my soul

With the idea of bungy jumping to the end of my rope

And bouncing in and out, in and out of the lagoon of hope.

Now I'm three – I'm Shadrach, Meshach and Abednego

And we won't bow the knee low to some King So-and-so.

Saying our God can save us from a grilling

And even if He doesn't, we're still not willing

To bow the knee low to some King So-and-so ...

... Then I'm David striding up hill toward Goliath of Gath

Grinning at the prospect of God's victory aftermath.

*Then I switch and I'm nine feet tall looking down
on it all,
    Laughing at this rumour of a tumour that's so
much smaller than me . . .
    . . . I'm peter soaking a sandal.
    Raring to start going overboard for my Lord,
    Daring to step out on a spiritual surfboard . . .
    . . . But then I'm Job renting his robe
    Reeling with pain, rocking with fury
    About the injustice of my so called jury.
    Then I'm Joseph staring at pharaoh's prison wall
    Having done nothing wrong at all,
    On the verge of escape to influence the future of
every Jacob son.
    No, the other Joseph daring to believe in a
miracle baby
    Having done nothing wrong at all,
    On the verge of stepping into step-fathering the
Anointed One.
    No, the other Joseph caring enough to risk his
Arimathea career
    To bury the one who'd done nothing wrong at all,
    On the verge of seeing the church emerge with
the resurrected Son.*

Rob Lacey, 2005

From: Rob Lacey
Sent: 28 October 2005 13:41
To: Prayer Shield
Subject: Prayer update
    Quick update,
    Thanks so much for all your prayers, Sandra and I
are amazingly positive, chirpy even—some would say

'fully alive' about 90% of the time and, yes, we both have occassional dips into 'what if' territory – but we always make the return trip ... so far!

We just enjoyed a great week's holiday in Germany with Sandra's family and got some amazing autumn colours into our memory banks from our walks in the forest behind Sandra's family home. We read and chatted and played a lot. We also got a sense of some structure for my semi-sabbatical until Christmas: I'll work about half a day a week to keep the admin ticking over and the rest of the time will be for reading, listening, walking, swimming, resting, scribbling, chatting and tickling (mainly Lukas, but possibly Sandra too).

Please pray that this time recharges the batteries of body, mind and spirit and that we keep on picking up the clues on this treasure hunt God seems to be leading us on. Please also pray that this carving out of time to mull things over would not produce introspection or depression but would take us to the next level of awareness of God's presence with us. On a physical level, please pray that the tumour in the bladder realises it cannot coexist with the Holy Spirit inside my body and that the pain and the bleeding stop for good as a result. A relief of the symptoms would be both very welcome and a boost to faith levels for all of us battling for this.

Thanks so much

Rob

From: Rob Lacey
Sent: 01 December 2005 14:14
To: Prayer Shield
Subject: Prayer update

This last two and a half weeks I've been shaken and kicked in the back by a real thug of a kidney infection. And just when I thought I was getting better the mugger came back with a vengeance and hit me even harder this weekend just gone till I was being sick every night and waking up feeling pretty overhung from the medication–I blame the extended licensing hours: he was obviously under the influence and had issues with his urinary tract being misplaced.

Still, this last two days I've been much better, catching up on both sleep and some fun scribbling of ideas. So thanks all of you who've been praying unprompted (by me) as God's really pulled us through this physical and mental battle–it's really a challenge to not slip into the mire of mental depression when you're feeling that ill and you've got cancer. I had to really take hold of my imaginative mind and brainwash it into thinking 'this is just a bad kidney infection, you know the symptoms by now, just tough it out and don't waste worry beads on thinking this is the cancer strengthening its hold'.

Now I'm out the other side it's easy to be back where I was before, which is–thanks to your prayers–pretty positive, chirpy, prolific with new ideas and, generally, up for an adventure with God. Please pray that I'll be able to make the most of this attempt at a sabbatical (which, I feel, hasn't quite started yet!) and that we'll be well enough to go to Sandra's family in Germany for our Christmas break–the last trip back from Germany in October was pretty horrific with blood issuing from places it had no business to be issuing from!

Thanks and please keep praying

Rob

From: Rob Lacey
Sent: 08 December 2005 12:33
To: Prayer Shield
Subject: Lacey Productions – health update

Basically, all we want for Christmas is a new bladder/kidney set for Rob plus all the urinary tract attachments – all nicely wrapped up with batteries included if necessary. Please keep praying. Oh, and we'd also need a new lymphatic system to go with that – the cancer has spread into two lymph nodes next to the old bladder. We've been asking the Father Of Christmas many times a day for this and we've even got our friends to ask him for us too. If you have influence in these areas please join the growing lobby group representing us to the Father Of Christmas. Basically, it's been a scary summer and autumn – but we're doing remarkably well… considering. Thanks for all your support.

All Lukas (now nearly 5) wants is a baby brother (or sister – he doesn't mind) and we happen to know that the Father Of Christmas has this amazing present already packed but Lukas will have to wait until Easter till he gets it. His mum and dad are really thrilled too!

Have a happy Christmas and a Liberated new year.

Cheers

Rob + Sandra = (Lukas + Baby)

From: Rob Lacey
Sent: 06 January 2006 12:07
To: Prayer Shield
Subject: Prayer update

Happy new year!

Thanks for your support prayers over
Christmas – I'm thrilled to be able to say I was NOT ill
and had a great rest: lots of lie-ins, lots of reading and
even a few Narniaesque snowy forest walks! Good for
the soul. Father Christmas did a good job for Lukas
but the Father of Christmas hasn't yet delivered the
new urinary system for me – he may've sent it, but it's
been delayed (see Daniel 10:12 – 14, go on, you know
you want to).

However, Sandra now has a really bad flu so she
could do with shifting that and carrying on with her
blooming lovely pregnant woman thing – 'suits you,
madam'. Meanwhile I'm busy compiling and crafting
the range of ideas for the hour long opening night
of each Spring Harvest week. Please pray I create
the right combination of words and images that God
shapes into something He can really use this coming
Easter. Pray also that I remain well enough to rehearse
and perform my part in the show which I'll be doing
with Lacey Theatre Company in the Minehead Big
Top.

Lots happening. Pray that I gain strength and
finally get delivery of the wholeness and vitality which
God has for me.

Thanks so much

Rob

From: Rob Lacey
Sent: 22 February 2006 14:59
To: Prayer Shield
Subject: Prayer update

Weather God Rains

(Imagine smiley weatherman delivering this weather report)

Well, things seem to have settled into a surprisingly predictable pattern in the land of Rob – not at all pleasant, but at least we can dress accordingly. Based on recent patterns the daily forecast for the foreseeable future has the days beginning with a very foggy outlook – which is only to be expected after the level of chemicals pumped into the body during the night in order to minimise the damage of the overnight pain storms. This of course also increases the likelihood of bouts of hail-like vomiting which can occur at any moment.

Once the early fog has lifted the late morning period can expect to see a window of slightly finer weather – make the most of this: if there are plans to go out at all, this would be the best time because by mid afternoon the outlook will grow gradually darker and a likelihood of an onset of painful fronts will dominate the body, with the only areas escaping the full onslaught of the elements being the far north – around the shoulders and above; and the southern areas – from the knees downward. The Midlands, I'm afraid, can expect a continued pattern of strong buffeting from chilling northerly winds blowing in from the Sea of Despond and beyond. There is also a strong possibility of lightning striking regularly in the bladder area and you may well have to endure a rumbling of thunder due to back pressure in the Kidneys.

And the long term outlook? All records would suggest not to expect any dramatic improvement in conditions during this winter season. Signs of Spring will still seem a long way off yet—but keep looking or even praying for the telltale signs of lower blood content in the bladder area and a thinning out of the general covering of light-blocking pain clouds to reveal blue skies and the prospect of growth and early fruit harvests. The main prospect of improved conditions is to hope for a change in wind direction and that the Southerly breezes would lessen the chill factor and make the winter temperatures seem almost pleasant for the season.

Official advice is that journeys are only made if deemed absolutely necessary—conditions will make any longer journeys quite hazardous and should only be undertaken with extreme caution and with close friends with whom you can share body warmth if stranded. In the mean-time, stay indoors and be sure to take regular doses of vitamin prayer to guard against any Bodily winter chills developing into something even more serious in the Mind and Spirit regions. That's the weather where Rob is.

So ... Prayer action points: Please pray for a change in symptoms for me—as something we can wrap our faith around and for a double dollop of grace to cope with the pain of it all in the meantime.

Please pray for Sandra as she approaches her delivery date of 17th April and as she rehearses a

replacement dancer into her part of her Final Cut
show which is being taken to Stuttgart in early March.
Particularly pray that she will not develop the pre-
eclampsia (high blood pressure) that she had with
Lukas' delivery.

Please pray for Lukas—now 5—as he deals with
Daddy having 'a baddie tummy' and mummy having 'a
big tummy'. Lot's of changes for the lad to handle!

Thanks for your continued support

Rob

From: Rob Lacey
Sent: 07 March 2006 14:07
To: Prayer Shield
Subject: Prayer update

'A more temperate climate for Rob's health:
Thanks for your prayers since the last update. Several
things have combined to improve symptoms a little—

a) I'm now 10 days into a course of steroids which
mask the symptoms a little. Slightly less blood from
the nether regions too.

b) I had 3 units of blood by transfusion last week
to replace what I've been losing, from said nether
regions, and this also picks me up energy wise.

These improvements were gratefully accepted
and wonderfully timed since Sandra was away last
weekend with her Dance Theatre Company for 4 days
in Stuttgart launching her new dance piece. With a
lot of help from friends and family I was able to cope
with looking after the boy wonder pretty well and,
although he missed his mama, we had a lovely time
together and I got all the cuddles normally allocated
to Sandra—result!

Sandra's piece went down a storm in Stuttgart and two reviewers were there who said they loved the piece. So it was very exciting and I was chuffed to be able to hold the fort at home.

Next prayer date is that I have a CT scan this Thursday 9th – It'll be a full 6 months since the last scan and it'd be so brilliant to hear the doctors have to admit that the tumours in the bladder and lymph node have stabilised/shrunk/disappeared (delete according to your faith levels). Please pray that if the news is in the opposite direction that we get extra dollops of grace to cope. Also pray that we'll handle the horrible 2 week waiting period between the scan and the results – I hate that ticking clock.

So, still creaking along, doing about half a days work per day and trying to take it easy. Very much sensing that God's around, grateful for an improvement in symptoms but aware that both the steroids and the blood transfusion are temporary bonuses and also have some side effects. Still getting some rough nights – when nurse morphine is required – but not throwing up as much so able to retain my weight (having lost a stone from the sickness in February).

Please pray that as the baby's arrival comes nearer (due date is April 17th) that God gets through to us and helps us prepare in body, mind and spirit for the next mind bogglingly bizarre combination of good, bad and ugly that is Lacey Life.

Thanks so much for standing/kneeling/hopping with us.

Rob

[That was the last email Rob wrote (or dictated to Danielle, his PA, personal assistant).]

From: Rob Lacey
Sent: 16 March 2006 13:25
To: Prayer Shield
Subject: Urgent prayer update
Importance: High

(Knee pads on please)

Rob was taken into hospital by ambulance early Monday morning with acute pain from a twisted intestine. Treatment has calmed the symptoms but being in hospital has sped up hearing the CT and MRI scan results, which are not good. There's been significant growth in the tumour since July 2005 and more lymph nodes are affected – one tumour by the kidneys is 10cm wide. They are not sure yet what the medics will propose, but they seem reluctant to put a timescale to it due to Rob's exceeding their expectations 4 years ago. Please pray for Rob in hospital and the doctors as they make decisions. Please pray for 36 weeks pregnant Sandra. Please pray for Lukas.

Many thanks for your continued praying support
Danielle
Danielle Lancaster PA to Rob Lacey

From: Rob Lacey
Sent: 24 March 2006 09:14
To: Prayer Shield
Subject: Prayer update – urgent
Importance: High

Things are getting desperate

After 4 days of freedom Rob is back in a different hospital, Velindre Cancer Hospital, with a continued obstructed intestine. Doctors assume the cancer

tumour is blocking the movement of the bowels/
intestine and therefore not allowing him to have any
bowel movements at all. Rob is very weary and has a
lot of discomfort in the abdomen from the build up
of food. Having tried the Nil by mouth rest approach,
the oncologist says chemo or surgery are the only
option to shift the blockage, i.e the tumour. Neither
option appeals this close to the baby arriving (Sandra
is 36 weeks), but if he can't process food he won't be
able to survive for long. We feel we have no option
but to accept chemo at this stage. Please pray that
the chemo will shrink the cancer quicker than it will
shrink Rob and that God intervenes miraculously
pretty damn quick.

Thanks for your prayers – we really need them!

Rob and Sandra Lacey

From: Rob Lacey
Sent: 24 March 2006 17:25
To: Prayer Shield
Subject: Prayer update

I have just spoken to Rob in hospital and the
latest news is that they are moving him to Heath
Hospital. This is because he is having nephrostomy
tubes fitted to drain his kidneys which are blocked
and enlarged. From previous experience Rob knows
that this is a very painful procedure. He thinks he
should be in Heath for a couple of days and then will
be moving back to Velindre. Please pray that this
improves his kidney function.

Please also pray for the double book launch which
is happening at The Gate on Sunday for Rob's new
book The Liberator. Rob will now no longer be able
to be at this event so please pray that it goes well

without him. Anyone who is Cardiff based please feel
free to come along.

Many thanks

Danielle

Danielle Lancaster PA to Rob Lacey

From: Rob Lacey
Sent: 28 March 2006 12:03
To: Prayer Shield
Subject: Prayer update

Thank you for your prayers for the book launch
which went well. Rob was able to come out of hospital
for the launch on Sunday which was really great but
had to go back in on Monday morning. He has a
kidney infection for which he is on antibiotics but so
far it looks as though he will not have to have the
nephrostomy tubes, which is a real answer to prayer.
He is improving slowly, but his kidney function is not
good enough at the moment for chemotherapy to
start. Please pray for the whole situation.

Please pray for strength for Sandra and Lukas and
for the right timing and safe arrival of the baby.

Many thanks

Danielle

Danielle Lancaster PA to Rob Lacey

From: Rob Lacey
Sent: 29 March 2006 12:40
To: Prayer Shield
Subject: Prayer update

During the last two days Rob has been feeling
worse due to his kidney function not improving
significantly enough and his intestine still being
obstructed. They are going to refit him today with

a gastric tube to drain off any excess bile from his stomach and to stop him from getting sick. Due to the continued sickness and not being able to hold food down he is feeling very weak and tired.

Please pray for his kidney function to improve and his intestine and bowels to keep moving. Pray for the cancer to shrink and health being restored in a miraculous way. Lord have mercy!

Thanks for your prayers.

Rob and Sandra Lacey

Danielle Lancaster PA to Rob Lacey

From: Rob Lacey
Sent: 04 April 2006 09:10
To: Prayer Shield
Subject: Urgent prayer update

Rob is getting weaker and more tired daily and the doctors are only able to provide pain control and try to keep the symptoms at bay. He gets intravenous sodium and glucose but is not able to eat anything or be fed artificially since his intestine is blocked by the tumour and therefore he is not able to digest anything. The doctors are suggesting to induce Sandra for the baby to arrive sooner and therefore to make sure that Rob will be able to be at the birth, which will be at the same hospital.

Please pray for
• Rob to be fully healed
• For the baby to arrive as soon as possible (without having to be induced) and God's timing in all of this
  • For a safe delivery
  • For strength and grace for all the family

8th April 2006, Lukas meets his one-day-old sister

Thanks for all your prayers and for fighting and standing with us!

Rob, Sandra, Lukas and baby Lacey!

Danielle Lancaster PA to Rob Lacey

From: Rob Lacey
Sent: 04 April 2006 11:13
To: Prayer Shield
Subject: Please pray
  Importance: High
  Sandra will be induced tomorrow (Wednesday)! Please pray for a safe delivery and that Rob will be able to be there. Please pray for Rob's miraculous healing.
  We need to see God break through – it's crunchtime! Lord have mercy!

Sandra, Rob, Lukas and baby Lacey
Danielle Lancaster PA to Rob Lacey

From: Rob Lacey
Sent: 10 April 2006 12:28
To: Prayer Shield
Subject: Prayer update

Magdelena Grace Lacey arrived at 6pm on Friday the 7th April weighing 5lb 6oz. Mother and daughter are both well and at home. Rob is also home from hospital but is still weak and prayers are urgently needed for his recovery and rebuilding. Particular need is that Rob's liver function improves as 'yellow just isn't his colour'!

Thank you for your continued prayers.
Danielle Lancaster PA to Rob Lacey

From: Rob Lacey
Sent: 10 April 2006 12:38
To: Prayer Shield
Subject: Thank you

With Rob and Sandra's permission and as leaders of the church they are part of we want to write to express our deep appreciation for the support and love that has been given to them by all of you. We shared communion with them this morning and we are very conscious that Rob is still very ill but in good spirit. We have advised them, and they agree, that for the next two weeks there should be no visits – this will enable them to enjoy the arrival of Magdelena as a family. We would encourage and urge you to keep praying for grace, strength and healing, particularly for the liver function and the shrinkage of the tumour.

If you have any questions please feel free to contact either Norman or Paul through Danielle.

Thank you.

Norman Adams and Paul Francis.

Danielle Lancaster PA to Rob Lacey

From: Rob Lacey
Sent: 25 April 2006 16:19
To: Prayer Shield
Subject: Prayer update

Y'all,

Thanks for all your prayers–please keep on going!

Rob's still very weary but at least he's at home recovering from a month in hospital.

Sandra's doing well but very weary after a 24 hour labour and the joys of breastfeeding.

Lukas is learning to adapt to having a little sister.

Thanks for Sandra's 'wunderparents'–two and a half weeks into a month long stay and supporting us so well. So too Rob's parents in Cardiff and church/family and friends–what an amazing community!

Still waiting for Rob's liver function to improve as his kidney function and digestive systems seems to be doing better. But he's still quite jaundiced, though improving (his colour me beautiful friends assure him).

Pray for the District Nurses' daily visits (9.30am)– that we'll learn to detox from the medical world's assumptions without being in denial as to the severity of the situation but balancing this with God's world of possibilities also.

Thanks and please keep on sending them up as God continues to bring his warmth into our lives.

Rob & Sandra = (Lukas x Magdalena)^2

Danielle Lancaster PA to Rob Lacey

From: Lacey Productions
Sent: 02 May 2006 10:47
To: Supporters & Prayer Shield
Subject: Sad news about Rob

It is with deep sadness that we write to you all today to let you know that Rob passed away yesterday at 11am. His death was peaceful and Sandra was able to be with him throughout it all. Over the weekend Rob's decline was very rapid and on Sunday a decision was made to move him to a hospice. Sandra and all of the family would like to sincerely thank you for fighting and standing with them in prayer. Your support has been essential over this difficult period.

We will be in touch to let you know the date and details of the funeral soon. We thank God for and celebrate the life of Rob, a dearly loved husband, father, son, brother, artist and friend.

Please continue to pray for Sandra, Lukas and Magdelena and also all of Rob's and Sandra's family over these next days and weeks to come.

Many thanks again for your heartfelt support.

Danielle Lancaster

Lacey Productions

So had that lagoon of hope drained dry? Revisiting these emails after so much time revives that palpable sense of hope that was ours every day while Rob still had breath. Whether it was being buoyed by refreshing waters of prayer or facing trial by cancer's fire, one story in particular continued to provide hope in full measure for us both during those months and weeks before his death. I'll let Rob tell the story.

> [King Nebuchadnezzar builds a] huge statue ... made of gold and standing about 30 metres (100 feet) high and 3 metres (9 feet) wide—just big enough to represent the king's ego! The idea is that whenever the band plays everyone has two options: bow down to the king's image or step into the blazing ovens. Not great options! 'Course Shadrach, Meshach and Abednego don't have an option—out of loyalty to God they stay standing ... The king's furious but they tell him ...
>
> 'If we're chucked into this blazing oven, the God we work for could pull us out alive. He'll rescue us from your cruelty, King. Even if he doesn't and we fry, you should still know, there'd be no regrets—no way are we bowing down to your gods or your overgrown gold Action Man.'
>
> The king turns up the heat on the oven dial from one to seven and has them thrown in. It's so hot it kills the soldiers doing the throwing! The king's looking in to gloat and he sees four guys strolling round, chatting—the fourth one looks like the son of a god. He calls them out and the three step out not even singed. They don't even smell like they've been to a barbeque! The king's so impressed with them and their God that he bans any bad press on the Jewish God, on pain of death. The three Jews get a well-earned promotion.
>
> The Word on the Street by Rob Lacey, page 221

Having passed through the furnace once, Rob was sure God could do it for him again, and I stood by him all the way. Our faith together was rock solid, and the knowledge that so many thousands of people were praying was extremely reassuring. Close friends surrounded us with love. Joy and Tim opened their home for a whole year before Rob's death for people to come and pray for us and with us. Kath and James are also faithful friends. They were at Lena's birth and always on the end of a phone as well as supporting us in prayer. Kath was my beacon of hope throughout Rob's final illness. (She and Rob had known each other from childhood, both playing cello in the youth orchestra.) It has been wonderful knowing that such good friends stood, and continue to stand, by us. All three families have enjoyed so many lovely times together: meals, the beach, art galleries, holidays, sledging, more meals – the list is very long indeed.

One last wonderful bit of silliness. Throughout our marriage, last thing at night, Rob and I would often take it in turns to switch off the light. Before doing so, the one who held the pull cord would pull a funny face and then turn off the light. The image of that face would then remain in the memory of the other, causing great laughter in the darkness. It was a wonderful way of ending the day on a happy note. Even when Rob was very ill, he would still do it every now and then so we could chuckle our way to sleep.

Rob stayed alive as long as he could for his son, his daughter and his wife. 'I win both ways,' he always said. 'Either I get to stay with my wife and children or I get to be with Jesus.' Although he was excited at the prospect of heaven, it was clear he didn't want to leave us. Eventually, with Lena on one arm and holding Rob with the other, all I could say to him was, 'Go and see Jesus.' He died with his eyes open, looking at me for the longest time. My world stood still. Even now I can close my eyes and see the image of his loving gaze. His last look.

Chapter 11

You've Surrounded Me

'Thank you for allowing me to be me.' My fingers worked quickly as the pen skidded across the slip of paper. 'Thank you for loving me for who I am, how I am.' The undertaker was waiting downstairs. 'I love you always.' Each phrase on a different slip. 'You allowed me to become who I am.' Quick thoughts, quick expressions. 'I'll look after the children, I'll be fine ...' Each bit of paper quickly folded and each tucked into a different pocket. The clothes had been ready to hand over, but the idea of all these little messages had only just occurred to me. 'Thank you for your creativity.' Another pocket in Rob's jeans; I kept finding pockets. 'Thank you for believing in me.' Open pockets, zip pockets. I just wanted Rob to be buried with these little phrases of love and gratitude all over him. More pockets, more phrases, more slips of paper. Soon I had filled every one, but I didn't want to stop, so I went around each one again. 'Thank you for all the funny faces.' 'Thank you for calling me your International Dancer/Choreographer.' I smiled at the thought that undertakers are the epitome of restraint, respect and patience. He could wait for another few minutes, surely that was in his job description. 'Thank you for loving my mum and dad.' On and on it went until I had lost count how many messages I had scribbled and stuffed into Rob's pockets. Finally, I handed the clothes over. But what about shoes? I caught sight of Rob's slippers. Rob's empty slippers. That was worse than all the other empty shoes. There was something about the slippers. They were Birkenstock, German ones, and very comfortable. Rob really liked them, especially as our house has stone floors. We both wore them and people often said, 'Ooh, his and hers ...' They seemed to be a hallmark of us.

'Rob's going to wear them in the coffin.' So the comfy brown slippers shod Rob's feet to match his casual clothes for his last relaxed journey.

The first night after Rob died, Lukas slept with me in my bed. I wanted him close to me. Lena was in the Moses basket next to me on the other side, so I was surrounded, sandwiched, by my children. My mum and dad almost tucked me in that night. That first night. Etched upon my memory. Life without Rob, our new chapter about to begin. That first night still stands by me somehow, those first hours of darkness emptied of Rob, as though a lone sentinel still keeps watch somewhere.

When I had come back from the hospice, Lukas, aged almost five and a half, had returned from a sleepover at Kath and James' and was upstairs playing. I had imagined this moment and now that it was here, I dreaded it. How does any mum tell her small child that he won't see his daddy again? Each step on each stair built up the moment in my heart. There would be two moments in the next few days that would prove the hardest of my life, and the placing of my feet that carried me upwards brought me to the first one.

'Lukas? Can I have a talk with you?' He looked up at me, a tiny Pichu toy in his hand. 'Daddy has died.' He stared. There was a small pause which held within it the loss of innumerable possibilities together with the arrival of so much sadness.

'Really?'

'Yes. Daddy has died in the hospice.' Confusion clouded his face, and I stroked his hair.

'But where's Daddy now? What does it mean?' We had talked

about it, about heaven ... I had bought a children's book a few weeks before, *All About Heaven*, with different passages from the Bible, all the questions a child might ask ... Do we have a house there? What does it look like? Do we wear clothes? It's easy illustrated rhyme form was helpful.

'Shall we find out about heaven? Shall we have a look at that new book?' So we read it. I could see his thoughts dawning, and it all seemed to make sense to him.

'Daddy's okay now. It's fine,' he said. His dad had been ill for so long, practically all his life. 'He has got no more pain. So that's good.'

I had been dreading this, but Lukas was very pragmatic. His acceptance seemed tangible. This is the way it is. You can't change it. Young children are used to having no control over events in their lives.

Those first few days loomed very large. Unreality ruled. The film that was my life slipped into intense slow-moving imagery. Powerful, stirring music. Long enigmatic silences. Unusual close-ups. Astounding long shots. Grainy monochrome. Saturated colours. Contradictory thoughts. Detached thoughts. Strong emotions that subverted thinking.

I seemed to float through a sea of flowers. Every day saw more bouquets arriving to add to the already large number still present from Lena's birth just three weeks before. The house took on the appearance of a florist's wholesale stockroom. We ran out of vases, and my mother improvised with whatever she could find ... as the doorbell rang once more and another bouquet demanded its respectful place. Funeral arrangements had to be made, and I wanted an amazing send-off for Rob to celebrate his life. It was a good focus for me. I was determined to do this well and hold it all together.

My friend Kath took me shopping to buy an outfit for the funeral. Strong contradictions kicked me once more. Normally shopping is a joy, but this was the last thing I wanted to do. Simply walking where people would be, doing their normal things, felt peculiar. Surely they could see my bereavement like a huge day-glow aura? Kath kept me going while my emotions turned somersaults. I wanted to look my best for Rob so he could say to me, 'You looked lovely today ... quite quite beautiful,' but, of course, I knew he wouldn't. He couldn't. None of it made sense. What did it matter what I wore? What was the point? My husband was dead.

But it did matter. Rob and I had talked about the funeral. We knew we didn't want black. We didn't want anyone to wear black. For a crazy moment, I wanted to wear a red dress. Extravagance. A burst of uncompromising colour. No, no, too much ...

But then there was Lena, I would need to breastfeed during the day. Practicality wrestled with longing which wrestled with futile hope, and it was Kath who helped me to surface from the turmoil. I chose a loose-fitting, green dress-type top over white linen trousers with a black and white polka dot coat and scarf. Without Kath, I would have never resolved the tumult raging inside. She helped me to feel ready, to feel feminine, to be who I am.

'You need to feel comfortable in your own skin, Sandra.' She put her arm round me. I was so grateful to her. It didn't matter what other people thought, this was going to be my official goodbye to the man who loved me with all his heart.

Rob's funeral was on 11th May 2006. Seven hundred and fifty people attended. There had to be a video link into a separate room at Glenwood Church. The cellist and friend Charlotte Eksteen played as a seemingly endless crowd came and took their seats. It was a sunny and very warm day. I carried Lukas into the church as he clung round my neck. I concentrated on not looking at anybody, otherwise I knew I would lose control.

When we sat down, Lukas just wanted to put his head under my top, and then he kept whispering, 'Is Daddy really in that long box, Mummy? Can we go and have a look?' I kept saying that daddy's body is there, but he is in heaven.

During the service, there was a video clip of Rob speaking his *Word on the Street* version of the Lord's Prayer. When Lukas heard his voice, he sat up and looked around, thinking Rob was on stage with everyone else. Rob finished the prayer with 'Absolutely' – his own version of an 'amen'. Lukas realised it was a video and rested his head on my chest again. I felt for his innocence, his vulnerability. But he had accepted the sad fact.

The minister, Paul Francis, spoke, and many people took part paying tributes to Rob and reading some of his poems. The music and singing was inspirational, and we all sang Rob's favourite classic Welsh hymn, 'All Is Well with My Soul.' Contributions also included this wonderful poem written for the occasion and read by Gerard Kelly.

ROB'S GOD
I want to follow Rob's God;
God-the-goal of my soul's education.
Rob's God is approachable, articulate and artful,
A glowing God, of graceful inclination.
Rob's God snowboards cloudscapes
And paints daisies on his toes,
While watching Chaplin re-runs
On his iPod.
He smiles at cats and children,
Jumps in puddles with his shoes on,
A 'where's-the-fun-in-fundamentalism?' God.
Rob's God doesn't shoot
His own wounded,
Or blame the poor for failing
At prosperity.
He doesn't beat the broken
With bruised reeds from their garden,

Or tell the sick that healing's their
Responsibility.
Rob's God is a poet,
Painting people as his poems;
A sculptor shaping symphonies from stone
A maker of mosaics
Curator of collages
Woven from the wounds and wonders
We have known
A furnace of forgiveness;
Rob's God radiates reunion
Pouring oil on every fight
We've ever started
A living lover
Loving laughter
Lending light
To the helpless and the harmed and heavy-hearted
Other Gods may claim more crowded churches
Higher profiles
Better ratings
Fuller phone-ins,
But in the contest for commitment
In the battle for belief
In the war to woo my worship,
Rob's God wins
In the fight for my faith's fervour,
In the struggle for my soul,
In the race for my respect
Rob's God wins.
Absolutely.

Gerard Kelly, 11th May 2006[*]

* Used with permission.

A big surprise was the spontaneous standing ovation as the coffin made its way out. This was amazing and very moving. Rob had always jokingly engineered standing ovations with his audiences at the end of his one-man version of *the street bible*. He wanted the audience to experience standing in God's presence as he described the final scene in heaven.

'Would you mind standing, please?' Rob would ask. The audience did so for the climax of the show. Applause naturally followed without the audience having had the chance to sit down again, and Rob took his bows. 'How else am I going to get a standing ovation?' he would chuckle. The audience loved it.

But now family, friends and fellow performers rose as one to applaud a life that had brought so much to so many. It was poignant and overwhelming, such an outpouring of love and gratitude for who Rob was. And for the first time, I looked at people. I wanted to look at them despite my tears.

That walk back through the crowd with Lukas by my side was the second hardest moment in my life. I saw faces, hundreds of faces. When any of us looks at another, when we face someone, face up to something, face the music, face the facts . . . it is an expression of honesty. No barriers. Nothing to hide behind. Faces. A sea of faces. I had to walk through them without grief's strange comfort keeping my head bowed. I had to look at everyone looking at me. I didn't want to avoid anyone's gaze or glance. I knew this was the truth, I was walking without Rob. I was living without Rob. My children were without their father. And I had to make that first journey of admission and truth. I was facing the facts. And I know now that all those faces were doing the same. It was my role in that loving gathering of humanity to be the focus for Rob that day. And his humour was still there. I imagined him saying, 'Don't worry, no one can see you properly anyway . . . they're all crying.' And it seemed as if everyone was, but their tears were joined by smiles too. Big smiles of gratitude.

Then we released hundreds of helium-filled balloons into the early summer sunshine. It was an easy choice, the right choice, to send Rob off with hundreds of balloons. He loved the idea when we had talked about it. Balloons seem to mark our life. We had balloons on the Trabant 'limousine' for our wedding, hundreds of balloons in Rob's *Prodigal Grandson* and even more, together with champagne, at a special party in Glenwood Church to celebrate his healing in 2002. Everyone attending the funeral was invited to write a message to Rob on a label tied to a balloon and to release it at a given signal. I tied three together for Lukas, Lena and myself with our own words of love. I wanted an aerial choreography to send Rob heavenward, an expression of release, a final dance of freedom. I wasn't disappointed. We couldn't have asked for a better day, and it was breathtaking to watch. I released our three balloons as the signal for everyone else to let go. And let go we did. It was so beautiful and so sad all at once. Rob was released into the blue above with so many words of love. A breathless blossoming dance made more powerful with words. We had always been a winning combination, he and I. People cheered and clapped. The exuberance and joy were just right. And, in the slight breeze, watching a huge cloud of balloons ascending effortlessly and spreading silently, I like to imagine Rob smiling at the thought of God calling him home and with just one word on his lips ...

'Absolutely!'

I turned earthward again. It was weird to see so many people I hadn't seen for ages, but there wasn't time for conversations, there was the burial itself to see to. Everyone apart from close family waited at the church while we went to the cemetery. The young ones stayed behind. I didn't want Lukas to see the coffin going into the ground; I wanted the image of the balloons to remain and for him to stay and play with his cousins and friends.

The sound of my rose landing on the coffin in the grave was shocking. Its simple hollow thump punctured me. I wept. Even now the strength of that memory shakes me inside. But Rob's dad gave a beautiful speech. There were horses and ponies in the adjacent field, birds were singing. It was peaceful. And yet I knew I had to leave. Despite wanting to stay, I realised that Lena needed feeding. It had been six hours since her previous feed, three hours overdue. It was a peculiar moment, both death and life beckoning me simultaneously.

I sat in the middle of the church breastfeeding Lena while dozens and dozens of friends gathered around me to offer comfort and sympathy but also to see Lena for the first time and to congratulate me. Another friend later commented that, from a vantage point slightly further away, this scene was reminiscent of Michelangelo's *La Pièta*, Mary holding Christ's body across her lap. Except this was life and not death ... and yet it was still my husband's funeral. It did feel very surreal breastfeeding with seven hundred and fifty mourners present. Afterwards the funeral director held my hand and told me that it had been the most beautiful funeral he had ever attended. Of course, he had experienced an extraordinary number of them. Yet he was very moved by all the love expressed, and it felt like he was a distant uncle rather than someone delivering a professional service. It was lovely of him to tell me.

The sand and the waves called me the next day, and I walked along the beach simply to engage with nature and with life's journey. My sister Katja stayed with me for another week after my parents and my brother and his family returned home. Then my good friend Tini, also from Germany, spent the following fortnight with me. My numbness and anger went hand in hand.

'Sandra, look after yourself.' My mum had made a point of ensuring I took this in before she left. 'Don't allow your milk to dry up because of grief. Look after yourself and the children.'

I knew I couldn't lose my breast milk or anything else my children needed. I had to keep on giving to them both. They had lost their dad, and I didn't want them to lose anything else. I knew

I needed to be strong. I pulled myself together and didn't allow the grief to kick in fully. I became immune. Tini was actually crying more than I was. After those first two days, I reined myself in for the sake of my children. Every night I played with Lukas and Lena, being silly and tickling like Rob did. I knew I would never replace him for Lukas, but I wanted to be the best I could be. Then, when everyone had finally gone and it was only the three of us, Lukas and Lena contracted chicken pox. Lukas especially was very ill, and a tangible awfulness threatened to drown me.

I decided to make some changes. Grief could wait a while longer, as I decided to have a three- or four-month break from everything. So in July we went on holiday to Spain with Katja, Rainer and Lukas's cousin Leon. In August we went to Ludwigsstadt. In September I decided to convert the attic into an office so the spare room could return to being a bedroom. And I took in a lodger. Looking at it now, and with the benefit of more recent counselling, I can see how I needed to push on and survive. To hold my world together. To make sense of everything for myself. The strategy worked, but I was in for a rougher ride than I had expected.

Spain proved to be just the right thing. Quite apart from cocktails with my sister sitting by the pool and Lukas and Leon revelling in each other's company, I bonded with Lena. For the first three weeks of her life, I had needed my own space to cope with Rob's illness. I hadn't given myself to her; cancer had stood between us. The Spanish people we encountered thought Lena was wonderful, and they cooed over her endlessly.

'*Hermosa niña!* She is so beautiful!' And I realised they were right! I had a wonderful daughter. A beautiful and gorgeous little girl. I was a mummy again, and Lena and I got to know each other. I fell in love with her.

And then I came home to the empty chair, the empty shoes, the empty car, the empty bed. My mum came over to help with Lena for a few weeks, and I got back into my career. Alongside running

Harnisch-Lacey Dance Theatre, I was working at The Gate, teaching dance and running a Saturday theatre school for six- to sixteen-year-olds. I also taught freelance at the Welsh College of Speech and Drama. Builders set about altering the attic. I had a mountain of stuff to organise and shift. A lot of Rob's clothing and possessions I simply packed into boxes for future sorting. Life without him felt like a mix of so many negative things. C. S. Lewis described the loss of one's life partner as trying to walk again with only one leg ... and a prosthesis that doesn't quite fit. Their absence is profoundly life changing. I pushed myself on, constantly working. But there were problems with The Gate, and my job as artistic director seemed to vaporise as a result of financial difficulties and a change of management. Losing that job felt like having my baby taken away from me. It hurt knowing how upset Rob would have been too. But Lacey Theatre Company carried on with Elin holding the reins. She worked at my home and was a constant support—which must have been very difficult for her. My lodger was Abby Guinness, who had also been in the theatre company and was now studying in Cardiff.

But I didn't see the danger signs. I became exhausted. A long, restful sleep was a distant memory. I still wasn't allowing myself to grieve for Rob. My focus was on my children and my work. I couldn't tell how close to a nervous breakdown I had come. I dreaded our traditional picture postcard German Christmas without Rob that year, but with my family by my side, it was okay, although I couldn't bring myself to go to church with the brass band playing in the snow after the service. It was Rob's favourite part of Christmas, but in Ludwigsstadt everyone knows everyone else's business, and I didn't want people regarding me as 'the poor widow'. Back in the UK, I jumped onto my treadmill once more.

Finally, good friends urged me to stop. I realised they had been telling me to do so for a long while; I simply hadn't heeded their advice. But in my heart I knew they were right. So I slowed down and tried to stop. After a restful Easter 2007, I was determined to sort out Rob's headstone and arrange a tree to be planted for him. I resolved to start afresh after having had a good break. Inevitably, my hours were filled with memories of Rob. The intensity of our life together could not be so easily assigned to the past. There was a lot to come to terms with ... not the least his workaholic tendencies.

My mind returned to how he had given himself so completely to his final work, *The Liberator*. His appetite to create something exciting and arresting was undiminished throughout that long period of writing and editing. It was staggering just how committed Rob was to it. Some might argue that it was as if his body would only last for the time it took to produce the book and see it on the shelves. I knew better. Rob loved his work, it excited him – but he stayed alive long enough to welcome his daughter into the world. I was privileged to witness at first-hand how much he wanted to be here for his family. And, of course, he didn't want to leave. His love for us was superb, selfless and complete. Right up to that very last weekend, we really did live in hope of healing. We knew God could do it again. It wasn't that we were avoiding the issue of being ready to die, it was simply that we had lived through it all once before and were keen to allow God's glory to break through again. But that same glory was to be expressed in another way, and Rob's body simply needed to shut down. How he managed to outlive his prognosis was itself a miracle, and we were more than aware just how much God had spoken and acted through his very weary servant.

On my way back from visiting friends in York the day before the first anniversary of Rob's death, my sister phoned me to say that my dad had been diagnosed with leukaemia. No. No. It could not be happening. Not my dad. My lovely, playful, supportive and wonderful father. Suddenly it felt as if my whole world was falling apart all over again. My dad and I had always been so very close. It rendered me speechless. What next? What if my dad dies? How many more losses must there be? When I eventually went to see him in hospital with all those chemo drips just like Rob had been,

I couldn't believe it was true. He was already very poorly, and he would have died, but he had sought help just in time. Literally one day longer, they said, and it would have been too late. My father's oncologist had never explained his symptoms to him, so he never knew the severity of the situation. My father did eventually die in November 2008. In just two and a half years, the two most important men in my life had gone.

The day of the first anniversary of Rob's death dawned, and I needed to focus. I turned off my mobile phone. Rachel joined me, and we went to the beach at Penarth, near to the hospice where Rob had been. Later we had a meal with friends as a celebration, and then watched videos of Rob and pored over pictures of him. I see now how my heart, my mind and my soul had been joined to a remarkable and beautiful man, but our time together had come to an end. The tantalising hope of heaven almost remains as much a reality now as it did when Rob was ready to embark on his final journey. The threshold between this life and the next seemed paper thin, so very flimsy at those times, and its legacy is mine to this day – as close as our breath, as tangible as thought, as compelling as an aroma that evokes a memory. Though I may not experience its emotional immediacy in the same way now, I still sense it.

Rob lives on in so many wonderful ways and for so many, many people. But, of course, there are two particular people in whom he lives on quite literally. For almost the first five and a half years of his life, Lukas had his dad to hold, tickle, jump on, play and laugh with ... and he also shared some of the frustrations and disruptions that Rob's illness brought. But Lukas already demonstrates how much like his father he is – witty, aware, good with words and always mindful of his audience. Some of his poetry has won him awards, he is a keen storyteller and his teachers talk about his talent with words and his love for reading and books. He is great at drawing, has a cheeky sense of humour and can often be heard talking in an American accent ... just for fun.

Lena too bears a remarkable resemblance to Rob, especially her eyes. Sometimes it is almost as though Rob looks back at me. As well as having a wicked laugh and highly developed social skills, she has a great love for people and soon has visitors exactly where she wants them. There will only ever be a few photographs of Lena and Rob together. But I am so glad they met when there was so much that might have prevented it happening. He met his little girl, and Lena often says, 'Daddy had been cuddling me every day when I was a baby.'

14th April 2006, Lena, seven days old

In Rob's blood-stained notebook that he had in hospital with him, written after Saturday night, 22nd April, and before he died just over a week later, there is this poem. It is his last one:

MAGDELENA'S OVERWHELMING WELCOME
Wow. Didn't even know I had a whelm to be overed.
Never mused on such a miracle.
Didn't know how becoming my coming could be.

Can't even see, smell, hear, touch, taste
    most of you yet.
And yet I can't forget the shades of pink,
    violet and amber you've surrounded me with.

                                        Rob Lacey, 2006

Rob's tree, a white meddler, is planted in a shady corner next to the rugby pitch in Roath Park, close to where we live, and bears the following inscription:

Rob Lacey
25/7/1962 – 1/5/2006
Well done – done good – good faith – faithful – fulfilment
Will be yours! We love you!

Appendix

The following was written by Rob in his notebook sometime in April 2006 while he was in hospital. As you will see from the final (future) entry, this timeline was probably intended to help get his next book started ... the story of his miraculous healing, an insight into how *the street bible* came about and, of course, our life together.

True CV – Me?

Why I'm unqualified, unreliable and probably unemployable ...
but things seem to get done!

1962 – 1979	School Cardiff, Head Boy Llanishen High
1980 – 1983	Canterbury University, Hons Degree – Economics
1983 – 1987	Management Trainee with Lloyds Bank, Cardiff
1987	Left bank to go pro with Trapdoor Theatre Co., touring community theatre
June 15th 1987	Married Kate
May 1991	Kate left me – I'd have left me if I could have
1991 – 92	Sold ethical insurance
Oct 1993 – June 1993	Mime and Physical Theatre with Desmond Jones, London
May 1994	Begin going out with Sandra
	Begin solo theatre / performance poetry touring
	1st full solo show 'People Like Me'
Sept 2nd 1995	Married Sandra in Germany
March 1996	1st Carcinoma in Situ in the bladder – all clear by summer '96

1997 – 1999	2nd solo story telling show 'Prodigal Grandson'
1998	Write and Direct 'Paradise Crushed'
1999	Write 'Grey Daze' Duo show, tour with Sandra Bill and Rach on tech desk
	Publish 'Are We Getting Through?' creative story/ poem resource book
March 2000	2nd bout of bladder cancer
May 2000	Try for a baby before treatment
Jan 2001	Lukas was born
	Begin with St B @ Job.
	Writing through pain and symptoms
March 2001	Family move to Cardiff
May 2001	Last performance of 'People Like Me'
Sept 2001	Op to remove bladder – find tumour behind bladder
	Stop 'street bible' writing – first draft done
Oct/Nov 2001	Mexico for alternative treatment and Toronto for Prayer conference – with Bill n Rachel
Dec 2001	Hospital Cdf. – Radio Therapy
	Cancer in lymphs and bones, weight loss down to 7st – walk on crutches/wheelchair
Feb 2002	Gaining strength despite chemo
March 2002	Restart 2nd draft of 'street bible'
May 2002	Recurrence of acute back pain – fear of end
July 2002	Test of bones – clear
Aug 2002	Test of lymphs – clear
Jan 2003	Deliver 'street bible' manuscript
March 2003	'street bible' published UK (2 yrs solid writing)
April 2003	Tour solo perf. of stb show with Bill n Rach on live music
	– live 'street bible' CD launched
Autumn 2003	Too tired to tour. Danielle begins as PA
March 2004	Published 'street life' study book with Nick Page

Spring 2004   Start writing 'The Liberator'.

Summer 2004   Tour festivals/conferences to launch 'Word on the Street' in USA

Summer 2004   Launch Lacey Theatre Co in UK

Sept 2004   Open Gate Arts + Training Centre in Cdf.
                          Sandra and Rob co-Artistic Directors with Kelvin Thomas

Autumn 2004   Weary – limiting live performances

Winter 2004/Spring/Summer 2005   Writing 'Liberator'

March 2005   Rebrand 'street bible' as 'Word on the Street' in UK

Summer 2005   Tests on bladder/kidneys etc.
                          Try for a baby

Sept 2005   Diagnosed cancer in lymph nodes decline chemo therapy

Autumn 2005   Complete 'Liberator' (18 months solid work)

Winter 2005/6 Relatively well with cancer

March 2006   Poisoned Pool Published in aid of Tearfund

March 2006   Rob into hospital with kidney and intestine trouble – obstructions from cancer tumours

April 2006   Baby Magdalena arrives
                          Let home with Magdalena from hospital

May 2006   Begin compiling 'Dramatic Enough?' book

Weight 10 stone

To be continued?

Afterword: Meeting Rob Lacey

Meeting Rob Lacey was a very memorable event for so many reasons. One was the date. Wednesday 21st December 1988. Pan Am flight 103 blew up over Lockerbie and the tragic news shocked us at the end of a very enjoyable evening. Rob had been juggling among an audience at a performance of a touring play I had directed. This was its last night at an arts centre in Newport, Wales. His superb juggling skills were matched only by his uncanny ability to engage with every single person for whom he performed, regardless of age. I could tell instantly that this man had something very special. As we said goodbye I hoped we would meet again.

January 1991. Four days with Trapdoor Theatre Company somewhere on the west coast of Wales. Rob had asked me to coach, encourage and devise with the company. On more than one occasion he and I sat up chatting after the others had gone to bed and we giggled and guffawed into the early hours whilst feeding a huge driftwood fire. We seemed to be kindred spirits, sharing outlook and humour and so much more. Meeting up over the following few years was a joy—I was always keen to spend time with Rob, if only to hear his latest sheep joke.

September 1997. Nottingham. On the first day of devising *Prodigal Grandson* together, we found ourselves talking about heroes. Who had inspired us? Who did we admire? I talked about two people who had continued to impress me and raise my sights higher, and then it was his turn. Did he have a hero? There was a pause. Then, with an impish look, he simply pointed at me. I laughed. But Rob was serious. I was his hero. I was flabberghasted, how on earth had I allowed this to happen? He really meant it and said so. After expressing a little more shock we fell into laughter, the default condition of our relationship, and I think I said I was determined to disabuse him of such a crazy notion. But Rob knew his own mind and for the rest of his life his precious gift to me was a respect and an admiration which was ennobling and humbling — as well being quite amusing.

September 2002. Rob was declared clear from cancer. My younger brother Mark was diagnosed with secondary skin cancer and died within two months. Among the people who came to me in my grief was Rob. He cried with me, he held me. But we still managed to laugh together. That was the Rob effect, embodying the teachings of Jesus. Mourning really could be turned into joy.

Saturday 8 April 2006. Heath Hospital, Cardiff. The last time I saw Rob. I had written a very short story for him about suffering and redemption, it was playful and tongue-in-cheek. His eyes filled with tears as he read it and then he sat back, smiling. He held out both hands in deference. "The master has spoken! Honestly, I spend two years of my life paraphrasing the Bible then another eighteen months writing the Liberator and you do it all in one short story!" We both giggled, me shaking my head vigorously. His generosity knew no limits. But, in truth, that one small gesture revealed so much to me. He had become the master. Rob the poet, Rob the artist, Rob the writer, Rob the Bard. It was an honour to witness the life of a friend blossom — no, explode — into such an expression of creativity. A life of utter abundance. A life that lived out the principles and teachings of a greater Master so completely. Who was the hero now? My finger will always point to Rob.

October 2007. Cardiff. I set up my video camera to interview Sandra for this book about Rob and their life together. She spoke and I went home with six one hour Mini DV tapes, all full. She was only just over halfway through their story.

May 2008. Cardiff. I video Sandra again. This time she filled five more Mini DV tapes and got to the end of her story.

December 2008 — October 2009. Using transcripts I wrote as Sandra in the first person, sending her chapters one at a time. Sometimes we met. Sometimes we phoned. We talked. A lot. And I began to understand Rob's greatness more wholly. Sandra was honest and open, giving all she could so that their story may be told effectively. I found myself continually amazed at this woman's creativity, perception, artistry, generosity and love. Without wishing in any way to downgrade Rob and all he was and did, it became very apparent to me that he was only half the story. The loud half. The loud laugh.

But Sandra does a good line in giggling too. Theirs was a joy filled partnership that emanated a certain magic. Each truly became part of the other, inseparable, perfectly balanced and symbiotic. Little wonder then that Sandra's grief has been so deep and so intense. But like her husband she bounces back and so, also like Rob, she demonstrates the word becoming flesh — the spirit of resurrection. I have had the privilege to spend many wonderful hours marvelling at the tenacity, energy, patience, creativity and sheer grace that is Sandra. I often find myself referring to her as Wonder Woman. My life has been enriched by her. Absolutely.

And finally ... This book has been written on my MacBook Pro laptop with a decidedly dodgy 'p' key. I have had to set the AutoCorrect feature in Microsoft Word to include a 'p' for every omission, of which there have been thousands. But AutoCorrect doesn't catch them all and I have often been heard complaining "I need a 'p'!" "If only my 'p' worked properly!" Rob would have loved this irony, given his urinary history.

Steve Stickley, Artistic Director, Footprints Theatre

Trust, Nottingham, March 2010

Acknowledgements

My biggest thank you goes to my two wonderful children, Lukas and Magdalena, who saw Mummy night after night on the computer or on the phone, talking to Steve about the book. Thanks for your patience when I was stressed and tired and couldn't tuck you in at night. Thanks for all the love and joy you bring to me.

A big thank you to Steve Stickley, who was an amazing listener and was able, through his sensitivity and wisdom, to create a space where I felt safe to open up — not to mention what a brilliant writer he is, managing to make my *Germlish* sound beautiful.

The love and support we received throughout the years of Rob's illness and the time since has been overwhelming. So many walked this journey with us and became part of 'Our Story'; without those people our lives wouldn't be the same. I would like to take this opportunity to express my heartfelt thanks to all of you.

To my mum and dad for all their wonderful love to us and practical support; my sister, Katja, who carried me through some of the darkest moments; my brother Frank; Rainer, Leon, Rob's mum and dad, who lovingly looked after my children again and again; Derek, Peter and Gill and their families, who loved and cared for us throughout all these years; our special friends Bill and Rachel; Kath and James and Tim and Joy who were always there, be it day or night. Thank you so much, words aren't enough to express what you did for us. Elin Kelly who single-handed steered the boat of Lacey Theatre Company through turbulent times, giving all she could to keep Rob's legacy alive. Rob's PA, Danielle Lancaster, who helped Rob stay sane; all the actors in Lacey Theatre company, sharing the many meals around our table; Alun Mathias and all the other trustees of Lacey Theatre Company who are committed to carrying on Rob's legacy; Donna Morris Lee who took the load off my shoulders and pushed Harnisch-Lacey Dance Theatre forward; all my wonderful friends and families from Roath Park Primary School: Pamela and Gareth, Rosie and Emil, Darja and Florian, Koko, Shona, Ruth and Louise and many more who loved and cared for all of us; my lodgers Abby Guinness, Dulcie Sellick and Kate Sadler for their friendship and support and their amazing love for my children; Ken and Queenie Ratcliffe, who child-minded Lukas and Lena; our neighbours Michele, Vince and Isaac Browne, who never grow tired of us popping in; Jeanette and Andy Gorringe, who always had a meal ready when I was too exhausted to cook; my friends back in Germany, Tini, Simone and Annett, who were always at the end of a phone; Glenwood Church, which supported us by providing meals, child care, friendship and spiritual support. From our time in London: thanks to Phil and Julie Stokes and everybody at The Well (Ichthus Camberwell), The Swans, The Bernardins, Sarah Fordham, Stefan (our Best Man), Dale, John and Carina Persson, Chantal, Roy and Jane Harvey, whose hospitality and support to us was tremendous; my dance friends from Laban Centre days: Barbara, Mara, Anne, Gail, Colin and Cristian; our friends from across the pond, Ben and Amanda Irwin, Cliff and Uli Guthrie, Paul Caminiti and Sheyna.

Thanks too to Sue Brower and everybody at Zondervan for their patience, genorsity and expertise; everybody at Spring Harvest for their continued commitment to support Rob's work; and, by no means least, everybody at The Gate Arts Centre for their ongoing support of Harnisch Lacey Dance Theatre.

There are too many loving and supportive people to thank, so please forgive me if I haven't mentioned you by name. Thanks to all of you, who carried us through prayer over all those years—we were and are truly grateful. Your prayers made such a difference to our lives and they still do.

Sandra

I would like to thank the fabulous Sandra, Lukas and Lena all of whom have inspired in full, and often playful, measure. Special thanks to my wife Janet for reading and crying and reading again! To Ben Irwin for great editorial insights and humour. I would also like to thank my daughters Daisy and Tilda for their wonderful support in helping to transcribe eleven hours of video interviews, and also to Enola Stevenson who finished off the task. And thanks to my son Joel for being my constant lexicon guide. Acknowledgement and thanks must also go to David and Ann Adeney, Liz Babbs, Sue Brower, Fi Burke, Sarah Churchill, Jonathan Etheridge for rescuing a Mini DV tape, Pete and Margaret Farley, Abby Guinness, Elin Kelly, Jackie Marks, Roy McCloughry, Robin Reece-Crawford, Mike and Fi Shouler, Anna Stickley, John Stickley, Pat and Ray Stickley, Theo Stickley, Michèle Taylor, Lucy Thampi, Simon Whittaker, Sarah Woodall, the Trustees of Footprints Theatre, and the staff at Risley Hall Hotel. Their support, knowingly or otherwise, has helped to get this story written. And for those whom I have ommitted, sorry. You can blame it on a proliferation of senior moments. I often do.

Steve

Look for *People Like Us* on Facebook

the word on the street

Rob Lacey

> "Rob helped me discover angry and sad voices in passages of the Bible that had left me indifferent, and he made me laugh at other passages so familiar that I had never seen the healthy irreverence, humor and irony they expressed."
>
> — Dr. David Trobisch, professor of New Testament Language and Literature, Bangor Theological Seminary

For those who've never read the Bible, and for those who've read it too much.

Rob Lacey's "dangerously real" retelling of Scripture vividly demonstrates that the Bible is packed full of stories/poems/images that resonate with the big issues of today. This fresh paraphrase with running commentary brings the text alive: Bible stories are retold as mini-blockbusters; psalms as song lyrics; epistles as emails; Revelation as a virtual reality.

Out with stale religious terms, here's a "Bible" that talks today's language—gritty, earthy, witty. Enough of starting at Genesis with good intentions but getting lost in Leviticus. Lacey succeeds in revitalizing a classic work by focusing on the big picture: fast-forwards through the "slow-moving" bits with pace, passion and energy to make the Bible a page-turner again.

What's more, Lacey's award-winning* tour de force was created during a remarkable personal journey through terminal cancer: the stuff the Bible stories are made of. This life-experience injects Lacey's take on Scripture with authenticity and authority—resonating with Bible characters who also wrestled with the big questions.

Purist alert: This is not THE Bible (capital B) ... but it might just get you reaching for one.

*Book of the year (2004), Christian Booksellers Convention Ltd. (UK)

Available in stores and online!

ZONDERVAN®
.com